THE QUINN & BODEN CO PRESS
RAHWAY, N. J.

CONTENTS

CHAPTER I

CHAPTER VI

CHAPTER VII

CHAPTER VIII

CHAPTER XI

A LIKELY STORY

CHAPTER I

" You'll have to light the gas, Sairah! " said an
Artist in a fog, one morning in Chelsea. For although summer was on the horizon, it was cold and
damp; and, as we all know, till fires come to an
end, London is not fogless—if, indeed, it ever is so.
This was a very black fog, of the sort that is sure to
go off presently, because it is only due to atmos-
pheric conditions. Meanwhile, it was just as well
to light the gas, and not go on pretending you could
see and putting your eyes out.

This Artist, after putting his eyes out, called out,
from a dark corner in his Studio, to something in a

dark corner outside. And that something shuffled into the room and scratched something else several times at intervals on something gritty. It was Sairah, evidently, and Sairah appeared impatient.

"They're damp, Sairah," said the Artist feebly. "Why do you get that sort? Why can't you get Bryant and May?"

"These *are* Bryant and May, Mr. Aching. You can light 'em yourself if it sootes you better. I know my place. Only they're Safety, and fly in your eye. Puttin' of 'em down to dry improves. I'd screw up a spell, only there's no gettin' inside of the stove. Nor yet any fire, in the manner of speaking."

The scratching continued. So did Sairah's impatience. Then the supply of the something stopped, for Sairah said: "There ain't any more. That's the hend of the box. And exceptin' I go all the way to the King's Road there ain't another in the house—not Bryant and May."

"Oh dear, oh dear!" said the Artist, in the lowest spirits. But he brightened up. "Perhaps there's a Vesta," said he.

Sairah threw the thing nearest to her against the thing nearest to it to indicate her readiness to search.

"Look in the pocket of my plaid overcoat, Sairah," he continued. "It was a new box Tuesday."

Sairah shuffled into another room, and was heard
to turn over garments. The Artist seemed to know
which was which, by the sound. For he called
out: "None of those! On the hook." Sairah
appeared to turn up the soil in a new claim, and
presently announced: "Nothing in neither pocket.
Only coppers and a thrip'ny!"

"Oh dear—I'm certain there was! Are you sure
you've looked? Just look again, Sairah." He
seemed distressed that there should be no Vesta in
his overcoat pocket.

"You can see for yourself—by lookin'," says
Sairah. "And then there won't be any turnin'
round and blamin' me!" Whereupon she appears,
bearing a garment. The reason she shuffles is that
she has to hold the heels of her shoes down on the
floor with her feet.

The owner of the overcoat dived deep into the
pockets, but found nothing. He appeared dumb-
foundered. "Well, now!" he continued. "Whatever can have become of my Vestas?" And
thereon, as one in panic on emergency, he put down
the sponge and brush he was using and searched
rapidly through all his other pockets. He slapped
himself in such places as might still contain forgotten pockets; and then stood in thought, as one
to whom a light of memory will come if he thinks
hard enough, but with a certain glare and distortion

of visage to say, in place of speech, how truly active
is his effort of thought. And then of a sudden he
is illuminated, and says of course!—*he* knows!
But he doesn't know, for, after leaving the room to
seek for his Vestas, and banging some doors, he
comes back, saying he thought they were there
and they aren't. Wherefore, Sairah must run out
and get some more; and look sharp, because they
must have the gas! But Sairah, who has not been
exerting herself, awakes suddenly from something
equivalent to sleep which she can indulge in upright,
without support, and says, nodding towards a thing
she speaks of, " Ain't that them on the stove ? "
And the Artist says, " No, it isn't; it's an empty
box. Cut along and look sharp ! " Sairah made no
response and time was lost in conversation, as
follows :

" That ain't an empty box ! "

" It *is* an empty box ! Do cut along and look
sharp ! "

" It ain't my idear of an empty box. But, of
course, it ain't for *me* to say nothin' ! "

" I tell you I'm quite *sure* it's empty. Perfectly
certain ! "

" Well ! It ain't for me to say anything. But
if you had a asted me, I should have said there
wouldn't any harm have come of looking inside of
it, to see. Of course I can *go*, if you come to

that! Only there's tandstickers in the kitchen, and for the matter of that, the fire ain't let out; nor likely when it's not the sweep till Wednesday."

"Get 'em out of the kitchen, then! Get the tandstickers or get anything. Anywhere; only look alive!" He seemed roused to impatience.

"Of course I *can* get them out of the kitchen. Or there's missuses bedroom candlestick stood on the landin', with one in, and guttered." Sairah enumerated two or three other resources unexhausted, and left the room.

When she had vanished, the Artist went and stood with his back to the stove, for it was too dark to work. Being there, he picked up the empty box and seemed to examine it. Having done so, he left the room, and called over the stair-rail, to a lower region.

"Sair-ah!"

"Did you call, Sir?"

"Yes—you needn't go! There's some here."

"'Arf a minute till I put these back."

And then from underground came the voice of the young woman saying something enigmatical about always wishing to give satisfaction, and there was never any knowing. But she remained below, because her master said: "You needn't come up again now. I'll light it myself." In an instant, however, he called out again that she must bring

the matches, after all, because the Vestas were all
stuck to, through being on the stove. When
Sairah reappeared, after a good deal of shuffling
about below, he asked her why on earth she couldn't
come at once. She explained, with some indignation, that she had been doing a little dusting in
the parlour: and, of course, the tandstickers, she
put 'em back in the kitchen, not bein' wanted, as
you might say. But all obstacles to lighting the
gas were now removed.

Illumination presented itself first as an incom-
bustible hiss; but shortly became a flame, and was
bright enough to work by. The Artist did not seem
very contented with it, and said that the pressure
was weak, and it was off at the main, and there
was water in the pipes, and the gas was bad and
very dear. But he worked for half-an-hour or so,
and then a young woman came in, of whom he took
no notice; so she must have been his wife. Of
whom anyone might have thought that she was
stopping away from a funeral against her will, and
resented the restraint. For she bit her lips and
tapped with her feet as she sat in the arm-chair
she dropped into when she entered the room. She
made no remark, but maintained an aggressive
silence. Presently the young man moaned.

"What *is* the rumpus?" said he plaintively.
"What *is* the everlasting rumpus?"

" It's very easy for you. Men can! But if you were a woman, you would feel it like I do. Thank God, Reginald, you are not a woman! "

" Good job I ain't! We might quarrel, if I was. You've got something to be thankful for, you see, Mrs. Hay." This way of addressing her, as Mrs. Hay, was due to the substitution of the initial for the whole name, which was Aiken.

" Oh, you *are* unfeeling," said she reproachfully. " You know perfectly well what I meant! "

" Meant that you thanked God I wasn't a woman." But this made the lady evince despair. " Well!— what *did* you mean, then? Spit it out."

" You are tired of me, Reginald, and I shall go for my walk alone. Of course, what I meant was plain enough, to any but a downright fool. I meant *you* were to thank God, Reginald—on your knees!— that *you* were a man and not a woman. The idea of my saying anything so silly! Wait till you are a woman, and *then* see! But if you're not coming, I shall go. I don't know why you want the gas. It all mounts up in the bills. And then *I* shall be found fault with, I suppose."

" I want the gas because I can't see without it."

After a phase of despair, followed by resignation, the lady said, speaking in the effect of the latter: " I think, Reginald, if you had any regard for the bills, you would just look out of the window, once in an hour or so, and not consume all those cubic feet of gas at three-and-ninepence. The fog's gone! There's the sun. I knew it would be, and it was perfectly ridiculous to put off going to the Old Water Colour."

"Suppose we go, then? Hay, Mrs. Hay? Get your hat, and we'll go." He turned the gas out.

"Oh no! It's no use going now—it's too late. And it's all so depressing. And you know it is! And I shall have to get rid of this new girl, Sairah."

"I thought she looked honest." This was spoken feebly.

She answered irritably: "You always think they look honest when they're ugly. This one's no better than they all are. It's not the honesty, though. It's she won't do anything."

"Why didn't you have that rather pleasin'-looking gyairl with a bird's wing on her hat?"

"That conscious minx! I really do sometimes quite wonder at you, Reginald! Besides, she wanted a parlourmaid's place, and wouldn't go where there wasn't a manservant kept. You men are such fools! And you don't give any help."

Mr. Aiken, observing a disposition to weep in these last words, seemed embarrassed for a moment; but after reflection became conciliatory. "Sairah does seem lazy. But she says she's not been accustomed."

"And then you give way! You might put that magnifying-glass down just for one moment, and pay attention! Of course, she says she's not been accustomed to anything and everything. They all do! But what can one expect when their master blacks his own boots?"

"What can *I* do, when she says she hopes she knows her place, and she ain't a general, where a boy comes in to do the rough work?"

"What can you *do?* Why, of course *not* carry your dirty boots down into the kitchen and black them yourself, and have her say, when you ask for the blacking, do you know where it's kept? I've no patience! But some men will put up with anything, except their wives; and then one's head's snapped off! '*Do you know where it's kept!*' The idea! . . . Well, are you coming, or are you not? Because, *if* you're coming, I must put on my grey tweed. If you're *not* coming, say so!"

But Mr. Aiken did not say so. So, after a good deal of time needlessly spent in preparation, the two asked each other several times if they were ready, shouting about the house to that effect. And then, when they reappeared in the Studio, having succeeded very indifferently in improving their appearance, the lady asked the gentleman more than once whether she looked right, and he said in a debilitated way, Yes!—he thought so. Whereon she took exception to his want of interest in her appearance, and he said she needn't catch him up so short. However, they did get away in the end, and Sairah came in to do a little tidin' up—not often getting the opportunity in the Studio—in pursuance of a programme arranged between herself and her mistress, in an aside out of hearing of her master, in order that the latter should not interpose, as he always did, and he knew it, to prevent anything the least like cleanness or order. How he could go on so was a wonder to his wife.

As for Sairah, the image of herself which she nourished in her own mind was apparently that of one determined to struggle single-handed to re-establish system in the midst of a world given over to Chaos. Whatever state the place would get into if it wasn't for her, she couldn't tell! The other inhabitants of the planet would never do a hand's turn; anyone could see that! In fact, the greater part of them devoted themselves to leavin' things about for her to clear up. The remainder, to gettin' in the way. When you were that worried, you might very easy let something drop, and no great wonder! And things didn't show, not when riveted, if only done careful enough. Or a little diamond cement hotted up and the edges brought to. There was a man they knew his address at Pibses Dairy, over a hivory-turner's he lived, done their ornamential pail beautiful, and you never see a crack!

But Sairah's alacrity, when she found herself alone in the Studio, fell short of her implied forecast of it. Instead of taking opportunity by the fore-lock, and doing the little bit of tidying up that she stood pledged to, she gave herself up to the con-templation of the Fine Arts.

Now, there were two Fine Arts to which this master, Mr. Reginald Aiken, devoted himself. One, the production of original compositions; which did not pay, owing to their date. Some of these days they would be worth a pot of money—you see if they wouldn't! The other Fine Art was that of the picture-restorer, and did pay. At any rate, it paid enough to keep Mr. Aiken and his wife—and at this particular moment Sairah—in provisions cooked and quarrelled over at the street-door by the latter; leaving Mrs. Aiken's hundred a year, which her Aunt Priscilla allowed her, to pay the rent and so on, with a good margin for cabs and such-like. Anyhow, as the lady of the house helped *with* the house, the Aikens managed, somehow. Or perhaps it should be said that, somehow, the Aikens managed anyhow. Mrs. Verity, their landlady, had her opinions about this.

This, however, is by the way; but, arising as it does from this Artist's twofold mission in life, it connects itself with a regrettable occurrence which came about in consequence of Sairah's not confining herself to tidying up, and getting things a bit straight, but seizing the opportunity to do a little dusting also.

Those on whom the guardianship of a picture recently varnished has fallen know the assiduous devotion with which it must be watched to protect it from insect-life and flue. Even the larger lepidoptera may fail to detach themselves from a fat, slow-drying varnish, without assistance; and who does not know how terribly the delicate organization of bettles' legs may suffer if complicated with treacle or other glutinous material. But beetles' legs may be removed with care from varnish, and leave no trace of their presence, provided the varnish is not too dry. Flue, on the other hand, at any stage of desiccation, spells ruin, and is that nasty and messy there's no doing anything with it; and you may just worrit yourself mad, and sticky yourself all over, and only make matters worse than you began. So you may just as well let be, and not be took off your work no longer; nursing, however, an intention of saying well now!—you declare, who ever could have done that, and not a livin' soul come anigh the place, you having been close to the whole time, and never hardly took your eyes off?

That sketches the line of defence Sairah was constrained to adopt, after what certainly was at least a culpable error of judgment. She should not have wiped over any picture at all, not even with the cleanest of dusters. And though the one she used was the one she kep' for the Studio, nothing warranted its application to the Italian half-length that had been entrusted to Mr. Aiken by Sir Stopleigh Upwell, to clean and varnish carefully, and touch up the frame, without destroying the antique feeling of the latter.

Mr. Aiken was certainly to blame for not locking the door and taking away the key. So he had no excuse for using what is called strong language when he and his wife came back from the Old Water Colour. She had not been in *ten minutes*—a period she laid great stress on—when she heard him shouting inside the Studio. And then he came out in the passage and shouted down the stairs.

"Good God, Euphemia! where are you? Where the Devil are you? Do come up here! I'm *ruined*, I tell you! . . . that brute of a girl! . . ." And he went stamping about in his uncontrollable temper.

His wife was alarmed, but not to the extent of forgetting to enter her protest against the strong language. "Reginald!" she said with dignity, "have I not often told you that if you say God and Devil I shall go away and spend the rest of the day with my Aunt Priscilla, at Coombe? Before the girl and all!"

But her husband was seriously upset at something. "Don't go on talking like an idiot," he said irritably. Then his manner softened, as though he was himself a little penitent for the strong language, and he subsided into "Do come up and see what that confounded girl has done." Those conversant with the niceties of strong language will see there was concession in this.

Mrs. Aiken went upstairs, and saw what the confounded girl had done. But she did not seem impressed. "It wants a rub," she said. Then her husband said, "That's just like you, Euphemia. You're a fool." Whereupon the lady said in a dignified manner, "Perhaps if I am a fool, I'd better go." And was, as it were, under compulsion to do so, seeing that no objection was raised.

But she must have gone slowly, inasmuch as she presently called back from the landing, "What's that you said?" not without severity.

"I said ' Call the girl.' "

"You said nothing of the sort. What was it you said before that?"

Now, what her husband had said was, "The idea of a *rub!* Idiotic barbarian!" He was unable to qualify this speech effectually, and his wife went some more stairs up. Not to disappear finally; a compromise was possible.

"Did you say 'idiotic barbarian,' or 'idiotic barbarians'? Because it makes all the difference."

"Barbarians. Plural. Don't be a fool, and come down."

Thereupon the lady came back as far as the door, but seemed to waver in concession, for she made reservations.

"I am not coming down because of anything," she said, "but only to remind you that that Miss Upwell was to come some time to see the picture, and I think that's her."

"What's her? I don't hear anyone at the door."

"It's no use gaping out of the front window. You know quite well what I mean. That's her in the carriage, gone to the Macnivensons' by mistake for us, as people always do and always will, Reginald, until Mrs. Verity gets the Borough Council to change the numbers. 'Thirty-seven A' is a mere mockery."

Mr. Aiken came out of the Studio, and went up to the side-window on the landing, commanding a view of the street in which thirty-seven A stood, his own tenancy being in the upper half of a corner house. "That's her," said he. "And a young swell. Sweetheart, p'raps! Smart set, they look. But, I say, Mrs. Hay . . ."

"Do come away from the window. They'll see you, and it looks so bad. *What* do you say?"

"What the Devil am I to do? I can't let her see the picture in that state."

"Nonsense! Just wipe the mess off. You are such a fidget, Reginald."

But the Artist could not have his work treated thus lightly. The girl must say he had been called away on important business. It was absolutely impossible to let that picture be seen in its present state. And it would take over an hour to make it fit to be seen. . . . Well, of course, it *was* difficult, Mr. Aiken admitted, to think what to say, all in a hurry! He thought very hard, and twice said, "I've an idea. Look here!" And his wife said, "Well?" But nothing came of it. Then he said, "Anyhow, she mustn't come into the Studio. That's flat! . . ." But when, in answer to inquiry as to how the difficulty of the position should be met, he riposted brusquely, "Who's to see her? Why, *you!*"—Mrs. Aiken said, in the most uncompromising way, No—that she wouldn't; the idea! If there were to be any fibs told, her husband must tell them himself, and not put them off on her. It was unmanly cowardice. Let him tell his own fibs.

But the colloquy, which threatened to become heated, was interrupted by a knock at the door. Warmth of feeling had to give way before necessity for action. Broadly speaking, this took the form of affectation, on the part of Mr. and Mrs. Aiken, of a remoteness from the Studio not favoured by the resources of their premises, and, on the part of Sairah, of a dramatic effort to which she proved altogether unequal. She was instructed to say that she didn't know if her master was at home, but would see, if the lady and gentleman would walk into the Studio. She was then to convey an impression of passing through perspectives of corridors, and opening doors respectfully, and meeting with many failures, but succeeding in the end in running her quarry down in some boudoir or private chapel. She failed, and was audible to the visitors in the Studio, within a few feet of its door, which didn't 'asp, unless pulled to sharp. She had not pulled it to sharp. And her words were not well chosen :—" I said to 'em to set down till you come, and you wouldn't be a minute." No more they were; but there are more ways than one of not being a minute, and they chose the one most illustrative—to Mrs. Aiken's mind— of the frequency of unexpected visits from the *élite*. "Don't go rushing in, as if no one ever came! " said she to her husband.

The young lady and gentleman did not sit down, but walked about the room, the former examining its contents. The gentleman, who was palpably an officer in a cavalry regiment, neglected the Fine

Arts, in favour of the lady, whom he may be said
to have gloated over at a respectful distance. But
he expressed himself to the effect that this was an
awful lark, straining metaphor severely. The young
lady, whose beauty had made Sairah's head reel,
said, "Yes—it's fun," more temperately. But
both looked blooming and optimistic, and ready to
recognize awful larks and fun in almost any combination of circumstances.

The first instinct of visitors to a Studio is to find
some way of avoiding looking at the pictures. A
good method towards success in this object is to
lean back and peep over all the canvases with their
faces to the wall, and examine all the sketch-books,
in search of what really interests you so much more
than finished work; to wit, the first ideas of the
Artist, fresh from his brain—incomplete, of course,
but full of an indefinable something. They are
himself, you see! But they spoil your new gloves,
and perhaps you are going on to Hurlingham.
These young people were; and that, no doubt, was
why the young lady went no further in her researches than to discover the rich grimy quality of
the dirt they compelled her to wallow in. It
repulsed her, and she had to fall back on the easels
and their burdens.

They glanced at " Diana and Actæon," unfinished,
the Artist's *capo d'opera* at this date, and appeared

embarrassed for a moment, but conscious that
something is still due to High Art.

"Why don't you say the drawing's fine, or the
tone, or something? You're not doing your duty,
Jack." Thus spoke the young lady, who presently,
to the relief of both, found an enthusiasm. "She's
perfectly lovely! But is *she* Mr. Malkin's work?
She isn't—*she's our picture!* She's Early Italian."
She clapped her hands and laughed with delight.
Oh dear!—how pretty she looked, transfixed, as it
were, with her lips apart opposite to the picture
Sairah had been attending to!

The young man took his eyes off her to glance at
the picture, then put them back again. "I don't
dislike 'em Early Italian," he said. But he wasn't
paying proper attention; and, besides, Sairah's little
essay towards picture-restoration had caught his passing glance. "What's all that woolly mess?" said he.

"Picture-cleaning, of course," said the lady.
"Mr. Malthus knows what he's about—at least, I
suppose so. . . . Oh, here he is!" Now this
young lady ought to have made herself mistress of
the Artist's real name before visiting his Studio.
Not having done so, his sudden appearance—he had
taken the bit in his teeth and rushed in as though
at most very few people ever came—was a little
embarrassing to her, especially as he said correctively, "Aiken." Thereon the young lady said she

meant Aiken, which may have been true, or not.
However, she got the conversation on a sound
footing by a little bit of truthfulness. "I was just
saying to Captain Calverley that the 'woolly mess,'
as he is pleased to call it, is what you are doing to
the picture. Isn't it, now?"

Mr. Aiken satisfied his conscience cleverly. He
smiled in a superior way—as a master smiles at one
that is not of his school—and said merely, "Something of the kind."

This young lady, Madeline Upwell, had never been
in a real picture-restorer's studio before, and could
not presume to be questioning anything, or taking
exceptions. So she accepted Sairah's handiwork
as technical skill of a high order. And Mr. Aiken,
his conscience at ease at having avoided fibs, which
so often lead to embarrassments, felt quite in high
spirits, and could give himself airs about his knowledge of Early Italian Art.

"A fine picture!" said he. "But not a Bronzino."

Miss Upwell looked dejected, and said, "Oh
dear!—isn't it? Ought it to be?" Captain
Calverley said, "P'raps it's by somebody else."
But he was evidently only making conversation.
And Miss Upwell said to him, "Jack, you don't
know anything about it. Be quiet!" Whereupon
Captain Calverley was quiet. He was very good

and docile, and no wonder; for the fact is, his inner soul purred like a cat whenever this young lady addressed him by name.

Mr. Aiken went on to declare his own belief about the authorship in question. His opinion was of less than no value, but he gave it for what it was worth. The picture was palpably the work of Mozzo Vecchio, or his son Cippo—probably the latter, who was really the finer artist of the two, in spite of Jupp. As to the identity of the portrait, he did not agree with any of the theories about it. He then, receiving well-bred encouragement to proceed from his hearers, threw himself into a complete exposition of his views—although he frequently dwelt upon their insignificance and his own —with such enthusiasm that it was with a wrench to his treatment of the subject that he became aware that his wife had come into the room and was expecting to be taken notice of, venomously. At the same time it dawned on him that his visitors had assumed the appearance of awaiting formal introduction. The method of indicating this is not exactly like endeavouring to detect a smell of gas, nor giving up a conundrum and waiting for the answer, nor standing quite still to try on, nor any particular passage in fielding at cricket; but there may be a little of each in it. Only, you mustn't speak on any account—mind that! You may say

"er"—if that indicates the smallest speakable
section of a syllable—as a friendly lead to the introducer.   And it is well to indicate, if you can, how
sweet your disposition will be towards the other
party when the introducer has taken action, like
the Treasury. But the magic words must be
spoken.

Miss Upwell was beginning to feel a spirit of
Chauvinism rising in her heart, that might in time
have become " Is *this* Mrs. Aiken ? " with a certain
gush of provisional joy, when the gentleman perceived his neglect, and said, " Ah—oh!—my wife,
of course! Beg pardon! " On which Mrs. Aiken
said, " You must forgive my husband," with an
air of spacious condescension, and the incident
ended curiously by a kind of alliance between the
two ladies against the social blunders of male mankind.

But the Artist's wife declined to fall in with
current opinion about the picture.   " I suppose it's
very beautiful, and all that," said she.   " Only
don't ask *me* to admire it! I never *have* liked
that sort of thing, and I never *shall* like it."   She
went on to say the same thing more frequently
than public interest in her decisions appeared to
warrant.

The young lady said, in a rather plaintive, disappointed tone, " But *is* it that sort of thing? "

She had evidently fallen in love with the picture, and while not prepared to deny that sorts of things existed which half-length portraits oughtn't to be, was very reluctant to have a new-found idol pitch-forked into their category.

The Artist said, "What the dooce you mean, Euphemia, I'm blest if *I* know!" He looked like an Artist who wished his wife hadn't come into his room when visitors were there.

The Captain said, "What sort of thing? I don't see that she's any sort at all. Thundering pretty sort, anyhow!"

Thereupon the Artist's wife said, "I suppose I'm not to speak," and showed symptoms of a dangerous and threatening self-subordination. The lady visitor, perceiving danger ahead, with great tact exclaimed: "Oh, but I do know so *exactly* what Mrs. Aiken means." She didn't know, the least in the world. But what did that matter? She went on to dwell on the beauty of the portrait, saying that she should persuade Pupsey to have it over the library chimneypiece and take away that dreary old Kneller woman. It was the best light in the whole place.

But her sweetly meant effort to soothe away the paroxysm of propriety which seemed to have seized upon the lady of the house was destined to fail, for the husband of the latter must needs put his word in,

saying, " I don't see any ground for it. Never
shall." This occasioned an intensification of his
wife's attitude, shown by a particular form of silence,
and an underspeech to Miss Upwell, as to one who
would understand, " No ground ?—with those arms
and shoulders! And look at her open throat—oh,
the whole thing!" which elicited a sympathetic
sound, meant to mean anything. But the young
lady was only being civil. Because she had really
no sympathy whatever with this Mrs. What's-her-
name, and spoke with severity of her afterwards,
under that designation. At the moment, however,
she made no protest beyond an expression of rap-
turous admiration for the portrait, saying it was
the most fascinating head she had ever seen in a
picture. And as for the arms and open throat, they
were simply ducky. The Artist's wife could find
nothing to contradict flatly in this, and had to content herself with, " Oh yes, the *beauty's* undeniable.
But that was how they did it."

The young officer appeared to want to say something, but to be diffident. A nod of encouragement
from Miss Upwell produced, " Why, I was going to
say—wasn't it awfully jolly of 'em to do it that
way?" The speaker coloured slightly, but when
the young lady said, " Bravo, Jack! I'm on your
side," he looked happy and reinstated.

But when could the picture be finished and be

sent to Surley Stakes? The young lady would never be happy till it was safe there, now she had seen it. Would Mr. Aiken get it done in a week? . . . no? —then in a fortnight? The Artist smiled in a superior way, from within the panoply of his mystery, and intimated that at least a month would be required; and, indeed, to do justice to so important a job, he would much rather have said six weeks. He hoped, however, that Miss Upwell would be content with his assurance that he would do his best.

Miss Upwell would not be at all content. Still, she would accept the inevitable. How could she do otherwise, with Captain Calverley's sisters waiting for them at Hurlingham?

"Quite up to date!" was the verdict of the Artist's wife, as soon as her guest was out of hearing.

"Who?" said the Artist. Then, as one who steps down from conversation to communication, he added in business tones: "I say, Euphemia, I shall have to run this all down with turps before the copal hardens, and I really must give my mind to it. You had better hook it."

"I'm going directly. But it's easy to say 'who?'"

"Oh, I say, do hook it! I can't attend to you and this at the same time."

"I'm going. But it *is* easy to say 'who?' And you know it's easy."

The Artist, who was coquetting with one of those nice little corkscrews that bloom on Artists' bottles, became impatient. "Wha-a-*awt* is it you're going on about?" he exclaimed, exasperated. "Can't you leave the girl alone, and hook it?"

"I can leave the room," said his wife temperately, "and am doing so. But you see you knew perfectly well who, all along!" Even so the Japanese wrestler, who has got a certainty, is temperance itself towards his victim, who writhes in vain.

Why on earth could not the gentleman leave the lady to go her own way, and attend to his work? He couldn't; and must needs fan the fires of an incipient wrangle that would have burned down, left to itself. "Don't be a fool, Euphemia," said he. "Can't you answer my question? What do you mean by 'quite up to date'?"

Now, Mrs. Aiken had a much better memory than her husband. "Because," she replied, dexterously seizing on his weak point, "you never asked any such question, Reginald. If you had asked me to tell you what I meant by 'quite up to date,' I should have told you what I meant by 'quite up to date.' But I shall not tell you now, Reginald, because it is worse than ridiculous for you to pretend you do not know the meaning of 'quite up to date,' when it is not only transparently on the surface, but obvious. Ask anyone. Ask my Aunt Priscilla. Ask Mrs. Verity." The lady had much better have stopped here. But she wished to class her landlady amongst the lower intelligences, so she must needs add, somewhat in the rear of her enumeration, in a quick *sotto voce*, " Ask the girl Sairah, for that matter ! "

" What's that ? " said her husband curtly.

" You heard what I said."

" Oh yes, I heard what you *said*. Well—suppose I ask the girl Sairah ! "

" Reginald ! If you are determined to make yourself and your wife ridiculous, I shall go. I do think that, even if you have no common sense, you might have a little good feeling. The girl Sairah ! The idea ! " She collected herself a little more— some wandering scraps were out of bounds—and went almost away, just listening back on the staircase landing.

Now, although an impish intention may have flickered in the mind of Mr. Reginald Aiken, he certainly had no definite idea of catechizing the girl Sairah about the phrase under discussion when he rang the bell for her and summoned her to the Studio. But his wife having taken him *au sérieux* instead of laughing at his absurdity, the impish intention flared up, and had not time to die down

before Sairah answered the bell. Would it have
done so if he had not been conscious that his wife
was still standing at pause on the staircase to keep
an eye on the outcome?

So, when Sairah lurched into his sanctum, asking
whether he rang—not without suggestion that
offence would be given by an affirmative answer—
his real intention in summoning the damsel wavered
at the instigation of the spirit of mischief that had
momentary possession of him; and instead of blow-
ing her up roundly for damaging his picture, he
actually must needs ask her the very question his
wife had said "The idea!" about. He spoke loud,
that his speech should reach that lady's listening
ears.

"Yes, Sairah: I rang for *you*. What is the
meaning of . . . ?" He paused a moment, to
overhear, if possible, some result of his words in the
passage.

"It's nothin' along o' me. *I* ain't done nothin'."
A brief sketch of a blameless life, implied in these
words, seemed to Sairah the safest policy. She
thought she was going to be indicted for the ruin
of the picture.

"Shut up, Sairah!" said the Artist, and listened.
Of course, he was doing this, you see, to plague his
wife. But he heard nothing, being nevertheless
mysteriously aware that Mrs. Aiken was still on the

landing above, taking mental notes of what she overheard. So he pursued his inquiry, regarding Sairah as a mere lay-figure of use in practical joking. "I expect you know the meaning of 'up to date,' Sairah," said he, and listened. But no sign came from without. If the ears this pleasantry was intended to reach were still there, their owner was storing up retribution for its author in silence.

It was but natural that this young woman Sairah, having no information on any topic whatever—for this condition soon asserts itself in young women of her class after their Board-School erudition has had time to die a natural death—should be apt to ascribe sinister meanings to things she did not understand. And in this case none the less for the air and aspect of the speaker, which, while it really was open to the misinterpretation that it was intended to convey insinuating waggery to the person addressed, had only reference to the enjoyment Mr. Aiken had, or was proposing to himself, from a mild joke perpetrated at his wife's expense. However, the young woman was not going to fly out—an action akin to the showing of a proper spirit—without an absolute certainty of the point to be flown out about. Therefore Sairah said briefly, "Ask your parding!" Briefly, but with a slight asperity.

The Artist, though he was in some doubt whether his jest was worth proceeding with, was too far com-

mitted to retreat. With his wife listening on the
stairs, was he not bound to pursue his inquiry?
Obviously he must do so, or run the risk of being
twitted with his indecision by that lady later on.
So he said, with effrontery, "Your mistress says
you can tell me the meaning of the expression 'up
to date,' Sairah."

Sairah turned purple. "Well, I never!" said
she. "Mrs. Aching to say that of a respectable
girl!"

Mr. Aiken became uncomfortable, as Sairah turned
purple. He began to perceive that his jest was a
very stupid one. As Sairah turned purpler, he
became more uncomfortable still. A panic-stricken
review of possible ways out of the difficulty started
in his mind, but soon stopped for want of materials.
Explanation—cajolery—severe transition to another
topic—he thought of all three. The first was simply
impossible to reasoning faculties like Sairah's. The
second was out of Mr. Aiken's line. If the girl had
been a *model* now! . . . And who can say that
then it might not have been ticklish work—yes!—
even with the strong personal vanity of that inscrutable class to appeal to? There was nothing
for it but the third, and Mr. Aiken's confidence in
it was very weak. Something had to be done,
though, with Sairah's colour *crescendo,* and probably
Mrs. Hay outside the door; that was the image his

mind supplied. He felt like an ill-furnished storm-
ing-party, a forlorn hope in want of a ladder, as he
said, "There—never mind that now! You've been
meddling with this picture. You know you have.
Look here!" Had he been a good tactician, he
would have affected sudden detection of the injury
to the picture. But he lost the opportunity.

Sairah held the strong position of an Injured
Woman. If she was to have the sack, she much
preferred to have it "on her own"—to wrest it, as
it were, from a grasp unwilling to surrender it—
rather than to have it forced upon her unwilling
acceptance, with a month's notice and a character
for Vandalism. So she repeated, as one still rigid
with amazement, "Mrs. Aching to say that of a
respectable girl!" and remained paralyzed, in dumb
show.

Mr. Aiken perceived with chagrin that he might
have saved the situation by, "What's this horrible
mess on the picture? *You've* been touching this!"
and a drowning storm of indignation to follow. It
was too late now. He had to accept his task as
Destiny set it, and he cut a very poor figure over it
—was quite outclassed by Sairah. He could
actually manage nothing better than, "Do let that
alone, girl! I tell you it was foolery. . . . I tell
you it was a joke. Look here at this picture—the
mischief you've done it. You *know* you did it!"

To which Sairah thus:—"Ho, it's easy gettin'
out of it that way, Mr. Aching. Not but what I
have always known you for the gentleman—I will
say that. But *such* a thing to say! If I'd a been
Missis, I should have shrank!"

The Artist felt that there was nothing for it but
to grapple with the situation. He shouted at the
indignant young woman, "Don't be such a confounded idiot, girl! I mean, don't be such an
insufferable goose. I tell you, you're under a complete misconception. Nobody's ever said anything
against you. Nobody's said a word against your
confounded character, and be hanged to it! Do
have a little common sense! A young woman of
your age ought to be ashamed to be such a fool."

But Sairah's entrenchments were strengthened,
if anything. "It's easy calling fool," said she.
"And as for saying against, who's using expressions,
and passing off remarks now?" Controversial
opponents incapable of understanding anything
whatever are harder to refute than the shrewdest
intellects. Mr. Aiken felt that Sairah was oak and
triple brass against logical conviction. Explanation
only made matters worse.

A vague desperate idea of summoning his wife
and accusing Sairah of intoxication, as a sort of
universal solvent, crossed his mind; and he actually
went so far as to look out into the passage for her,

but only to find that she had vanished for the moment. Coming back, he assumed a sudden decisive tone, saying, " There—that'll do, Sairah! Now go." But Sairah wasn't going to give in, evidently, and he added, " I mean, that's enough! "

Whether it was or wasn't, Sairah showed no signs of concession. *She* was going, no fear! She was going—ho yes!—she was going. She said she was going so often that Mr. Aiken said at last, " Well, go! " But when the young woman began to go vengefully, as it were—even as a quadruped suddenly stung by an ill-deserved whip—he inconsequently exclaimed, " Stop! " For a fell purpose had been visible in her manner. What, he asked, was she going to do?

What was she going to do? Oh yes!—it was easy asking questions. But the answer would reach Mr. Aiken in due course. Nevertheless, if he wanted to know, she would be generous and tell him. She wasn't an underhand girl, like the majority of her sex at her age. Mean concealments were foreign to her nature. She was going straight to Mrs. Aching to give a month's warning, and you might summing in the police to search her box. All should be above-board, as had been the case in her family for generations past, and she never had experienced such treatment all the places she'd been in, nor yet expected to it.

It was then that this Artist made a serious error of judgment. He would have done much more wisely to allow this stupid maid-of-all-work to go away and attend to some of it in the kitchen, while he looked after his own. Instead of doing so, he, being seriously alarmed at the possible domestic consequences of his very imperfectly thought out joke—for he knew his wife accounted the finding of a new handmaid life's greatest calamity—must needs make an ill-advised attempt to calm the troubled waters on the same line that he would have adopted, at any rate in his Bohemian days, with Miss de Lancey or Miss Montmorency—these names are chosen at random—whose professional beauty as models did not prevent their suffering, now and again, from tantrums. And cajolery, of the class otherwise known as blarney, might have smoothed over the incident, and the whole thing have been forgotten, if bad luck had not, just at this moment, brought back to the Studio the mistress of the house, who had only been attracted by a noise in the street to look out at a front-window. She, coming unheard within hearing, not only was aware of interchanges of unusual amiability between Reginald and that horrible girl Sairah, but was just in time to hear the latter say, "You keep your 'ands off of me now, Mr. Aching!" without any apparent intention of being taken at her word.

And, further, that the odious minx brazened it out,
leaving the room as if nothing had happened, before
the gentleman's offended wife could find words to
express her indignation. At least, so this lady told
her Aunt Priscilla that evening, in an interview
from which we have just borrowed some telling
phrases.

As for her profligate husband, it came out in the
same interview that he looked "sheepish to a
degree, and well he might." He had tried to cook
up a sort of explanation—"oh yes! a *sort*"—which
was no doubt an attempt on the misguided man's
part to tell the truth. But we have seen that he
was the last person to succeed in such an enterprise;
and, indeed, self-exculpation is tough work, even
for the guiltless. Fancy the fingers of reproachful
virtue directed at you from all points of the compass. And suppose, to make matters worse, you
had committed something—not a crime, you would
never do that; but something or other of a com-
mittable nature—what on earth could you do but
look sheepish to some degree or other? Unless,
indeed, you were a minx, and could brazen it out,
like that gurl.

Such a ridiculous and vulgar incident would not
be worth so much description, but that, like other
things of the same sort, it led to serious conse-

quences. A storm occurred in what had hitherto
been a haven of domestic peace, and the Artist's
wife carried out her threat, this time, of a visit to
her Aunt Priscilla. That good lady, being a spinster
of very limited experience, but anxious to make it
seem a wide one, dwelt upon her knowledge of mankind and its evil ways, and the hopelessness of un-
divided possession thereof by womankind. She had
told her niece " what it was going to be," when she
first learned that Mr. Aiken was an Artist. She
repeated what she had said before, that Artists'
wives had no idea what was going on under their
eyes. If they had, Artists would very soon be un-
provided with the raw material of proper infidelity.
They would have no wives, and would go on like in
Paris. This tale is absolutely irresponsible for Miss
Priscilla's informants; it only reports her words.

Now, Mrs. Euphemia Aiken, in spite of a severe
ruction with her husband, had really not consciously
imputed to him any transgression of a serious nature
when—as that gentleman worded it—she " flounced
away " to her Aunt Priscilla with an angry report
of how Reginald had insulted her. She had much
too high an opinion of him to form, on her own
account, a mental version of his conduct, such as
the one her excellent Aunt jumped at, in pursuance
of the establishment of a vile moral character for
Artists and nephews-in-law generally, with a con-

crete foundation in the case of an Artist-nephew—a
Centaur-like combination with a doubt which half
was which. But nothing is easier than to convince
any human creature that any other is twice, thrice,
four times as human as itself, in respect of what is
graceless or disgraceful—spot-stroke barred, of
course; meaning felony. So that after a long interview with Aunt Priscilla, this foolish woman cried
herself to sleep, having accepted the good lady's
offered hospitality, and was next morning so vigor-
ously urged to do scriptural things in the way of
forgiveness and submission to her husband—so Mil-
tonic, in fact, did the prevailing atmosphere become
—that she naturally sat down and wrote a healthily
furious letter to him. The tale may surmise that
she offered him Sairah as a consolation for what it
knows she proposed—her own withdrawal to a
voluntary grass-widowhood. For she flatly refused
to return to her deserted hearth. And, indeed, the
poor lady may have felt that her home had been
soiled and desecrated. But it was not only her
Aunt's impudent claim to superior knowledge—she
was still Miss Priscilla Bax, and of irreproachable
character—that had influenced her, but the recollection of Sairah. It would not have been half as
bad if it had been a distinguished young lady with
a swoop, like in a shiny journal she subscribed for
quarterly. But Sairah! That gurl! Visions of

Sairah's *coiffure;* of the way Sairah appeared to be
coming through, locally, owing to previousness on
the part of hooks which would not wait for their
own affinities, but annexed the very first eye that
appealed to them; of intolerable stockings she
overlooked large holes in, however careful she see
to 'em when they come from the Wash; of her
chronic pocket-handkerchief—all these kept floating
before her eyes and exasperating her sense of insult
and degradation past endurance. Perhaps the
worst and most irritating thought was the extent to
which she had stooped to supplement this maid's
all-work by efforts of her own, without which their
small household could scarcely have lived within
its limited means. No!—let Reginald grill his own
chops now, or find another Sairah!

It was illustrative of the unreality of this ruction
that the lady took it as a matter of course that
Sairah would accept the sack in the spirit in which
it was given; for official banishment of the culprit
was her last act on leaving the house. No idea
entered her head that her husband had the slightest
personal wish to retain Sairah.

As for him, he judged it best to pay the girl her
month's wages and send her packing. He removed
her deposit of flue from the picture-varnish, and in
due time completed the job and sent it off to its
destination. He fell back provisionally on his old

bachelor ways, making his own bed and slipping
slowly down into Chaos at home, but getting well
fed either by his friends or at an Italian restaurant
near by—others being beyond his means or fraught
with garbage—and writing frequent appeals to his
wife not to be an Ass, but to come back and be jolly.
She opened his letters, and read them, and more
than once all but started to return to him—would
have done so, in fact, if her excellent Aunt had not
pointed out, each time, that it was the Woman's
duty to forgive. Which she might have gone the
length of accepting, but for its exasperating sequel,
" and submit herself to her husband."

But neither he nor either of the other actors in
this drama had the slightest idea that it had been
witnessed by any eyes but those of its performers.

CHAPTER II

OLD Mr. Pelly is the little grey-headed wrinkled man with gold spectacles whom you have seen in London bookshops and curio-stores in late August and early September, when all the world has been away; the little old man who has seemed to you to have walked out of the last century but one. You may not have observed him closely enough at the moment to have a clear recollection of details, but you will have retained an image of knee-breeches and silk stockings; of something peculiar in the way of a low-crowned hat; of a watch and real seals; of a gold snuff-box you would have liked to sell for your own benefit; and of an ebony walking-stick with a silver head and a little silk tassel. On thinking this old gentleman over you will probably feel sorry you did not ask him a question about Mazarine Bibles or Aldus Manutius, so certain were you he would not have been rude.

But you did not do so, and very likely he went back to Grewceham, in Worcestershire, where he lives by himself, and you lost your opportunity that time. However that may be, it is old Mr. Pelly our story has to do with now, and he is sitting before a wood-fire out of all proportion to the little dry old thing it was lighted to warm, and listening to the roaring of the wind in the big chimney of the library he sits in.

But it is not his own library. That is at Grewceham, two miles off. This library is the fine old library at Surley Stakes, the country-seat of Sir Stopleigh Upwell, M.P., whose father was at school with Mr. Pelly, over sixty years ago.

Mr. Pelly is stopping at " The Stakes," as it is called, to avoid the noise and fuss of the little market-town during an election. And for that same reason has not accompanied Sir Stopleigh and his wife and daughter to a festivity consequent on the return of that very old Bart. for the County. They will be late back; so Mr. Pelly can do no better than sit in the firelight, rejecting lamps and candles, and think-ing over the translation of an Italian manuscript, in fragments, that his friend Professor Schrudengesser has sent him from Florence. It has been supposed to have some connection with the cinque-cento por-trait by an unknown Italian artist that hangs above the fire-blaze. And this portrait is the one the story

saw a little over six months since, in the atelier
of that picture-cleaner, who managed to brew a
quarrel with his wife by his own silliness and bad
taste.

It is only dimly visible in the half-light, but Mr.
Pelly knows it is there; knows, too, that its eyes
can see him, if a picture's eyes can see, and that its
laugh is there on the parted lips, and that its
jewelled hand is wound into the great tress of gold
that falls on its bosom. For it is a portrait of a
young and beautiful woman, such as Galuppi Bal-
dassare wrote music about—you know, of course!
And Mr. Pelly, as he thinks what it will look like
when Stebbings, the butler, or his myrmidons bring
in lights, feels chilly and grown old.

But Stebbings' instructions were distinctly not to
bring in lights till Mr. Pelly rang, and Mr. Pelly
didn't ring. He drank the cup of coffee Stebbings
had provided, without putting any Cognac in it, and
then fell into a doze. When he awoke, with a start
and a sudden conviction that he indignantly fought
against that he had been asleep, it was to find that
the log-flare had worn itself out, and the log it fed
on was in its decrepitude. Just a wavering irresolute flame on its saw-cut end, and a red glow, and
that was all it had left behind.

" Who spoke ? " It was Mr. Pelly who asked the
question. But no one had spoken, apparently.

Yet he would have sworn that he heard a woman's voice speaking in Italian. How funny that the associations of an Italian manuscript should creep into his dream!—that was all Mr. Pelly thought about it. For the manuscript was almost entirely English rendering, and no one in it, so far as he could recollect, had said as this voice did, "Good-evening, Signore!" It was a dream! He polished his spectacles and watched the glowing log that bridged an incandescent valley, and wondered what the sudden births of little intense white light could be that came and lived on nothing and vanished, unaccounted for. He knew Science knew, and would ask her, next time they met. But, for now, he would be content to sit still, and keep watch on that log. It must break across the middle soon, and collapse into the valley in a blaze of sparks.

Watching a fire, without other light in the room, is fraught with sleep to one who has lately dined, even if he has a pipe or cigar in his mouth to burn him awake when he drops it. Much more so to a secure non-smoker, like Mr. Pelly. Probably he *did* go to sleep again—but who can say? He really believed himself wide-awake, though, when the same voice came again; not loud, to be sure, but unmistakable. And the way it startled him helped to convince him he was awake. Because one is never surprised at anything in a dream. When one finds oneself at Church in a stocking, and nothing more, one is vexed and embarrassed, certainly, but not surprised. It dawns on one gradually. If this *was* a dream, it was a very solid one, to survive Mr. Pelly's start of amazement. It brought him out of his chair, and set him looking about in the half-lighted room for a speaker, somewhere.

"Who are you, and *where* are you?" said he. For there was no one to be seen. The firelight flickered on the portraits of Sir Stephen Upwell, the Cavalier, who was killed at Naseby, and Marjory, his wife, who was a Parliamentarian fanatic; and a phenomenal trout in a glass case, with a picture behind it showing the late Baronet in the distance striving to catch it; but the door was shut, and Mr. Pelly was alone in the library. He was rather frightened at his own voice in the stillness; it sounded like delirium. So it made him happier that an answer should come, and justify it.

"I am here, before you. Look at me! I am La Risvegliata—that is what you call me, at least." This was spoken in Italian, but it must be translated in the story. Very likely you understand Italian, but remember how many English do not. Mr. Pelly spoke Italian fluently—he spoke many languages—but *he* must be turned into English, too, for the same reason.

"But *you* are a picture," said he. "You cannot speak." For he understood then that his hallucination—as he thought it, believing himself awake—was that the picture-woman over the mantelpiece had spoken to him. He felt indignant with himself for so easily falling a victim to a delusion; and transferred his indignation, naturally, to the blameless phantom of his own creation. Of course, he had *imagined* that the picture had spoken to him. For " La Risvegliata "—the awakened one—was the name that had been written on the frame at the wish of the Baronet's daughter, when a few months back he brought this picture, by an unknown artist, from Italy.

"I can speak "—so it replied to Mr. Pelly—" and you can hear me, as I have heard you all speaking about me, ever since I came to this strange land. Any picture can hear that is well enough painted."

"*Why* have you never spoken before? " Mr. Pelly was dumbfounded at the unreasonableness of the position. A speaking picture was bad enough; but, at least, it might be rational. He fell in his own good opinion, at this inconsistency of his distempered fancy.

"Why have you never listened? I have spoken many a time. How do I know why you have not heard? " Mr. Pelly could not answer, and the voice

continued, "Oh, how I have longed and waited for
one of you to catch my voice! How I have cried
out to the wooden *Marchese* whose *Marchesa* will
not allow him to speak, and to that beautiful Signora
herself, and to that sweet daughter most of all.
Oh, why—why—have they not heard me?" But
still Mr. Pelly was slow to answer. He found something to say, though, in the end.

"I can entertain no reasonable doubt that your
voice is a fiction of my imagination. But you will
confer a substantial favour on me if you will take
advantage of it, while my hallucination lasts, to tell
me the name of your author—of the artist who
painted you."

"*Lo Spazzolone* painted me."

"*Lo* . . . who?"

"*Lo Spazzolone.* Surely, all men have heard of
him. But it is his nickname—the big brush—from
his great bush of black hair. Ah me!—how beautiful it was!"

"Could you give me his real name, and tell me
something about him?" Mr. Pelly took from his
pocket a notebook and pencil.

"Giacinto Boldrini, of course!"

"Ought I to know him? I have never heard his
name."

"How strange! And it is but the other day that
he was murdered—oh, so foully murdered! But

no!—I am wrong, and I forget. It is near four
hundred years ago."

Mr. Pelly was deeply interested. The question
of whether this was a dream, a hallucination, or a
vision, or the result of exceeding by two ounces his
usual allowance of glasses of Madeira, he could not
answer offhand. Besides, there would be plenty of
time for that after. His present object should be
to let nothing slip, however much he felt convinced
of its illusory character. It could be sifted later.
He would be passive, and not allow an ill-timed
incredulity to mar a good delusion in the middle.
He switched off scepticism for the time being, and
spoke sympathetically.

"Is it possible? Did you know him? But of
course you must have known him, or he could
scarcely have painted you. Dear me!" Mr. Pelly
checked a disposition to gasp; that would never
do—he might wake himself up, and spoil all. The
sweet voice of the picture—it was like a voice, mind
you, not like a gramophone—was prompt with its
reply:

"I knew him well. But, oh, so long ago! One
gets to doubt everything—all that was most real
once, that made the very core of our lives. Sometimes I think it was a dream—a sweet dream with
terror at the end—a nectar cup a basilisk was
watching, all the while. Four hundred years!

Can I be sure it was true? Yet I remember it all —could tell it now and miss nothing."

Mr. Pelly was silent a moment before answering. He reflected that if his reply led to a circumstantial narrative of events four hundred years old, it would be a bitter disappointment to be waked by the return of the family, and to have it all spoiled. However, it was only ten o'clock, and they might be three hours yet. Besides, it was well known that dreams have no real duration— are in fact compressed into a second or so of waking. He would risk it.

"I have a keen interest, Signora," said he, "in the forgotten traditions of antiquity. It would indeed be a source of satisfaction to me if you would consider me worthy of your confidence, and entrust to me some portion at least of your family history, and that of your painter. I can assure you that no portion of what you tell me shall be published without your express permission. No one can detest more keenly than myself the modern American practice of intrusion into private life. . . ." He stopped. Surely that sound was a sigh, if not a sob. In a moment the voice of the picture came again, but with even more of sadness in it than before:

"Was it antiquity, then, in those days? We did not know it then. We woke to the day that

was to come—that had not been, before—even as
you do now; and the voices of yesterday were not
forgotten in our ears. We flung aside the thing of
the hour; as you do now, with little thought of
what we lost, and lived alone for hope, and the
things that were to be. I cannot tell you how
young we were then. And remember! I am
twenty now; as I was then, and have been, ever
since."

"I see," said Mr. Pelly. "Your original was
twenty when you were painted. And you naturally
remained twenty." He felt rather prosaic and dry,
and to soften matters added, "Tell me of your
first painting, and what is earliest in your recollection."

"Then you will not interrupt me?" Mr. Pelly
gave a promise the voice seemed to wait for, and
then it continued, and, as it seemed to the listener,
told the tale that follows, which is printed as continuous. The only omissions are a few interruptions of Mr. Pelly's, which, so far as they were
inquiries or points he had not understood, are made
up for by very slight variations in the text,
which he himself has sanctioned, as useful and
explanatory.

Whether he was awake or dreaming, he never
rightly knew. But his extraordinary memory—
he is quite a celebrity on this score—enabled him

to write the whole down in the course of the next day or two, noting his own interruptions, now omitted.

The most rational way of accounting for the occurrence undoubtedly is that the old gentleman had a very vivid dream, suggested by his having read several pages—this he admits—of the manuscript translation, in which a too ready credulity has detected a sequel to the story itself. None knows better than the student of alleged supernatural phenomena how frequent is this confusion of cause and effect.

CHAPTER III

You ask me to tell you what is earliest in my
recollection. I will do so, and will also endeavour
to narrate as much as I can remember of the life of
the lady I was painted from; whose memory, were
she now living, would be identical with my
own.

The very first image I can recall is that of my
artist, at work. He is the first human being I ever
saw, as well as the first visible object I can call to
mind. He is at work—as I am guided to under-

stand by what I have learned since—upon my right
eye. It is a very dim image indeed at the outset,
but as he works it becomes clearer, and at last I see
him quite plainly.

He is a dark young man, with hair of one thick-
ness all over, like a black door-mat, and a beautiful
olive skin. As he turns round I think to myself
how beautiful his neck is at the back under the hair,
and that I should like to kiss it. But that is
impossible. I can recall my pleasure at his fixed
gaze, and constant resolute endeavour. Naturally
I want him to paint my other eye. Then I shall see
him still better.

I am not surprised at his saying nothing—for
remember!—I did not know what speech was then.
He had painted my mouth, only, of course, I did
not know what to do with it. Needless also to say
that I had not heard a word, for I had no ear at all.
I have only one now, but it has heard all that has
been spoken near it for four hundred years. I
heard nothing then—nothing at all! I only gazed
fixedly at the fascinating creature before me who
was trying his best to make *me* beautiful too—to
make me as beautiful as something that I could not
see—something his eyes turned round to at intervals,
something to my right and his left. What I recall
most vividly now is my curiosity to know what this
thing or person was that took his eyes off me at

odd moments; to which he made, now and again, slight deprecatory signs and corrective movements with his left hand; from which he received some response I could not guess at, which he acknowledged by a full-spread smile of grateful recognition. But always in perfect silence, though I saw, when his brush was not in front of my incomplete eye, that his lips moved, showing his beautiful white teeth; and that he paused and listened—a thing I have learned about since—with a certain air of deference, as towards a social superior. Oh, how I longed to see this unseen being, or thing! But I was not to do so, yet awhile.

My recollection goes no farther than the fact of this young artist, working on in a strange, systematic way, quite unlike what I have since understood to be the correct method for persons of genius, until at the end of some period I cannot measure, he paints my other eye, and I rejoice in a clearer image of himself; of the huge bare room he works in; of the small window, high up, with its cage of grating against the sky; of the recess below it, in which, at the top of two steps, an old woman sits plaiting straws, and beside her a black dog, close shaved, except his head, all over. But I get no light upon the strange attraction that takes my creator's attention off me, until after a second experience, as strange as my first new-found phenomenon of sight—to wit, my hearing of sound. As he painted my ear, it came.

At first, a musical, broken murmur—then another, that mixes with it. As one rises, the other falls; then both together, or as the threads of a cascade cross and intersect in mid-air. Then a third sound, a sound with a musical ring that makes my heart leap with joy—a sound that comes back to me now, when in the early mornings of summer, I hear, through the window of this room opened outwards to let in the morning air, the voice of the little brown bird that springs high into the blue heaven, and unpacks its tiny heart in a flood of song. And then I think to myself that *that* is the language in which I too should have laughed, had laughter been possible to me.

For what I heard then from behind the easel I stood on as the young artist painted me was the laughter of Maddalena Raimondi, from whom he was working; whom I may describe myself as being. For ought not the name written on the frame below me to be hers also, with the date of her birth and death? Are not my eyes that I see with now hers? Is not the nostril with the lambent curve—that is what a celebrated Art-Critic has called it—hers, and the little sea-shell ear hers that heard you say, but now, that my original cannot have been more than twenty? . . .

More than twenty! No, indeed!—for in those days a girl of twenty was a woman. And the girl that one day a little later came round at a signal from behind the panel, to see the portrait that I now knew had received its last touch from its maker, was one who at eighteen had been threatened, driven, goaded into harness with an old Devil of high rank, to whom she had been affianced in her babyhood; and who is now, we may hope, in his proper Hell, as God has appointed. Yet it may well be he is among the Saints; for his wealth was great, and he gave freely to Holy Church. But to Maddalena, that was myself—for was I not she?— he was a Devil incarnate.

For mark you this: that all she had known I too knew, in my degree, so soon as ever I was completed. Else had I been a bad portrait. It all came to my memory at once. I remembered my happy girl-hood, the strange indifference of my utter innocence when I was first told I was destined to marry the great Duke, whose vassal my father was, and how my marriage would somehow—I am, maybe, less clear about details than my original would have been—release my father from some debt or obligation to the Raimondi which otherwise would have involved the forfeiture of our old home. So ignorant was I that I rejoiced to think that I should be the means of preserving for my family the long

stretches of vine-clad hills and the old Castello in the
Apennines that had borne our name since the first
stone was laid, centuries ago. So ignorant, innocent,
indifferent—call it what you will!—that the moment
I was told my destiny I went straight to Giacinto,
the page, with whom I had grown from infancy, to
tell him the good news, that he might rejoice too.
But he would not rejoice at my bidding, and he
was moody and reserved, and I wondered. I was
but twelve and he thirteen. Although a girl may
be older than a boy, even at those years, her eyes are
not so wide open to see some things, and it may be
he saw plainer than I. I know not.

This, then, was what had happened to the beautiful
creature that came round into my sight on that day
that I first saw and heard and knew her for myself,
and hoped I was well done, and very like. And
thus, also, it all came back to me, so soon as I was
finished and was really Maddalena Raimondi, how
the great Venetian artist, Angelo Allori, whom
they called *Il Bronzino,* came to the Castello to
paint my mother, and how he took a fancy to
Giacinto, and would have him away to his studio,
and taught him how to use brushes and colours, and
how to grind and prepare these last, and to make
canvas ready for the painter. And it ended by his
taking him as an apprentice, at his own wish and
Giacinto's. And they went away together to

Venice, and I could recall now that Maddalena had
not seen Giacinto after that for six years.

That is to say: she had not seen him till he came
to the Villa Raimondi in the first year of her unhappy marriage, an unhappy bride with all the
deadly revelation of the realities of life that an
accursed wedlock must needs bring. The girl was
no longer a girl; she knew what she had lost. And
I knew it too, and all that she had known up to the
moment of that last brush-touch, when Giacinto said,
" Now, *carissima Signora,* you may come round and
see ! "

And the ringing laugh came round, and *she* came
round, that had been me. Then I too saw what I
had been—what I was still. And after that, I will
tell you what I saw and heard—but presently!

For I want you first to know what Maddalena
was when her old owner told her that he had com-
manded a young Venetian artist, of rising fame, to
come at once, under penalty of his displeasure, to
paint her portrait in a dress of yellow satin brocade
well broidered in gold thread, and a *gorgiera* of fine
linen turned back over it, that had belonged to his
first wife, Vittoria Fanfani, who was much of the
size and shape of la Maddalena, as who could
tell better than he ? And for this portrait she was
to sit or stand, as the painter should arrange, in
front of the tapestry showing Solomon's Judgment

in the *Stanza delle Quattro Corone;* which is, as you
would say, The Room of the Four Crowns, so called
because it was said four Kings had met there in old
days, three of whom had slain the fourth, which
was accounted of great fame to the Castello Raimondi.   And the time for this painting was to be
each day after the sun had passed the meridian;
for the room looked southeast, and one must study
the sun.   And Marta Zan would always be in
attendance, as a serious person who would keep a
check on any pranks such young people might
choose to play.   For as I too now knew and could
well remember, it was a wicked touch of this old
birbante's character that he was never tired of a
wearisome pretence that this young Maddalena,
whose heart was truly broken if ever girl's heart
was, was still full of joyousness and youth and
kittenish tricks.   And he would rally her waggishly
before his retinue for pranks she had never played,
and pretended youthful escapades she could have
had no heart for.   For in truth she was filled up
with sorrow, and shame of herself and her kind, and
intense loathing of the old man her master; but
she was forced to reply to his unwelcome *badinage*
by such pretence as might be of gaiety in return.
And this, although she knew well all the while that
there was not a scullion among them all but could
say how little she loved this eighty-year-old lord

of hers; though none could guess, not even the women, what good cause she had to hate him.

But the sly old fox knew well enough; and when he made his edict that Marta Zan—an old crone, who had been, some said, his mistress in his youth —should keep watch and ward over his young wife's demeanour with this new painting fellow, he knew too that in the thick wall of the *Stanza delle Quattro Corone* was a little, narrow entry, where one might lie hid at any time, approaching from without, and see all that passed in the chamber below. And so he would see and know for himself; for he knew Marta Zan too well to place much faith in her.

You may guess, then, that Maddalena, when *il Duca* first informed her of his gracious pleasure about the portrait, was little inclined to take an interest in that, or any other scheme of his Highness; but to avoid incurring his resentment, she was bound to affect an interest she did not feel, and in this she succeeded, so far as was necessary. But my lord Duke was growing suspicious of her; only he was far too wily an old fox to show his mistrust openly. Be sure that when, after Maddalena's first sitting with my young artist, he noticed that the roses had returned to her cheeks, and that her step was light again upon the ground, he said never a word to show his thought, and only resolved in

his wicked old heart to spy upon the two young
people from his cyrie in the wall.

It was little to be wondered at that Maddalena
should show pleasure when she saw who after all
was the young Venetian painter; who, still almost
a boy, had climbed so high in fame that it was
already held an honour to be painted by him. For
he was her old friend Giacinto, and she in her languid
lack of interest in all about her, had never asked
what was the actual name of *Lo Spazzolone*. For
by this nickname only had he been spoken of in her
presence, and it may easily be he was known by no
other to the old *Duca* himself, so universal is the
practice of nicknaming among the artists of Italy.
But he was Giacinto himself, sure enough!—only
grown so tall and handsome. And you may fancy
how gladly the poor Maddalena would have flung
her arms round the boy she had known from her
cradle, and kissed her welcome into his soul—only
there! was she not a wife, and the wife too of the
thing men called the Duke? What manner of
thing was he, that God should have made him, there
in the light of day?

But if it was difficult for Maddalena to keep her
embrace of welcome in check, you may fancy how
strong a constraint my young painter had to put on
himself when he saw who the great lady was whom
he was come to paint. For none had told him,

and till she came suddenly upon him in all the beauty of her full and perfect womanhood, he had no idea that she would be la Maddalena—*la sua sorellaccia* (that is, his ugly sister), as he would call her in jest in those early days—because there was no doubt of her beauty, and the joke was a safe one. Only mind you!—this would be when they were alone, as might be, in the court of the old Castello, looking down into the deep well and dropping stones to hear them splash long after, or gathering the green figs in the *poderi* when the great heat was gone from August, and they could ramble out in the early mornings. When her sisters or brothers were there, she was *la Signorina* Maddalena. *I* can remember it all now! One does not lightly forget these hours —the hours before the ugly dawn of the real World. Nor the little joys one takes as a right, without a rapture or a thought of gratitude; nor the little pangs one thinks so hard to bear, and so soon forgets.

If you should ask me how it came about that the two of them should have so completely parted during all those six years, that la Maddalena should not even have known the nickname of the young painter, nor his fame, I must beg that you will remember that these were not the days of daily posts, of telegraphs, and railways; nor of any of the strange new things I hear of now, and find so hard to understand. Moreover, my own opinion is that the parents of Maddalena judged shrewdly that this young stripling was no friend to be encouraged for a little daughter that was to be the salvation of their property. The less risk, the less danger! The fewer boys about, the fewer fancies of a chit. They managed it all, be sure of that! It was for the girl's own best interest.

But—dear me! *—if you know anything of life in youth, and of the golden thread of Love that is shot through it in the weft, and starts out somewhere always, here or there, whatever light you hold it in—if you know this, there is no more to be said of why, when they met again, in the *Stanza delle Quattro Corone,* each heart should leap out to meet the other, and then shrink back chilled, at the thought of what they were now that they were not once, and of what perforce they had to be hereafter. But the moment was their own, and none pauses in the middle of a draught of nectar because, forsooth, the cup will soon be empty. La Maddalena became, in one magic instant, a Maddalena whose laugh rang out like the song of the little brown bird I told you of but now, and filled the wicked old room with its music. And as for our

---

* Probably the words Mr. Pelly heard were "*Dio mio!*" which some consider the original of the English "Dear me!" Many of the expressions are evidently literal translations.—EDITOR.

poor Giacinto—well!—are you a man, and were you ever young? He could promise the withered old *Duca* that he would make a merry picture of *la Duchessa;* none of your sinister death's-head portraits, but with the smile of *sua Altezza.* For all Maddalena's heart was in her face, and that face wore again the smile of the old, old days, the days long before her bridal. And you see that face before you now.

Now, if only this old shrunken mummy will begone! If he will only go away to count over his gold, to rack his tenantry for more than his share of the oil-crop, to get absolution for his sins, or, better still, to go to expiate them in the proper place! If he will only take his venerable presence and his cold firm eye away—if it be but for an hour! . . .

He went—sooner than we had hoped. And then when he was quite, quite gone, and the coast was clear, then the laughter broke out. And Marta Zan wondered was this really the new *Duchessa?* —she who had brought from her bridal no smile but a sad one, no glance unhaunted by the memory or the forecast of a tear, no word of speech but had its own resonance of a broken heart. The beldam chuckled to herself, and saw money to come of it, if she winked skilfully enough, and at the right time. But in this she was wrong, for she judged these

young people by her bad old self; and indeed they
thought no harm of her sort. Neither could she
see their souls, nor they hers. But the laughter
and the voices filled the place, and each felt a child
again, and back in the old Castello in the hills.

"And was it really you, Giacinto? You, your
very self—the little Giacintino grown so great a
man! *Dio mio,* how great a man you have grown!"

"And was the *Duchessa* then *la nostra* Maddalena,
grown to be a great Signora! Was it all true?"

And then old Marta scowled from the steps below
the window, for was not this saucy young painter
bold enough to kiss the little hand her mistress let
him hold so long; and most likely she was ready
enough to guess that the poor boy had much ado
to be off kissing the lips that smiled on him as well.
But then, when the Maddalena saw through his
heart, and saw all this as plain as I tell it you now,
she flinched off with a little sigh, and a chill came.
For now, she said, they were grown-up people,
responsible and serious, and must behave! And
Marta Zan would not be cross; for look you, Marta
cara, was not this Giacinto, her foster-brother, and
had they not been rocked to sleep in the same
cradle? And had they not eaten the grapes of a
dozen vintages at her father's little castle on the
hill, and heard the dogs bark all across the plain
below in the summer nights?

So Marta, though she looked mighty glum over it, kept her thoughts for her own use, with due consideration how she might get most profit from what she foresaw, and yet keep her footing firm with her great Duke. She was a cunning old black spot, was Marta, and quick to scheme her own advantage, for all she was near seventy. But she saw no reason for meddling to check her young *Duchessa's* free flow of spirits, and she invented a good apology for letting her alone. *She* was not going to mar the portrait by making the sitter cry and look sulky: red eyes and swelled cheeks were no man's joy. So she told her employer. And she thought to herself, see how content the old man is, and how clever am I to hoodwink him so!

Be sure, though, that she did not know how he was passing his time, more and more, in that little chapel of knavery in the wall, but a few yards from the two happy young folk, as they laughed and talked over their old days. Only in this, you may believe me, that never a word passed between them —for all that so many came to the lips of both and were disallowed—that might not have been spoken, almost, in the presence of the gracious Duke himself —nay, quite!—if he had not been so corrupt and tainted an old curmudgeon that he would have found a scutch on the leaf of a lily new-blown, and read dishonour into innocence itself. So there he

sits in his evil eyrie, day by day, hatching false
interpretation of every word and movement, but
all silence and caution, for come what may he will
not spoil the portrait. It will be time enough when
it is quite done. Time enough for what? We shall
see. Meanwhile, as well to keep his eye on them!
Small trust to be placed in Marta Zan!

So, all this while, I grew and grew. And the
laugh that you see on my lips is Maddalena's as she
sat looking down on her young painter, and the joy
and content of my eyes are her joy and content;
and the loose lock of hair that ripples, a stream of
golden red, over the red-gold of the brocaded
gilliflower on the bosom of my bodice, is the lock of
hair Maddalena had almost told Giacinto he might
cut away and take, to keep for her sake. But she
dared not, because of that dried old fig, old Marta,
and the grim eye of her owner. Yet she might
never see Giacinto again! She suspected, in her
heart, that he would be schemed away from her once
more, as before.

But I grew and grew. And now the hour is near
when no pretence can prolong the sittings that have
been the happiness—the more than happiness—of
six whole Autumn weeks. How quick they had
run away! Could it be six weeks! Yes, it was.
And there was an ugly, threatening look in the
Duke's old eye; but he said little enough. No

doubt *Messer il Pittore* knew best how long was
needed to paint a portrait; but he had said three
weeks, at the outset. So it must needs be. And
this, to-day, was the last sitting; and the picture
—that was I—would be complete, and have a
frame, and hang on the wall in the great room of
state, where already were hanging the two portraits
of the former wives of his Excellency; whereof the
last one died three years before, and left the old
miscreant free to affiance himself to the little Maddalena, who was then too young to marry, being but
fourteen years old. So at least said her mother,
and his Excellency was gracious enough to defer
his nuptials, in spite of his years. And our most
Holy Father Pope Innocent was truly convinced
by this that the charge of the Duke's enemies made
against him of having poisoned his second wife was
groundless. For with so young a bride in view,
would not any man have deferred poisoning a lady
who was still young and comely, at least until the
object of his new passion was old enough to take
her place? So said his Holiness, and for my part
I think he showed in this his penetration and his
wide insight and understanding of his fellow-men.
For man is, as saith Scripture, created in the Image
of God, and it is but seemly and reasonable that
His Vicar on Earth should know the inner secrets
of the human heart; albeit he may have small

experience himself of Love, as is the manner of Ecclesiastics.

I will now tell you all I saw on that day of the last sitting, being now as it were full-grown and able to see and note all; besides being, as I have tried to show, able to feel all the lady Maddalena had felt and to follow her inmost thought.

When they were come to the end of the work I could see that both were heavy at heart for the parting that was to come; and I knew of myself that Maddalena had slept little, and I knew, too, that this was not because *sua Eccellenza* the Duke snored heavily all night, for had that been so, poor Maddalena would have been ill off for sleep at the best of times. No!—she had lain awake thinking of Giacinto; and he of her, it may be. But what do I know? I could see he was not happy: could you expect it? And his hand shook, and he did no good to me. And he would not touch my face and hands with the colour, and I well knew why.

Therefore, when he had tried for a little and could not work to any purpose, my lady *la Duchessa* says, as one who takes courage—for neither had yet spoken of how they must part—"Come, my Giacinto, let us be of better cheer, and not be so downcast. For who knows but the good God may let us meet again one happy day when His will is?

Let us be grateful for the little hour of our felicity, and make no complaint now that it was not longer. But you cannot work, my Giacinto, and are doing no good to the beautiful picture. Leave it and come and sit here by me, and we will talk of the old days, the dear old time. And as for the old Marta, she is sound asleep and snoring; only not so loud as my old pig of a husband all last night!" Indeed, it was true of old Marta, but for my own part I think she was only pretending to be asleep, for my Maddalena had talked to her of how this would be the last time, and softened her, and given her ten Venetian ducats and a cap of lace. But, for the snoring of the old Duke, it had done some service; for the little joke about it had made Maddalena speak more cheerfully, and Giacinto could find a laugh for it, though he had little heart to laugh out roundly at anything. La Maddalena went near to make him, though! For she talked of how thirteen little puppies all came at once of three mothers, and she christened them all after the Blessed Apostles and Judas Iscariot, and every one was drowned or given away except Judas Iscariot; and how she would hold up Judas for Giacinto to kiss, saying he was a safe Judas this time, as how could he be else with that little fat stomach, and not a month old.

So I was finished, and Giacinto would have put his signature in one corner had he not thought it

best to wait until *sua Eccellenza* the Duke had seen
it, for who could say he would not have it altered?
Messer Angelo Allori had finished a portrait of *la
Principessa* Gonzaga and just as he was thinking
to sign it, what does her ladyship do but say she
would rather have been painted in her *camorra di
seta verde,* and thereat he had to paint out the old
dress and paint in the new, for none might say nay
to *la Principessa.* So that is how it comes that
this picture—that I am—is unsigned; and that the
Art Critics, for once, are not unanimous about who
was the author.

But *I* know who that author was, and I can see
him still as he sits at the feet of his lady, *la Duchessa*
Maddalena, and his thick, black hair that had got
him the nickname of *Spazzolone;* which is, or
would be as speech goes now, the scrubbing-brush.
And I can see his beautiful olive-tinted throat,
more fair than tawny, like ivory, and his great black
eyes, like an antelope's. I can see her, la Maddalena,
seated above him—for he is on the ground—her
two white hands encircling her knees, with many
rings on them, one a great opal, the one you see on
my finger now; and her face, with the red-gold hair,
you see on my head, but somewhat fallen about it,
for it had shaken down; and the face it hedged in
was white—so white! It was not as you see me
now; rather, indeed, the face of the sad Maddalena

before ever she saw *Lo Spazzolone,* than mine as I
have it before you. Look awhile upon my face,
and then figure it to yourself as it would be if the
lips wanted to tremble, and the eyes to weep,
but neither would do so, from sheer courage and
strength of heart against an evil cloud. Then you
will see la Maddalena as she sat there with eyes
fixed on Giacinto, knowing each minute nearer the
end; but all the more taking each minute at the
most, as one condemned to die delays over his last
meal on earth. The gaoler will come, and the
prison-guard, and he knows it.

How long, do you ask me, did the pair sit thus,
the eyes of each devouring the face of the other;
the lips of each replying to the other in a murmured
undertone I could not have heard from where I
stood on my easel, had it not been that I too, myself,
was la Maddalena, and spoke her words and heard
his voice? I can only tell you the time seemed too
short—though it was none so short a time, neither!
But I do not know. I do know this, though—and
I wish you too to know it, that you may think no
thought of blame of my Maddalena—that never a
word passed her lips that any young wife might not
fairly and honestly speak to her husband's friend.
And scarce a word of his in return that might not
have been fairly and honestly spoken back; and
for such a slight forgetfulness, as it seemed to me,

of what was safe for both—will you not forgive the
poor boy? Remember, he was but a boy at best,
for all his marvellous skill. And was not his skill
marvellous? For look at my lips, and see how they
are drawn! Look at my eyes and say, have they
moved or not—or will they not move, in an instant?
Look at the little bright threads of gold in my cloud
of hair! And then say, was he not a wondrous
boy?

But a boy for all that! And to my thinking it
was *because* he was a boy, or was only just a man
having his manhood forced painfully upon him by
sorrow, that he gave the rein for one moment to his
tongue. And it was such a little moment, after all!
Listen and I will tell you, if you will not blame him.
Promise me!

They had talked, the two of them—or of us, as
you choose to have it—over and over of the old
days at the Castello, of the old Cappellano who
winked at all their misdeeds, and stood between
them and the anger of her parents, many a time.
How they had frightened him half to death by
making believe they had the Venetian plague upon
them, by dropping melted wax on their skins with
little strawberries in the middle. And how Giacinto
undeceived him by eating the strawberries. And
what nasty little monkeys they were in those days,
to be sure! That made them laugh, and they were

quite merry for a while. But then they got sad
again when la Maddalena told how Fra Poco—
that was what they called *il padre* Buti the Cappellano, for he was a little man—was the only one of
them all that had had a word to say against her
marriage, and how he had denounced her father one
day as for a crime, and invoked the vengeance of
God upon the old Duke's head for using his power
to defraud a young virgin of her life, and saying let
him have the lands and enjoy them as he would,
and rather go out and beg on the highways for alms
than sacrifice his own flesh and blood. And how
she had overheard all this speech of Fra Poco, and
had said to herself that, come what might, she would
save the old domain for her father and her brother.
And how that very day her brother, who was but
young, had beaten her with her own fan, and then
run away with it; and little he knew what she was
to suffer for him! But in truth *she* knew little
enough herself, for what does a girl-chit know!

And it may have been *her* fault, too, or mine, for
talking thus of her marriage, and none of the boy's
own, that my Giacinto should have, as I say, half
forgotten himself. For it was but just after she
had spoken thus, and they had sat sad and silent
for a space, that the big bells of San Felice hard by
must needs clang out suddenly in the evening air,
and then they knew their parting had come, too

soon, and that then they might never meet again.
And on that my Giacinto cried out as one whose
heaviness of heart is too sore to be borne, *" O sorellaccia mia! Mia carina—mio tesoro!* Oh, if it
might but be all a dream, and we might wake and
find it so, at the old Castello in the hills, and hear
the croaking of the frogs and the singing of the
nightingales when the sun had gone to bed, and be
punished for staying out too late to listen to them!
Oh, Maddalena *mia!*—the happy days when there
were no old Dukes! . . ." But la Maddalena
stopped him in his speech, saying, but as one says
words that choke in his throat, " Enough—enough,
Signore Giacinto! Remember what we are now—
remember what I am!—what you are!" For this,
said she, was not how *sua Eccellenza* the Duke should
be spoken of in his own house. And then the great
bells, that were so near they went nigh to deafen
you, stopped jangling; but the biggest had something to say still, a loud word at a time, and far
apart. And what he said was, that now the hour
had come, and they should meet no more. And
then he paused, and they thought he was silent.
But he came back suddenly once again, to cry out
" Never!" and was still.

Then comes the old Marta from her corner, rubbing
her eyes, for she had been very sound asleep. And
her mistress, as one who will not be contradicted,

points her on in front, and she passes out, and her black dog. Then says my Maddalena to the painter, " And now, farewell, my friend," and holds out her hand for him to kiss, for is she not the Duchess? And he kisses it without speech, but with a sort of sob, and she gathers up her train, and turns to go. But as she reaches the door, she hears behind her the voice that tries to speak, but cannot.

Then she turns, and her despair is white in her face. And Giacinto's eyes are in his hands—he dares not look up. But she goes back and he hears her, and his name as she speaks it. And then he looks up, and see!—they are locked in each other's arms, as though never to part. And then Maddalena knows, and I know with her, what Love is, and what Life might have been. To think now, at such a moment, of the abhorred caresses that must be endured, later! No, my Maddalena, nothing to be thought of now, nothing said, nothing seen nor heard, just for that few moments that will never come again!

That was so, and therefore neither of these imprudent young people heard the gasp or snarl of anger that came through the little slot in the wall above. Down comes my lord, unheard; reaches the room, unheard. But not alone! For there are behind him two of his retinue, rough troopers, buff-jerkined and morion-capped with steel, ready for any crime at their master's noble bidding. So silently have they come that the first sound that rouses the young artist and his *sorellaccia* from their little moment of rapture—for which I for one see little reason to blame them—and brings them back to conscious life and the knowledge of their lot, is the slight ring of the short sword-dagger one of them draws from the scabbard. Their eyes are opened now, and *Lo Spazzolone* sees his executioners; while Maddalena and I see a cold, hard old face to which all pleading for mercy—if there had been a crime—would have been vain; and which would make a crime, inexorably, of what was none, from inborn cruelty and jealous rage. It is all over!

All over! Yes, for any chance of life for Giacinto, for any chance of happiness for la Maddalena for the rest of her term of life. But it may give pleasure to you to know—as it gives me pleasure—however little!—that our young painter, who was strong and active as a wild cat, got at the old man's wicked throat and wellnigh choked him before his assassins could cover the three or four steps between them; and before the one whom Maddalena did not stop —for she flung herself bodily on the man with the sword—could strike with a mace he had. And the blow fell on the olive-tinted neck I had loved so well, and the poor Giacinto fell with a thud and

lay, killed or senseless. But the old Devil had felt
his grip with a vengeance, and the two men-at-arms
looked pleased, and lifted up and bore away the
seeming dead Gacinto with admiration. The old
man choked awhile, and la Maddalena remained
marble-white as a new cut block at Massa Carrara,
and as motionless, until her old owner had drunk
some wine and done his choking; and then he
pinched her tender white wrist savagely—I could
show you where he made his mark, but I cannot
move—and drew her away, saying, "You come
with me, young mistress!" But first he goes and
stands opposite the picture, still gripping her wrist.
Then says he, "*Non c'e male*"—not bad—and leads
her away, dumb. And they leave me alone in the
Stanza delle Quattro Corone, and I hear the door
locked from the outside. And the night comes, and
I hear the voices of the frogs in the flat land, and
think of the boy and girl that heard them together
in that other old Castello I remember so well, but
have never seen. And the sun comes again and
shines upon some blood upon the floor. It is not
Giacinto's—it is Maddalena's, where she cut herself
on the man with the sword.

After that I remember no more till two men came
to measure for the frame I now have on. They
came next day, accompanied by the old Marta, who
unlocked the door. But her little dog came with

them, too, and no sooner had he run once all round
the room, to see for cats or what might be else, than
he goes straightway to the blood-mark on the floor.
And so shrewd is he to guess what it is—remember,
he had gone away with Marta when all the riot came
about—that he looks round from one to the other
for explanation, and tries hard to speak, as a dog
does. Whereat each of the three also looks to the
other two, and makes believe the dog is gone mad,
to be making little compassionate whines and cries,
and then, going to each one in turn to tell of it,
touching them with his fore-paws, and then back
again to the blood. But none would give him a
good word, and as for la Marta, she must needs
slap him, to the best of her withered power, on his
clean-shaved body; which very like hurt but little,
but the poor dog cried out upon the injustice! For
he knew well this that he smelt was blood. As I
believe, so did the three of them; however, in that
household each knew that blood, anywhere, was best
not seen by whoever wished to keep his own in his
veins. So they took the measure for my frame,
and went their way. And presently, when they
have gone, back comes the old woman, but no dog,
and brings with her burnt wood-ash, such as the
fire leaves in the open grate, quite white and dry.
And she makes a heap on the blood-stain with it,
and water added, and goes away again and locks

the door without, as before. After which the sun
goes many times across the brick floor, stopping
always to look well upon the blood-spot; and the
night comes back, and I see a little sharp edge of
silver in the sky, beyond the window-grating, and I
remember that it was the new moon, in the days of
the old Castello, and I say to myself, now I shall
see it grow again, as it grew in those old days when
Giacinto watched it with me. And it grows to
be a half-moon before la Marta comes again and
gathers up the ashes, and leaves the floor clean.
But then I know they will soon come with the
frame. So it happens; and then I am in my frame
and am carried away to the great old Castle in the
Apennines, and hanged upon the wall in the State
banqueting-room; and after a while, I know not
how long, the old Duke comes to see, and is pleased
to approve. And my Maddalena comes, or rather
he leads her, stark dumb, and white as the ashes
that dried up the drops of her blood upon the
floor.

And then day follows day, and each day my lord
leads a thinner and a whiter Maddalena to the head
of his board, and each day she answers him less
when he speaks to her, which he does with an evil
discourtesy when none other is there to check it;
and a courtesy, even worse to bear, when they are
in the presence of the household, or of noble guests

on a visit. He sees, as I see, that her eyes are
always fixed on me, as I hang behind his chair, for
well he knows she would not be giving him her eyes
—not she! So he tells the *primo maggiordomo,* who
is subservient, but dropsical, and goes on a stick,
to see that I am moved to a place in a bay to the
left of his mistress; the old Devil having indeed
chosen this place cleverly so that la Maddalena
might not easily see me by turning her eyes only;
but when she gives a little side turn to her head as
well, then she may see me plainly. And, of course,
it fell out as the cunning fox had foreseen, and the
poor Maddalena's eyes wandered more and more to
her picture, and then, as they came back, they
would be caught in the cold gaze that came at her
from the other table-end, and would fall down to
look on the food she was fain to send away un-
tasted. This goes on awhile, and then my Duke
speaks out when they are alone. *He* knows, he
says, what all these sly glances mean—all this
furtive peeping round the corner—we are hankering
after that old lover of ours, are we not? And there
are things it is not easy to forget—ho, ho! And
he laughs out at the poor girl and her sorrow. But
she is outspoken, as one in despair may well be, and
says to her old tormentor that if he means by the
word "lover" that she has in any way whatever
made light of her wifely duty to his lordship, it is

false, and he knows it; for the boy was no more to her than any foster-brother might have been, brought up with her from the cradle. Only, let him not suppose, for all that, that she held him, husband as he was, and all his lands and hoarded wealth, and titles from his Holiness the Pope, one tithe as dear as the shoelace or the button on the coat of the boy he had murdered. On that his *Eccellenza* sniggered and was amused. "I should have thought so much," says he, "from the good round buss you gave him at parting. But who has told you your so precious treasure is dead? None has said so to me, so far. When last I heard of him, he was down below, beneath your feet, '*con rispetto parlando*,'" which is a phrase folk use in Tuscany, not to be too plain-spoken for delicacy about feet and the like.

But now I must tell you something the old miscreant meant when he said this, and pointed down below the great table, which else might be hard to understand. For this great table stood over a trap or well-hole in the floor, and this well-hole went straight down to the dungeons under the Castle, where, if all tales told were true, there was still living a very old man who was first incarcerated forty years since, and had lived on, God knows how! And others as well, though little was known of them by those above in the daylight. But this old man

had made some talk, seeing that he was first confined there in the days of the old Duke, our Duke's
father, a just man and well-beloved, for a crime
committed near by, on the evidence of his wife and
his brother. Of whom, having lived some while *par
amours,* the brother having died by poison, and the
woman having died in sanctity as Mother Superior
of the nuns of Monte Druscolo in Umbria, it was
known that the latter made confession on her death-
bed that her paramour was truly, but unknown to
her, the author of the crime for which his brother
was condemned. Now, this came to her knowledge
by a chance, later. On which she, learning with
resentment the concealment of this from herself, and
seeing that the victim of this crime had been a
young girl under her care and charge, had com-
passed the death of the real culprit for justice' sake,
but had not thought it well to proclaim the truth
about her husband's innocence, for she might have
found it hard to look him in the face. So he was
left where he was, the more that it was thought he
might die if brought out into the sun; and, indeed,
he was very old, and the Holy Abbess in extreme
old age when she made her confession. But he is
not in my tale, nor she, and I speak of him only
because of the chance by which he made known to
me the existence of this same well-hole beneath my
lord's dining-table. For it was the telling of this

story at the banquet that caused it to be spoken of, and also how in old days its use was to be opened after the meal, that the guests might of their *gentilezza* throw what they had not cared to eat themselves to the prisoners below. And the Prince Cosmo dei Medici, who was graciously present, was pleased to say it would have been a pretty tale for the great Boccaccio—or perhaps our good Ser Bojardo would try his hand upon it?

But now you may see, plain enough, what the wicked old man meant when he pointed down in that way. He thought to make his young wife believe that her lover—as he would call him; though he knew the word, as he used it, was a lie— was still living, and that, too, underground, where a ray of light might hardly penetrate at high-noon; and almost surely, too, the victim of starvation and tortures she shuddered to think of; even for witches or Jews—aye, even for heretics! She could see the whole tale in the cruelty of her princely husband's eyes; except, indeed, his victim was really dead, slain by the cruel blow she herself had seen; and seeing it, what wonder was it that she longed only to know that he was dead; for then she could die too? But to slip away and leave Giacinto still alive!—in a damp vault with the old bones of those who had died and been buried there, so that none should know of them; and neither

day nor the coming of night, but only one long
darkness, and not one word from her, and ignorance
of whether she herself still lived or died. Surely,
if she were to die and leave him thus in ignorance,
her ghost would rise from the grave to be beside
him in the darkness of his dungeon; and then how
her heart would break to speak with him, and be
—as might chance—half-heard, and serve only to
add a new terror to his loneliness.

Such things I could guess she felt in her heart. I
could not feel them now myself, not being la Maddalena as she was at this moment. I am still, as I was
then, the Maddalena as she laughed back, from the
dais she sat on, her delight in response to the
pleasure in her young painter's eye; and all she
became after is—to me—like a tale she might have
heard, or some sad pretty ballad one gives a tear
to and forgets. But I can fancy, and maybe you
can too, how her whole young soul was wrenched
as she flung herself at her old tormentor's feet, and
besought him in words that I would myself have
wept for gladly—had God not made me as I am—
to tell her truly, only to tell her, was he living or
dead? She would ask no more than just that much
of his clemency. What wrong had she done him?
—what had Giacinto?—that he should make her
think the sun itself a nightmare; for it would shine
on her, but never reach the black pit below them,

where, for all she knew, Giacinto might be now, at this very moment? Oh, would he not tell her? It was so little to ask!

But the old miscreant had not paid her yet for that kiss, and he would have his account discharged in full. So he takes her face in his two old hands, and pats her on the cheek, and tells her, smiling, to be of good cheer, for she will never know any more of the young *maestro,* nor whether he be alive or dead. But if she wishes to throw down some dainty titbits from the dinner-leavings, on the chance they shall reach the lips she kissed, why it is but telling Raouf and Stefano to lift the trap. It may be a bit rusty, but if it were oiled on the hinges this time, the less trouble the next! At this *la Duchessa* gave a long shriek, holding her head tight on, on either side, and then fell backward on the floor, and lay so, stark motionless. And then my great Duke seats himself on the nearest chair; and he has in his hand his crutched stick, to lean on against the gout in his foot. He takes it in his left hand, and just digs with it at the girl's body on the ground, either to rouse her or see if she be dead. But she does not move, and he has her carried away to bed; and his face is contented, as is that of a man who has worked well and deserved his fee.

I wish I could remember more of this old tale of four hundred years ago, but I had no chance to do

so, for after the scene I have just described the
noble Duke, hobbling a short space about the hall,
brings up short just facing the bay where I have
been hanged by his orders, to spite la Maddalena;
and then, after choking a little—as indeed he often
did since that fierce grip of my young *maestro, Lo
Spazzolone*—he calls out to his fat *maggiordomo,*
and bids him to see that I am removed to his own
private room and hanged under the picture of
Ganymede. But now he must only take it down
and remove it to the old stone chamber, where the
figs are put to dry on trays, and so leave it, to be
hanged in his room when he is away at Rome, as
will be shortly. So he hobbles away and I hear
him getting slowly up the little stair that goes to
his private room, and his attendants following him.
The dropsical *maggiordomo* stays to see that another
man should come, with a ladder and a boy, to help,
and they get me down from my hooks, and carry
me off; and I can smell the dried figs, and the *stoia*
that is rolled up in a stack, and the empty wine-
flasks. But I can see nothing, for they place me
with my face against the wall, and cover me over
with a sacking; and I can hear little more; and
then the great door clangs to and is locked, and I
am alone in the dark, without feeling or measure-
ment of time, and only catching faint sounds from
far-off.

I could guess, rather than hear, the sound of a footstep when one came, rarely enough, in the long corridor without. I could feel its rhythm in the shaken floor, but I could be scarcely said to hear it. I was aware of a kind of scratching close to me, that may have been some kind of beetle or scorpion, but of course it was quite invisible. There was one sort of *scaraffaggio* that would come, even between me and the wall one time, and make a noise like a thousand whirlwinds, and beat against me with his wings, and I should have liked to be able to ask him to come often. But he seemed not to care about me; and I could just hear him boom away in the darkness, joyous at heart and happy in his freedom. Oh, if he could have known how different was my lot! I thought of how he would float out into the sunlight, whirring all the while like the wheels of the great *orologio* at the old Castello when Fra Poco let it run down at noon so that he might reset it fair from the sundial on the wall in the Cortile where the well was—*our* well!

It may have been days, or it may have been weeks or months, before a change came, and I again heard human voices. But it would not be longer than two or three months at most; seeing that it was immediately, as far as I could judge, on the top of a little chance that is dear to my memory now, after—so I gather—some four hundred years.

For a sweet firefly came, by the blessing of God,
between me and the dry wall, and paused and hung
a moment in the air that I might get a sight of his
beauty. You have seen them in the corn, how they
stop to think, and then shoot on ahead, each to seek
his love, or hers: so it is taught by those who say
they know, and may be truly. This one also must
needs go on, though I would have prayed him to
stay, that *I* might be his love. Yet this could not
be, for neither did I know his tongue, nor was aught
else fitting. So he went away and left me sad-
hearted. He was a spot of light between a gloom
behind and a gloom before, even as the Star of
Bethlehem.

But about this that I was telling of. I had a
sense of half-heard turmoil without. Then the lock
in the door, and the imprecations of a man that
could not turn the key. He swore roundly 'at him
who made it, and at all locksmiths soever, as persons
who from malevolence scheme to exclude all folk
from everywhere; and I wished to rebuke him for
his injustice, for how can a locksmith do less than
make a key? And it was for him to choose the right
key, not to keep on twisting at the wrong one, and
swearing, which is what he was doing. But he was
a noisy, blustering person, for when he did get in,
being helped to the right key by a clever young boy
who saw his error, he was much enraged with that

boy for telling him; and he was ill-satisfied with such a place as this to stow away the furniture, but he supposed they must make it do.

Then came much moving in of goods. And I could gather this, but no more, from the conversation of those who brought it in—that it was the furniture of some one who was little loved, and only spoken of as "he" or "*il Vecchiostro*"—that he was gone on a journey, and much they cared how soon he arrived at the end of it. The boy, who was young and inquisitive, then asking whither this was that he had gone, they told him with a laugh that it was to his oldest friend, another like himself; to whom he had given his whole soul, and who would not care to part with him in a hurry. They hoped he would have a cool bed to sleep in. And when the boy hoped this too, they were very merry. But they worked hard, and brought in a great mass of furniture, which they stacked against the wall where I was, so that I was quite hidden away. There would be new fittings all through the Castle now, they said. But one said no—no! it would only be in the *Vecchiostro's* own private rooms. "'Tis done that he should be soonest forgotten," said one of them. But it was only just when they had brought in the last of it that this same one said that if ever he—this *Vecchiostro*—came back from Hell there would be all his gear ready for him. And then I

saw this was some dead man's property that his
successor would have put out of his sight.

Then says my young boy to his father, who was
the man who had sworn at the key, why did they
not take the Signora's portrait down instead of
leaving it there, because everyone loved her; and
for his part, she kissed him once, and said he was
carino. Then says his father, what portrait?
And he answers, " In there—behind." For he had
peeped in round my frame thinking he knew me
again; being in fact the same that had helped to
get me down in the banqueting-hall, how long since
I could not say. But his father calls him a young
fool not to say so before it was too late; and as for
him, it was time for his supper and bed, and whoever
else liked the job might move all the chairs and
tables again to fish her ladyship out. And as all
were of one mind they laughed over this and went
noisily away. And the door was locked and I
heard no more. And the darkness was darker still
and the silence deeper. And I longed for the
scaraffaggio to come and whirr once more, and for
the sweet light of the *lucciola*. But there was none
such for me. And my Maddalena must be surely
dead, I thought, else that young boy would tell her
I was here, and she would come to find the
picture Giacinto painted of her in that merry time.
But I waited for her voice in vain, and had

nothing for myself but the darkness and the silence.

Just as the diver holds his breath and longs for the sudden air that he must surely meet—in a moment—in another moment!—so I held as it were the breath of expectation, and believed in the coming of those who could not but seek me; for at first I felt certain they would come. They would never leave me here, to decay! But there came no voice, no glimmer of light, and I fell into a stupor in which all memory grew dim, even that of my Maddalena.

What I suffered through that long period of silence and darkness I cannot tell, nor could you understand. The prisoner in his solitude is grateful for each thing that enables him to note the flight of time; and the fewer such things are the drearier is the sameness of his lot. Can you imagine it if they were *all* removed—a condition of simple existence in black space, with no means of marking time at all? Would you become, on that account, unconscious altogether of weariness from the long unalleviated hours? No, indeed! Take my word for it. Rather, you would find it, as I found it, a state of bondage such as one would long and pray might be the lot of such as had been, in this life, devils against the harmless; but going on through all eternity, no nearer the end now than when it started countless ages ago, an absolute monotone of dulled sense without insensibility—even pain itself almost an alleviation.

That is what my life, if you can call it life, was to me through all that term; but, as thought is dumb, though I know the time goes on, how long it goes on I know not. When I next hear human speech, the voices are new and the words strange and barbarous. Also, when I am taken from the wall and turned round to the light, I can see nothing, and I know not why. Perhaps it is all dark here at all times, and they have brought no light. I shall see, though, well enough when I am hanged up under Ganymede, and see my bad old Duke again, and even my other self, my Maddalena. I have a longing on me to see her once more, and to see her more like me, if it may be. It seems so long! So much longer than the time when I was left alone in the *Stanza delle Quattro Corone*. But what you may find hard to understand is this, that though I could not know how long this dreadful waking sleep had been, neither could I be sure it had not been a few hours only. I now know, for I have learned since, that it was over three hundred years. Yet when the end came it found me not without a hope of Maddalena; or if not Maddalena, at least the Duke.

But I do not see them, either of them. Nor old Marta Zan and her little dog. Nor the dropsical old *maggiordomo*. That there is no Giacinto is little wonder to me. For I believe him dead, killed by that fell blow on the olive neck I loved so well, just behind the ear. I wonder, though, that I see none of the others. But indeed I have much ado to see anything. All is in a mist of darkness.

Also, I am presently stunned by the clash of many voices. I can catch from the words of those who speak Maddalena's language, the tongue that I can follow, that there is a great wranglement over me and my sale price. For I am to be sold, and the foreigners who wish to buy me are loud in their dispraise of me; so much so that I do not understand why they should wish to possess me at all. In fact, they do actually go away after much heated discussion, speaking most scornfully of pictures as things no man in his senses would ever buy, and of pictures with frames like mine as the most valueless examples. I gather all this from repetitions made by others, in Maddalena's tongue, nearly but not exactly.

Presently back comes one of them to say he will go to six hundred francs, but not a penny more. Then says a woman's voice, "Ah, Signore! Six hundred and fifty!" Then he, six hundred and twenty-five. And then some price between the

two. And so we are agreed at last. And I am to
be put in a box and sent to a place whose name I
have never heard, that sounds like L'Ombra, a name
that frightens me, for it sounds like the Inferno of
the great poet, Dante.

But I should tell you that, before this riot, and
noise, and disputation over me and my price, I had
heard the unpacking and removal of the great stack
of furniture that hid me. Only, as the persons who
removed it have no interest for us, and did not seem
from their conversation to be especially cultivated
or intelligent, but rather the reverse, I have not
said anything of them, nor of their valuations in
lire of each article as it was brought to light. Their
voices were the very first that I heard; but though
their words sounded strange to me, they only made
me think that maybe they were from Milan or
Genoa or some other place in Italy. I should not
have guessed them Tuscans; that is all. Indeed,
I hardly distinguished much of what they said until
they had removed the last of the furniture and I
was turned round to the light. Then I saw things
in a cloud, and heard indistinctly. I made out,
however, that I was thick with dust, and must be
brought out and cleaned before anyone could see
what I was like. Then I was carried away down
some stairs, and in the end I was aware, but dimly,
as in a dream, that I was again in the great chamber

where I last saw la Maddalena lying on the ground
insensible, while the old Duke prodded at her with
a stick. I could see there were many people in the
room, talking volubly. But I could not catch their
words well until a Signora, who seemed to take the
lead, wiped my face over with a wet sponge; and
then I heard more. Her voice was clearest, and
what she said was "*Ecco, Signori!* Now you can
see the ear quite plain. *Ma com'e bella! Bella
bella!*"—And then it was I came to hear all the
clamour of voices of a sudden.

Then follows all the bargaining I told you of.
The Signora's husband would not sell an old picture
—not he!—for a thousand pounds in gold; not till
all the dirt was off and he could see it fairly. All
applauded this, and said in chorus neither would
they! Who could tell what might not be, under
the dirt? However, they knew so little about it
that they would not mind buying this one, on the
chance. But for a decently reasonable price—say
five thousand Italian *lire.* On which the owner
said, "*Come mai! E pochissimo!*" Then the
Signori Inglesi took another tone, and would have
none of the picture, nor any picture, at any price!
They would not know where to hang it. They did
not like pictures on their walls. All the walls were
covered with pictures already, all favourites, that
must not be moved. But why need I tell you all

this? You have heard folk make bargains, and the lies they tell.

The English Signori departed, having bought me for six hundred and fifty English pounds. And then my lady and gentleman are mightily delighted, and dance about the room with joy. Now they will go to Monte Carlo and win back all they lost last year. Then I hear them talking in an undertone, thus:—

(He) "I hope they never suspected it was none of ours——"

(She) "*Ah, Dio mio!* And I had told them we were only *inquilini*"—that is, tenants.

(He) "*Non ti confondi?* Don't fret about that. *They* don't know what *inquilini* means. They can only say '*mangia bene, quanto costa!*"

(She) "*Speriamo!* But what a fine lot of old furniture! Couldn't we sell some of it, too?" And this young Signora, who was very pretty and impudent, and what I have since heard called *svelte,* danced about the room in high glee. But the good gentleman stopped her.

(He) "*Troppo pericolo!* The fat old Marchesa would find out. No, no! The picture is quite another thing——"

(She) "*Perche?*"

(He) "Can't you see, thickhead? If the old *strega*"—the old witch, that is—"had known the

picture was there, do you suppose she wouldn't have
had it out, long ago? And that other picture in
front of it, with the eagle. . . . Don't dance, but
listen!"

(She) ". . . Picture in front of it, with the
eagle . . . yes, go on!" But she won't quite stop
dancing, and makes little quick tiptoe movements,
not to seem over-subservient and docile.

(He) "I would have sold that, too, only it's too
big for safety. This one will go in a small case.
The *famiglia* will have to be well paid. What was
it la Filomena told you first of all about the room
and the furniture? Do stop that dancing!"

(She) "There, see now, I've stopped! But you
have been told, once!"

(He) "Then tell again!"

(She) "It wasn't la Filomena. It was that old,
old Prisca who knows all about the Castello—more
than the Marchesa herself. She told me there was
an old room in the great tower that had not been
open for hundreds of years, as no one dared to go
near it for fear of the wicked old Duke's ghost. I
told her we were *liberi pensatori*"—that is to say,
free-thinkers—"and he would not hurt us, and
where was the key? We would not touch anything
—only look in!"

(He) "Won't she tell about it all?"

(She) "Not till we go! Besides, she doesn't

know. La Filomena won't tell her; she knows I
know all about her and Ugo Pistrucci. And she's
the only person that goes near the old Prisca, who
hasn't been off her bed for months. Oh no!
She's all right. As for the man, I told them
la Prisca said the *mobiglia* was to be taken out
and dusted and placed in the passage. *Stia tranquillo, mio caro!*"

(He) "What a happy chance these pig-headed
rich milords happened to come in just as we got it.
They might have gone before we found it! Only
to think of it! *Seicento e cinquante lire . . .!*"

And so they went on rejoicing, and thinking of
new schemes, and how they would get me packed
off the very next day, and not a soul in the Castle
would ever know I had ever been there. They were
certainly very bad, unprincipled adventurers. You
should have heard them talk of what fun they would
have telling the old Marchesa about the great discovery of treasures they had made, and the care
they had taken nothing should be lost. And then
who knows but she might trust them to get a sale
for all her old rubbish in England, and what a lot
of money they might make, with a little discretion.
If I had remained there I should have been longing
always for a chance of telling the old *strega,* as they
called her, what a nice couple she had let her Castle
to for the summer months. For I am convinced,

not only that they were thieves, but that they were
not even lawfully married. However it may have
been, I saw no more of them. For next day the
same man that had done the removal of the furniture came with a box, and I was carefully packed,
and saw nothing more, and distinguished little
sound, for weeks it may have been, even months.
As the solidity of the box absorbed all sight and
hearing, and I knew nothing till I found myself on
an easel in a sort of Studio in a town that I at once
perceived to be L'Ombra. For what else could it
have been?

At this point Mr. Pelly, who had been listening
intently, interrupted the speaker. " I think you
have got the name of the place wrong," he said. " I
imagine it must have been London—*Londra*—the
English Metropolis—not L'Ombra. The sounds are
very similar, and easy to mistake."

" Possibly I was misled by the darkness. It made
the name seem so appropriate. But it was not
exactly night. There was a window near me, and
I could see there was a kind of yellow smoke over
everything. But there was music in the street,
and children appeared to be running and shouting.
Other things gave me the impression the time had
been intended for morning, but that something had
come in the way. It was a terrible place, much
like to that dark third circle in Hell, where

Dante and Virgilio saw the uncouth monster Cerberus.

"But let us forget it! Why should such a place be remembered or spoken of? I was there for no great length of time: long enough only for the picture-cleaner, in whose workshop I was, to remove the obscurations of four hundred years, and safeguard me with a glass from new deposits. For I understood him to say that I should be just as bad as ever in a very short space of time, in this beastly sooty hole, but for such protection.

"And yet this place was not entirely bad, nor in darkness at all times, for at intervals a phenomenon would occur which I supposed to be a peculiarity of the climate, causing the lady of the house to say, 'There—the sun's coming out. I shall get my Things on. Are you going to stay for ever in the house, and get fustier and fustier, or are you going to have a turn on the Embankment? You might answer me, instead of smoking, Reginald!' But I noticed that this phenomenon, whatever its cause, never seemed to attain fruition, the lady always saying she knew how it would be—they had lost all the daylight. I only repeat her words. I observed another thing worthy of remark, that it very seldom held up. I am again repeating a phrase that was to me only a sound. I have no idea what 'it' was, nor what it held up, nor why.

I am only certain that the performance was a rare one, however frequently it was promised. But the gentleman who restored me seemed to have confidence in its occurrence, conditionally on his taking his umbrella. Otherwise, he said, it was cocksure to come down cats and dogs, and they would be in for a cab, and he only had half-a-crown.

"These persons were of no interest in themselves, and I should never remember or think of them at all but for having been the unwilling witness of a conjugal misunderstanding, which may quite possibly have led to a permanent breach between them. It is painful to think that the whole difference might have been made in the lady's jealous misinterpretation of her husband's behaviour towards a maiden named *la Sera*—who, as I understood, came in by the week at nine shillings, and always had her Sunday afternoons, whatever those phrases mean; no doubt you will know—if I had been able to add my testimony to her husband's disclaimer of amorous intent. For it was most clear that the whole thing was but an innocent joke throughout, however ill-judged and stupid. I saw the whole from my place on the easel, and heard all that passed. I cannot tell you how I longed to say a word on his behalf, when, some days later, two friends paid him a visit, who had evidently been taken into his confidence, but who seemed to think that he had withheld

something from them, not treating them so frankly
as old friends deserved. Whereupon he warmly
protested that his wife had no solid ground of complaint against him, having gone off, unreasonably,
in what he called 'a huff'; but that he had just
paid *la Sera* her wages and sent her packing, so
that now he had to make his own bed and black
his own shoes.

"I am sorry to say that these two friends showed
only an equivocal sympathy, winking at each other,
and each digging the other in the ribs with strange
humorous sounds, as of a sort of fowl. Also, they
shook their heads at their friend, though not, as
I think, reproaching him seriously, yet implying
thus, as by other things said, that he was of a gay
and sportive disposition that might easily be misled
by the fascinations of beauty, which they were
pleased to ascribe to *la Sera*. This was, however,
scarcely spoken with an earnest intent, since this
maiden, despite the beauty of her name—for one
might conceive it to ascribe to her the tender
radiance and sad loveliness of the sunset—was
wanting in charm of form and colour, and had not
successfully cultivated such other fascinations as
sometimes make good their deficiency; as sweetness
and fluency of speech, or a quick wit, or even the
artificial seductions of well-ordered dress. I de-
rived, too, a most unfavourable impression from a

comment of her employer—to the effect that if, when she cleaned herself of a Sunday morning, she couldn't do it without making the whole place smell of yellow soap, she might as well chuck it and stop dirty.

"But I should grieve to think that this Signore's wife should have left him permanently for so foolish a quarrel. For, though their lives seemed filled with a silly sort of bickering, I believed from what I saw that there was really a sort of love between them, and I cannot conceive that they will be any happier apart. Indeed, had she been indifferent to her husband, could she have felt a trivial inconstancy, implying no grievous wrong, of such importance? But, indeed, it is absurd to use the word *inconstancy* at all in such a case, though we may condemn the ill-taste of all vulgar trifling with the solemn obligations of conjugal duty. I wish I might have spoken, to laugh in their faces and make a jest of the whole affair. But silence was my lot.

"I have hung here, as I suppose, for six months past, and have often striven to speak, but none has heard me till now. Think, dear Signore, how I have suffered! Think how I have longed to speak and be heard, when my Madeline, my darling—who loves me, and says she loves me—has talked to her great dog of her lover that was killed in the war. . . ."

Mr. Pelly interrupted. "Are you referring to young Captain Calverley?" he said. "Because, if so, it is not certain that he *is* dead. Besides, I suppose you know that Miss Upwell and the Captain were not engaged?" And then the old gentleman fancied he heard a musical laugh come from the picture.

"How funny and cold you English are!" said the voice. "Was *I* engaged to my darling, my love, that only time he pressed me to his bosom; that only time I felt his lips on mine? Was I not the bond-slave for life to the evil heart and evil will of that old monument of Sin, soaked deep in every stain of Hell? Was I not called his *wife?* Yet my heart and my soul went out to my love in that kiss, and laughed in their freedom in mockery of the laws that could put the casket that held them in bond, and yet must perforce leave them free. And when that young soldier tore himself away from my Madeline—I saw them here myself; there by the shiny fish, in the glass case—was their parting kiss less real than ours was, that hour when I saw him last, my own love of those years gone by?"

"A—it isn't a subject I profess to understand much about," said Mr. Pelly. He blew his nose and wiped his spectacles, and was silent a moment. Then, he said, "But whatever the sentiment of the young lady herself may be, there can be no doubt about her mother's. In fact, she has herself told me that she is most anxious that it should not be supposed that there was any engagement. So I trust—if you ever do have the opportunity of speaking to anyone on the subject—that you will be careful not to give the impression that such was the case. I do not, perhaps, fully realize the motives that influence Lady Upwell—a—and Sir George,—of course it's the same thing. . . ."

Mr. Pelly stopped with a jerk. He found himself talking uncomfortably and inexplicably to space, beside the embers of a dying fire, and in the distance he could hear the carriage bringing the absentees back through the wintry night, and the ringing tread of the horses on the hard ground.

"Poor Uncle Christopher all by himself, and the fire out!" said the first comer into the Library. It was the young lady who came to see the Italian picture at the restorer's Studio in Chelsea, a little over six months past. She had changed for the older since then, out of measure with the lapse of time. But her face was beautiful—none the less that it was sad and pale—in the glow as she brought the embers together to make life worth living to one or two more faggots, just for a little blaze before we went to bed.

"I was asleep and dreaming," said the old gentleman. "Such a queer dream!"

"You must tell it us to-morrow, Uncle Christopher. I like queer dreams." This young lady, Madeline Upwell, always made use of this mode of address, although the old gentleman was no uncle of hers, but only a very old friend of the family who knew her father before she was born, and called him George, which was his Christian Christian-name, so to speak, "Stopleigh" being outside family recognitions—a mere Bartitude!

But the picture, which might reasonably have protested against Mr. Pelly's statement, remained silent. So, when his waking judgment set the whole down as a dream, it was probably right.

CHAPTER IV

A RETROSPECTIVE CHAPTER. HOW FORTUNE'S TOY AND THE SPORT
OF CIRCUMSTANCES FELL IN LOVE WITH ONE OF HIS NURSES.
PROSE COMPOSITION. LADY UPWELL'S MAJESTY, AND THE
QUEEN'S NO ENGAGEMENT. THE AFRICAN WAR, AND JUSTI-
FIABLE FRATRICIDE. CAIN. MADELINE'S BIG DOG CÆSAR.
CATS. ORMUZD AND AHRIMAN. A HANDY LITTLE VELDT.
MADELINE'S JAPANESE KIMONO. A DISCUSSION OF THE NA-
TURE OF DREAMS. NEVER MIND ATHENÆUS. LOOK AT THE
PROPHET DANIEL. SIR STOPLEIGH'S GREAT-AUNT DOROTHEA'S
TWINS. THE CIRCULATING LIBRARY AND THE POTTED SHRIMPS.
HOW MADELINE READ THE MANUSCRIPT IN BED, AND TOOK
CARE NOT TO SET FIRE TO THE CURTAINS

THE story of Madeline, the young lady who is going one day to inherit the picture Mr. Pelly thought
he was talking to last night, along with the Surley
Stakes property—for there is no male heir—is an
easy story to tell, and soon told. There were a
many stories of the sort, just as the clock of last
century struck its hundred.

Whether the young Captain Calverley, whom the
picture alluded to, was a hero because, when, one
day in the hunting-field, our young heiress and her
quadruped came to grief over a fence, he made his
horse swerve suddenly to avoid disastrous complica-
tions, and thereby came to greater grief himself,
Mr. Pelly, at any rate, could form no judgment. It

107

was out of his line, he said. So, according to him, was the sequel, in which the sadly mauled mortal portion of the young soldier, with a doubt if the immortal portion was still in residence, was carried to Surley Stakes and qualified—though rather slowly—to resume active service by the skill of the best of surgeons and the assiduity of an army of nurses. But, hero or not, he was credited with heroism by the young lady, with all the natural consequences. And no doubt his convalescence was all the more rapid that he found himself, when he recovered his senses forty-eight hours after his head struck the corner of a stone wall in his involuntary dismount, in such very delightful company, with such opportunities of improving his relations with it. In fact, the scheme for his removal must have developed very soon, to give him a text for a sermon to the effect that he was Fortune's Toy and the Sport of Circumstances, that he accounted concussion of the brain and a fractured thigh-bone the only real blessings his lot had ever vouchsafed to him, and that happiness would become a Thing of the Past as soon as he rejoined his regiment. He would, however, devote the remainder of his life to treasuring the memories of this little hour of unalloyed bliss, and hoping that his cherished recollections would at almost the rarest possible intervals find an echo somehow and some-

where that his adoration—badly in love as he was—
failed in finding a description for, as the climax of
a long sentence. And perhaps it was just as well
that his resources in prose composition gave out
when they did, as nothing was left then but to
become natural, and say, "You'll forget all about
me, Miss Upwell, you know you will. That's what
I meant "—the last with a consciousness that when
we are doing prose composition we are apt to say
one thing and mean another.

Madeline wasn't prepared to be artificial, with
this young dragoon or anyone else. She gave him
the full benefit of her large blue eyes—because, you
see, she had got him down, as it were, and he couldn't
possibly become demonstrative with a half-healed
fracture of the thigh—and said, " I hope I *shan't*.
I shall try not to, anyhow." But this seemed not
to give entire satisfaction, as the patient said, rather
ruefully, *" You could,* if you tried, Miss Upwell! "
To which the young lady, who was not without a
mischievous side to her character, answered, " Of
course I could! " but immediately repented, and
added, " One can do anything one likes, if one tries
hard enough, you know! "

It would only be the retelling of a very old
story, the retreading of very old ground, to follow
these young people through the remainder of their
interview, which was interrupted by the appearance

of Madeline's mamma; who, to say the truth, had
been getting apprehensive that so many *têtes-à-tête*
with this handsome patient might end seriously.
And though his family was good, he was only a
younger son; and she didn't want her daughter to
marry a soldier. Fancy "Mad" being carried off
to India! For in the bosom of her family this
most uncomfortable of namelets had caught on
naturally, without imputation of Hanwell or Colney
Hatch.

However, her ladyship was too late, this time. No
clinical practice of any Hospital includes kissing or
being kissed by the patient, and "Mad" and her
lover were fairly caught. Nothing was left for it
but confession at high tension, and throwing ourselves on the mercy of the Court. But always with
the distinct reservation that neither of us could ever
love another.

Lady Upwell, a very beautiful woman in her day,
was indulging in a beautiful sunset, and meant to
remain fine till midnight. There was a gleam of
the yellow silver of a big harvest moon in the hair
that had been gold. She was good, but very
majestic; in fact, *her* majesty, when she presented
her daughter to her Queen, competed with that of
the latter, which has passed into the language. To
do her justice, she let it lapse on hearing the full
disclosure of these two culprits, and had the presence

of mind to ask them if they had no suspicion that
they might be a couple of young fools, to fancy they
could know their own minds on so short an acquaintance, etc. For this was barely seven weeks after
the hunting-field accident. "You silly geese!" she
said. "Go your own way—but you'll quarrel in
a fortnight. See if you don't!" *She* knew all
about this sort of thing, though Mr. Pelly didn't.

The latter was right, however, and prudent, when
in his dream he laid stress on the wish of Madeline's
parents that there should be "no engagement."
This stipulation seemed to be accounted by both
of them—but especially by the Baronet—as a sort
of panacea for all parental responsibilities. It could
not be reiterated too often. The consequence was
that there were two concurrent determinations of
the relative positions of Madeline and the Captain;
one an esoteric one—a sort of sacramental service of perpetual vows of fidelity; the other the
exoteric proclamations of a kind of many-headed
town-crier, who went about ringing his bell and
shouting that it was "distinctly understood that
there was no engagement." Mr. Pelly's repetition
of this in his dream may have had an intransitive
character; but he was good and prudent, just the
same. How we behave in dreams shows whether
the high qualities we pride ourselves on are more
than skin-deep.

But all the efforts of the exoteric town-crier were
of no avail against the esoteric sacramental services.
The most unsettling condition lovers can have im-
posed upon them—that of being left entirely to their
own devices, and never stimulated by so much as a
hint of a *chaperon*—failed to bring about a coolness.
And when within a year after his accident Jack
Calverley was ordered away with his Company to
South Africa, where war had already broken out,
the ᴖsacramental service the picture—or someone—
had witnessed, just by the glass case with the big
fish in it, was the farewell of a couple of heart-
breaks, kept under by the upspring of Hope in
youth, that clings to the creed that the stricken
classes, the mourning classes, are Other People, and
that to them pity shall be given from within our
pale of well-fenced security. It was a wrench to
part, certainly, but Jack would come back, and be
a great soldier and wear medals. And the Other
People would die for their country.

And then came the war, and the many unpleasant discoveries that always come with a war,
the most unpleasant of all being the discovery of
the strength of the enemy. The usual recognitions
of the obvious, too late; and the usual denunciations
of everybody else for not having foreseen it all the
time. The usual rush to the money-chest of unexhausted Credit, to make good with pounds

deficiencies shillings spent in time would have supplied; the usual storms of indignation against the incompetence in high places that never spent, in time, the shillings we refused to provide. The usual war-whoops from sheltered corners, safe out of gunshot; and the usual deaths by scores of men on both sides who never felt a pang of ill-feeling to each other, or knew the cause of quarrel—yes, a many of whom, had they known a quarrel was pending, would have given their lives to avert it! The usual bearing, on both sides, of the brunt of the whirlwind by those who never sowed a wind-seed, and the usual reaping of a golden harvest by the Judicious Investor, he who buys and sells, but makes and meddles not with what he sells or buys, measuring its value alone by what he can get and must give for it. And a very respectable person he is, too.

The history of Madeline's next few months made up for her a tale of anxious waitings for many mails: of pangs of unendurable tension over journals that, surrendered by the postman, would not open; that, opened at last, seemed nothing but advertisements; that, run to earth and convicted of telegrams, only yielded new food for anxiety. A tale of these periods of expectation of letters from Jack, by every mail. The first of expectation fulfilled; of letters full of hope and confidence, of forecast of victories easily won and a triumphant quick return. The second of expectation damped and thwarted; of victories revised; of Hope's rebukes to Confidence, the coward who fails us at our need; of the slow dawn of the true horrors of war—mere death on the battle-field the least of them—that will one day change the reckless young soldier to an old grave man that has learned his lesson, and knows that the curse of Cain is on him who stirs to War, and that half the great names of History have been borne by Devils incarnate. And then the third—a weary time of waiting for a letter that came not, for only one little word of news to say *yes* or *no* to the question we hardly dare to ask:—" Is he dead ? " For our poor young friend, after distinguishing himself brilliantly and yet coming almost scathless out of half-a-dozen actions, was *missing*. When the roll was called after a memorable action from which the two opponent armies retreated simultaneously, able to bear the slaughter by unseen guns no longer, no answer came to the name—called formally—of Captain Calverley. The survivors who still had breath to answer to their names already knew that he was missing—knew that he was last seen apparently carried away by his horse, having lost control over it—probably wounded, said report. That was all—soon told! And then followed terrible hours that should have brought more news and did not.

And the hearts of those who watched for it went sick with the fear that no news would ever come, that none would ever know the end of that ride and the vanished rider. But each heart hid away its sickness from its neighbour, and would not tell.

 And so the days passed, and each day's end was the grafting of a fresh despair in the tree nourished in the soil of buried hopes; and each morning Madeline would try to reason it away and discover some new calendar rule, bringing miscalculation to book—always cutting short the tale of days, never lengthening them. She talked very little to anyone about it, for fear her houses of cards should be shaken down by stern common sense; or, worse still, that she should be chilled by the hesitating sympathy of half-hearted Hope. But her speech was free to her great dog Cæsar, when they were alone together.

Cæsar was about the size of a small cart-horse, and when he had a mind—and he often had—to lie on the hearthrug, and think with his eyes shut, he was difficult to move. Not that he had an opposive or lazy disposition, but that it was not easy to make him understand. The moment he knew what was wanted of him he was only too anxious to comply. As, for instance, if he could be convinced of Cats, he would rise and leave the room abruptly, knocking several persons down, and leaving behind him the trail of an earthquake. But his heart was good and pure, and he impressed his admirers somehow that he was always on the side of Ormuzd against Ahriman: he always took part with the Right.

So Madeline, when she found herself alone with Cæsar, in those days, would cry into his fur as he lay on the rug, and would put sentiments of sympathy and commiseration into his mouth, which may have been warranted by the facts, only really there was nothing to show it. In these passages she alleged kinship with Cæsar, claiming him as her son.

"Was he," she would say, "his own mamma's precious Angel? And the only person in the house that had any real feeling! All the other nasty people keep on being sorry for her, and he says he knows Jack's coming back, and nobody need be sorry at all. And when Jack comes home safe and well, his mamma's own Heavenly Angel shall run with the horses all over Mousehold Common—he shall! And he shall catch a swallow at last, he shall, and bring it to his own mamma. Bless him! Only he mustn't scratch his darling head too suddenly; at least, not till his mamma can get her own out of the way, because she's not a bull or an elephant, and able to stand anything. . . . That's right, my pet! Now he shall try and get a little sleep, he shall." This was acknowledgment of a deep sigh, as of one who had at last deservedly found rest.

But it called for a recognition of its unselfish nature, too. "And he never so much as thought of going to sleep till he'd consoled his poor mamma—the darling!" And really her interviews with Cæsar grew to be almost Madeline's only speech about her lost lover; for her father and mother, though they talked to each other, scarcely dared to say a word to her, lest their own disbelief in the possibility of Jack's return should show itself.

And so the hours passed and passed, and the days grew to weeks, and the weeks to months; and now, at the time of the cold March night when Mr. Pelly dreamed the picture talked, the flame of Hope was dying down in the girl's tired heart like the embers he sat by, and none came bringing fuel and a new lease of life.

But the way she nursed the flame that flickered still was brave. She kept up her spirits entirely on the knowledge that there was no direct proof of Jack's death. She fostered a conception in her mind of a perfectly imaginary Veldt, about the size of Hyde Park, and carefully patrolled day and night. They would have been certain to find him if he were dead—was her thought. What a handy little Veldt that was!—and, oh, the intolerable leagues of the reality! But it did help towards keeping her spirits up, somehow or other.

Her father and mother ascribed more than a fair

share of these kept-up spirits to their great panacea.
They laid to their souls the flattering unction that
if there *had* been a regular engagement their
daughter would have given way altogether. Think
what a difference it would have made if she had had
to go into mourning! Lady Upwell took exception
to the behaviour of Jack's family at Calverley Court,
who had rushed into mourning six weeks after his
disappearance, and advertised their belief in his
death, really before there was any need for it. Her
daughter, on the contrary, rather made a parade of
being out of mourning. Perhaps it seemed to her
to emphasize and consolidate her own hopes, as well
as to rebuke dispositions towards premature despair
in others.

Therefore, when this young lady came upon old
Mr. Pelly, just aroused from his dream, she was
certainly not clad in sackcloth and ashes. She had
on her heliotrope *voile de soie;* only, of course, Mr.
Pelly didn't see it until she took off her seal-colour
musquash wrap, which was quite necessary because
of the cold. And the third evening after that,
which was to be a quiet one 'at home for Mr. Pelly
to read them the memoranda of his dream in the
Library, she put on her Jap kimono with the em-
broidered storks, which was really nearly as smart
as the *voile de soie;* and, of course, there was no need
to fig up, when it was only Mr. Pelly. And what-

ever tale her looks might tell, no one could have guessed from her manner she had such a sorrow at heart, so successfully did she affect, from fear of it, a cheerfulness she was far from feeling; knowing perfectly well that if she made any concession, she must needs break down altogether.

"Fancy your being able to remember it all, and write it out like that!" said she to Mr. Pelly when they adjourned into the Library after dinner.

"We must bear in mind," he replied, "that the story is a figment of my own mind, and therefore easier to recall than a communication from another person. Athenæus refers to an instance of . . ."

"Never mind Athenæus! How do you know it is a figment of your imagination?"

"What else can it be?"

"Lots of things. Besides, it doesn't matter. Look here, now, you say it was a dream, don't you?"

"I certainly think so."

"Well!—and aren't dreams the hardest things to recollect there are? Look at the Prophet Daniel, and Nebuchadnezzar." Mr. Pelly thought to himself that he would much sooner look at the speaker. But he only said, "Suppose we do!" To which the reply was, "Well, then—of course! . . ."

"Of course what?"

"Why—of course when you can recollect things that proves they're not dreams."

"Then, when Daniel recollected—or, I should rather say, recalled his dream to Nebuchadnezzar—did that prove that it wasn't a dream?"

"Certainly not, because he was a Prophet. The Chaldeans *couldn't* recollect, and that proved that it was."

The Baronet and his Lady remained superiorly silent, smiling over the heads of the discussion. The attitude of Debrett towards human weaknesses —such as Philosophical Speculation, or the Use of the Globes—was indicated.

When Mr. Pelly had finished reading his account of the dream—on which our relation of it, already given, was founded—discussion ensued. It embodied, intelligently enough, all the things that it is dutiful to say when we are disconcerted at the inscrutable.

The Baronet said we must guard ourselves carefully against being carried away by two or three things; superstition was one of them. It did not require a Scientific Eye to see that there was nothing in this narrative which might not be easily ascribed to the subconscious action of Mr. Pelly's brain. It was quite otherwise in such a case as that of his great-aunt, Dorothea, whose wraith undoubtedly appeared and took refreshment at Knaresborough Copping at the very time that she was confined of twins here in this house. The testimony to the truth of this had never been challenged. But when people came and told him stories of substantial tables floating in the air and accordions being played, he always asked this one question, "Was it in the dark?" That question always proved a poser, etc., etc.—and so forth. From which it will be seen that Sir Stopleigh belonged to that numerous class of persons which, when its attention turns towards wondermongering of any sort, loses its head promptly, and runs through the nearest available gamut of accepted phrases.

Her ladyship said she was not the least surprised at anything happening in a dream. She herself dreamed only the other night that Lady Pirbright had gone up in a balloon shaped like a gridiron, and the very next day came the news that old Canon Pirbright, at Trenchards Plaistowe, had had a paralytic stroke. It was impossible to account for these things. The only wonder to her was that Mr. Pelly should have recollected the whole so plainly, and been able to write it down. She would give anything to recollect that dream about the Circulating Library and the potted shrimps. Her ladyship discoursed for some time about her own dreams.

Mr. Pelly entirely concurred in the view that the whole thing was a dream. In fact, it would be absurd to suppose it anything else. When he got an opportunity to read Professor Schrudengesser's translation of the Italian MS. to his friends, they would readily see the source of most of the events his mind had automatically woven into a continuous narrative for the picture-woman to tell. He would rather read it to them himself than leave them the MS. to read, as there were points that would require explanation. He could not offer to do so till he came back from his great-grandniece Constance's wedding at Cowcester. A little delay would not matter. They would not have forgotten the dream-story in a fortnight. To this, assent was given in chorus.

But Madeline was not going to have the story pooh-poohed and made light of. "I believe it was a *ghost,* Uncle Christopher," said she. "The ghost of the woman in the picture. And you christened her after me by subconscious thingummy. *Maddalena's* Italian for Madeline. But they never give their names right. Ask anyone that has phenomena." Then she lit candles for all parties to go to bed, and kissed them all, including her alleged uncle, who laid stress on his claim for this grace in duplicate, as he had no one to kiss him at home. "Poor Uncle Christopher," said she, "he's been shut up in the dark with a ghost. . . . Oh yes!—I'm in earnest, and you're all a parcel of sillies." Then she borrowed his written account of the dream to re-read in bed, and take care the lamp didn't set fire to the curtains. She said she particularly wanted to look at that last sentence or two, about when the picture was in Chelsea.

CHAPTER V

THE story's brief reference to Mr. Aiken's life
after his good lady forsook him, may be sufficient for
its purposes, but the author is in a certain sense
bound to communicate to the reader any details
that have come to his knowledge.

Mr. Aiken's first step was to take an intimate
friend or two into his confidence. But his intimate
friend or two had a quality in common with Mr.
Pickwick's bottle or two. An intimate friend or
six would be nearer the mark—or even twelve.
He did not tell his story separately to each; there
was no need. If the mention of a private affair

within the hearing of cat or mouse leads to its
being shouted at once from the top of the house—
and that was the experience of Maud's young man
who went to the Crimea—how much more public
will your confidences become if you make them to
a tenant of a Studio that is one of a congeries.
Pimlico Studios was a congeries, built to accommodate the Artists of a great age of Art, now pending, as though to meet the needs of locusts. For
there can be no doubt that such an age is at hand,
if we are to judge by the workshop accommodation
that appears to be anticipating it. An ingenious
friend of the author—you must have noticed how
many authors have ingenious friends?—has been
able to determine by a system of averages of a most
irresistibly convincing nature, that the cubic area
of the Studios in Chelsea and Kensington alone
exceeds that of the Lunatic Asylums of the Metropolis by nearly seven and a quarter per cent. This
gentleman's researches on the subject are consequent upon his singular conviction that the output
of the Fine Arts, broadly speaking, is small in
proportion to the amount of energy and capital
devoted to them. We have reasoned with him in
vain on the subject, pointing out that the Fine Arts
have nothing in common with the economies of
Manufacture, least of all in any proportions between
the labour expended and the results attained.

Were it otherwise, the estimation of a painter's
merit would rise or fall with his colourman's bill
and the rent of his studio. This gentleman—
although he is a friend of the author—has no Soul.
If he had, the spectacle of the life-struggle which
is often the lot of Genius would appeal to him, and
cause him to suspend his opinion. It is always,
we understand, desirable to suspend one's opinion.
And he would do so, for instance, in the case of an
Artist, a common acquaintance of ours, whom at
present he condemns freely, calling him names.
This Artist has five Studios, each of them full of
easels and thrones. The number of his half-used
colour tubes that won't squeeze out is as the sands
of the sea, while his bundles of brushes that only
want washing to be as good as new, may be likened
to corn-sheaves, in so far as their stems go—a mere
affair of numeration. But their business ends are
another pair of shoes altogether; for, in the former,
the hairs have become a coagulum as hard as agate,
calling aloud for Benzine Collas to disintegrate them
—in the tune, this Artist admits, of threepence
each—whereas the ear of corn yields to less drastic
treatment. Contrivances of a specious nature in
japanned tin and celluloid abound, somewhat as
spray abounds on oceans during equinoxes, and
each of these has at one time fondly imagined it
was destined to become that Artist's great resource

and stand-by, the balustrade his genius would not
scorn to be indebted to. But he has never drawn
a profile with the copying-machine that has legs,
nor availed himself of the powers of the grapho-
scope—if that is its name—that does perspective,
nor done anything with the countless wooden
figures except dislocate their universal joints; nor,
we fear, for a long time paid anything on account
of the quarterly statements that flutter about, with
palette-knives full of colour wiped off on them, that
are not safe to sit down upon for months. But no
impartial person could glance at any of the in-
augurations of pictures on the thousand canvases
in these five Studios without at once exclaiming,
" This is Genius ! " The Power of the Man is everywhere visible, and no true lover of Art ever regrets
that so few of them have been carried into that
doubtful second stage where one spoils all the
moddlin' and the colour won't hold up, and somehow you lose the first spirit of the Idear and don't
get any forwarder. It never occurs to any mature
Critic to question the value of this Artist's results,
even of his least elaborated ones. And, indeed, an
opinion is current among his friends that restriction
of materials and of the area of his Studios might
have cramped and limited the free development of
a great mind. They are all unanimous that a
feller like Tomkins must have room to turn round,

or where are you! And, if, as we must all hope, the
growth of genius such as his is to be fostered as it
deserves, no one should look with an ungenerous
eye upon such agglomerations of Art-workshops as
the Pimlico Studios, or sneer at them as uncalled
for, merely because a Philistine Plutocracy refuses
to buy their produce, and has no walls to hang it on
if it did. We for our part can only note with regret
that any Studios should be so badly adapted to their
purpose, and constructed with so little consideration
for the comfort of their occupants, as these same
Pimlico Studios.

We have, however, been tempted away from our
subject, which at present is the community of
Artists that occupied them; and must return to it
to say that these very drawbacks were not altogether
without their compensations. For though these
Studios were unsound, like the arguments of Dis-
sent, being constructed to admit rainwater and
retain products of combustion, each of its own
stove and the Studio beneath it; these structural
shortcomings were really advantages, in so far as
they promoted interchange of social amenities between the resident victims of the speculative builder
who ran up the congeries. Sympathy against their
common enemy, the landlord, brought all the occupants of Pimlico Studios into a hotchpot of broth-
erly affection, and if the choruses of execration in

which they found comfort have reached the ears for which they were intended, that builder will catch it hot, one of these odd-come-shortlies. This expression is not our own.

When Mr. Reginald Aiken, with his domestic perplexity burning his tongue's end and crying aloud for utterance, called upon the Artist from whom we have borrowed it, that gentleman, Mr. Hughes, one of his most intimate friends, was thinking. He had been thinking since breakfast—thinking about some new aspects of Nature, which had been the subject of discussion with some friends the evening before. They were those new Aspects of Nature which have been presented so forcibly by Van Schronk and Le Neutre; and of which, in this Artist's opinion, more than a hint is to be found in Hawkins. He was thinking deeply when Mr. Aiken came in, and not one stroke of work had he done, would that gentleman believe him, since he set out his palette. Mr. Aiken's credulity was not overtaxed.

Mr. Hughes wanted to talk about himself, and said absently, "You all right, Crocky?" addressing Mr. Aiken by a familiar name in use among his intimate friends. He was not well disposed towards a negative answer when Mr. Aiken gave one; an equivocal one certainly, but not one to whose meaning it was possible to affect blindness. The

words were "Middlin'—considerin'!" But Mr.
Hughes was not going to be too coming.

"Wife well?" said he, remotely.

Mr. Aiken sprang at his inattentive throat, and
nailed him. "Ah, that's it," said he. "That's
the point."

Mr. Hughes was forced to inquire further, and
stand his Idea over, for later discussion. But he
might just as well have let it alone—better, if you
come to that. He really was a stupid feller, Hughes,
don't you know? "I say," said he, "don't you
run away and say I didn't tell you what would
happen." For he had interpreted his friend's
agitated demeanour and equivocal speech as the
result of a recent insight into futurity, showing him
in the position of a detected and convicted parent,
without the means of providing for an increasing
family. For they do that, families do.

"Don't be an ass, Stumpy," said he, using a
familiar name no fact in real life warranted. "It's
not that sort of thing, thank God! No—I'll tell
you what it is, only you mustn't on any account mention it."

"All right, Crocky! I never mention things.
Honest Injun! Go ahead easy." Mr. Hughes was
greatly relieved that his surmise had been wrong.
Good job for Mr. Aiken, as also for his wife! Mr.
Hughes desired his congratulations to this lady, but

withdrew them on second thoughts. Because, you
see, her escape from the anxieties of maternity was
entirely constructive. Mr. Hughes felt that he had
put his foot in it, and that his wisest course would
be to take it out. He did so. But Mr. Aiken had
something to say about his wife, and made it a
corollary to her disappearance from the conversation.

" She's bolted ! " said he lugubriously. " Went
away Thursday and wrote to say she wasn't coming
back, Friday. It's a fact."

Mr. Hughes put back his foot in it. " Who's she
bolted with ? Who's the feller ? "

Mr. Aiken flushed up quite red, like any turkey-
cock. " Damn it, Stump ! " said he, " you really
ought to take care what you're saying. I should
like to see any fellow presume to run away with
Euphemia. Draw it mild ! " He became calmer,
and it is to be hoped was ashamed of his irritability.
But really it was Mr. Hughes's fault—talking just
as if it was like in a novel, and Euphemia a character.

" I beg your pardon," said that offender humbly.
" It was the way you put it. Besides, they are
generally supposed to."

Mr. Aiken responded, correctively and loftily:
" Yes, my dear fellow, on the stage and in novels."
He added, with something of insular pride, " Chiefly
French and American."

"What's her little game, then?" asked Mr.
Hughes. "If it's not some other beggar, *what* is
it she's run away with?"

"She has not run away with anybody," said Mr.
Aiken with dignity. "Nor anything. Perhaps I
should explain myself better by saying that she has
refused to return from her Aunt's."

"Any reason?" said Mr. Hughes, who wanted to
get back to his Idea.

"I'm sorry to say it was my fault, Stumpy,"
came very penitently from the catechumen.

Interest was roused. "I say, young man," said
Mr. Hughes, with a tendency of one eye to close,
"what have you been at?"

"Absolutely nothing whatever!"

"Yes, of course! But along of who! Who's the
young woman you *haven't* been making love to? Tell
up and have done with it."

"You don't *understand,* Stump. Really *nobody!*"

Mr. Hughes thought a moment, as though he
were at work on a conundrum. Then he pointed
suddenly. "Fanny Smith!" said he, convictingly.

Mr. Aiken quite lost his temper, and got demonstrative. "Fanny Smith—Fanny grandmother!"
he exclaimed, meaninglessly. "How can you talk
such infernal rot, Stumpy! Do be reasonable!"

"Then it was *somebody,*" said his tormentor, and
Mr. Aiken felt very awkward and humiliated.

However, he saw inevitable confession ahead, and braced himself to the task. " Really, Stump," said he, " it would make you cry with laughing to know who it was that was at the bottom of it. I said ' Fanny grandmother,' just now, but at any rate Fanny Smith's a tailor's wife with no legs to speak of, who sits on the counter, and a very nice girl if you know her. I mean there's no fundamental absurdity in Fanny Smith. This was." Which wasn't good speechwork, but, oh dear, how little use accuracy is!

" Who was it then ? " Mr. Hughes left one eye shut, under an implied contract to reopen it as soon as the answer came to his question.

" Well ! " said Mr. Aiken reluctantly. " If you must have it, it was Sairah ! " He was really relieved when his friend looked honestly puzzled, repeating after him " Sairah ! What!—the gurl ! " in genuine astonishment. It was now evident that the Idea would have to stand over.

Mr. Hughes said farewell to it, almost audibly; then said " Stop a minute ! " and lit a pipe; then settled down in a rocking chair to listen, saying, " Now, my boy !—off you go." He was a long and loose-limbed person who picked his knees up alternately with both hands, as though to hold his legs on. Whenever he did this, the slipper in that connection came off, with the effect of bringing its

owner's sock into what is called keeping with the
rest of the Studio, one which many persons would
have considered untidy.

After which Mr. Aiken went off, or on—whichever you prefer. "Of course I don't expect you
fellers to do anything but chaff, you know. But
it's jolly unpleasant, for all that. It was like this,
don't you see? A young female swell had brought
her sweetheart—I suppose, unless he was her cousin
—to see a picture I'm cleaning for her parent, who is
a Bart. In Worcestershire. Know him? Sir Stopleigh Upwell."

Mr. Hughes didn't, that he could call to mind,
after a mental search which seemed to imply great
resources in Barts.

"Well—she was an awfully jolly girl, but quite
that sort." Mr. Aiken tried to indicate, by gesture,
a fashionably dressed young lady with a stylish
figure, and failed. But Mr. Hughes, an Impres-
sionist Artist, could understand, and nodded prompt
appreciation. So Mr. Aiken continued:

"When they cleared out, Euphemia said the
young woman was 'up-to-date.' And I suppose she
was. . . ."

"Oh certainly—quite up to date—not a doubt
of it!"

"Well—I made believe not to know the meaning
of the expression, just to take a rise out of Euphemia.

And you know she has just *one* fault—she's so matter-of-fact! She said everyone knew the meaning of ' up-to-date,' that knew anything. Ask anybody! Ask her Aunt Priscilla—and I certainly wasn't going to do that; just like bearding a tigress in her den with impertinent questions!— or Mrs. Verity the landlady. Or, for that matter, ask the gurl, Sairah! That's where *she* came in, Stump." Mr. Aiken seemed to hang fire.

" But," said Mr. Hughes, " she only comes in as an abstraction, so far. I can't see her carcass in it." From which we may learn that Mr. Hughes thought that abstract means incorporeal; or, at least, imponderable. It is a common error. " What did *you* say ? " he asked.

" I said ' Suppose I ask Sairah! ' and rang for her, for a lark. Euphemia was in an awful rage and pretended to go, but stopped outside to listen." The speaker's hesitation appeared to increase.

" Well—and when she came ? . . ."

" Why, the stupid idiot altogether misunderstood me. Damn fool! What the doose she thought I meant, I don't know. . . ."

" What did you say? Out with it, old chap! " Mr. Hughes seemed to be holding intense amusement back, with a knowledge that it would get the bit in its teeth in the end.

Mr. Aiken, seeing this, intensified and enlarged his

manner. " I *merely* said—No, really it's the simple
honest truth, every word—I *merely* said, ' Your
mistress says you know the meaning of "up-to-
date," Sairah.' And what does the beast of a girl
do but turn vermilion and stand staring like a stuck
pig."

Mr. Hughes began shaking his head slowly from
side to side. But he did not get to the direction
accelerando, for he stopped short, and said abruptly,
" Well—what next ? "

Mr. Aiken assumed a responsible and mature
manner, rather like that of a paterfamilias on his
beat. " I reasoned with the girl. Pointed out that
her mistress wouldn't say things to turn vermilion
about. I tried to soothe her suspicions. . . ."

Mr. Hughes interrupted. "I see. No tong-
dresses, of course ? "

Mr. Aiken explained that that was just where the
misapprehension had come in. If his wife had
been *inside* the room instead of on the *stairs,* she
would have seen that there was absolutely *nothing.*
Mr. Hughes looked incredulous.

, " There must have been somethin', old chap, to
set your missis off. Don't tell me ! "

But Mr. Aiken *would* tell Mr. Hughes—would
insist on doing so. " It was the horrible, shameless
brute's diabolical malice ! " he shouted. " Nothing
more nor less ! What does she do but say out loud

just as my wife was coming into the room, 'You keep your 'ands off of me, Mr. Aching!' and of course, when Euphemia came in, she thought I had just jumped half a mile off. And it was rough on me, Stump, because really my motive was to save my wife having to get another house-and-parlour-maid."

"Motive for what?" said Mr. Hughes shrewdly. He had touched the weak point of the story. "Did you, or did you not, young man, take this young person round the waist or chuck her under the chin?"

"My dear Hughes," said Mr. Aiken, with undisguised impatience, "I wouldn't chuck that odious girl under the chin with the end of a barge-pole. Nor," he added after reflection, "take her round the waist with one of the drags in readiness at the Lodge." The barge-pole had conducted his imagination to the Regent's Canal, and left it there.

Mr. Aiken had had no intention when he called on his friend Hughes to take the whole of Pimlico Studios into his confidence. But what was he to do when another Artist dropped in and Mr. Hughes said, "You won't mind Triggs? The most discreet beggar *I* ever came across!" What could he say that would arrest the entry of Mr. Triggs into the discussion of his family jar that would not appear to imply that that gentleman was an indiscreet beggar? And what course was open to him when Mr. Hughes told yet another Artist, whose name was Dolly, that he might come in, but he wasn't to listen? And yet another, whose name was Doddles?

Even if there had been no other chance visitors to the Studio during the conclave on Mr. Aiken's private affairs, there would have been every likelihood of complete publicity for them in the course of a day or two at most. For nothing stimulates Rumour like affidavits of secrecy. It's such fun telling what is on no account to go any farther. But as a matter of fact more than one gentleman who would have resented being called a *flâneur,* looked in at Mr. Hughes's Studio casually that morning to talk over that gentleman's Idea, mooted yesterday at The Club, and found himself outside a circle whose voices subsided to inaudible exchanges of postscripts to finish up. As each newcomer acted upon this in the sweet and candid manner of this community, saying unaffectedly " What's the fun? " and some friend of his within the circle usually said to him " Shut up! Tell you after! " and as moreover it was invariably felt that a single exclusion only embarrassed counsel, no opportunity was really lost of making Europe acquainted with the disruption of Mr. Aiken's household. And it was a pity, because so much gossip doesn't do any good. Besides, the time might have been profitably employed ventilating Mr. Hughes's Idea, and getting a sort of provisional insight into the best means of carrying it out. As it was, when, some time after midday, someone said, "I say, Stump, my boy, how about that Idea of yours we were talking about at The Club yesterday?" everyone else looked at his watch, and said it was too late to get on to that now; we must have lunch, and have a real serious talk about it another time. Then we went to lunch at Machiavelli's, and it was plenty early enough if we were back by three.

Mr. Aiken received a good deal of very sound advice from his friends as to how he might best deal with his emergency. He turned this over in his mind as he turned himself over on his couch when he got home about three in the morning, and was rather at a loss to select from it any samples from different Mentors which agreed upon a course. In fact, the only one thing they had in common was the claim made by their respective promulgators to a wider and deeper knowledge of that mysterious creature Woman than Mr. Aiken's inexperience could boast. One said to him—speaking as from long observation of a Sex you couldn't make head or tail of—that depend upon it she would come round, you see if she didn't. They always did.

Another, that this said Sex was obstinacy itself, and you might depend upon it she would stick out. They always did. Another, that a lot the best thing for a husband in like case to do was to go and cosset the offended lady over with appropriate caresses, before which she would be sure to soften. They always did. Another, that if you could convince her by some subtle machinations that you didn't care a twopenny damn how long she stayed away, back she would come on the nail. They always did. In the multitude of counsellors there is Wisdom, no doubt, but when the multitude is large enough to advise every possible course, it is just as easy to run through all the courses open to adoption by oneself, and choose one on the strength of its visible recommendations. More particularly because so many advisers insist on your taking their advice, and go on giving it, cataballatively, if you don't. Mr. Aiken felt, when he retired for the night, like the sheet Aunt Sally hangs up behind her being folded up at the end of a busy day on Epsom Downs.

It was a great pity that Mr. Aiken's domestic upset did not occur a few days later, because then Mr. Hughes's Idea would have had such a much clearer stage for its début. As it was, what with one thing and what with another, the mature discussion of this subject was delayed a full week. Next day

Triggs had to go to Paris, and of course it was nonsense to attempt anything without him—for look at the clearness of that man's head! Then, when Triggs came back, a day later than expected, his Aunt must needs invite her nephew down to Suddington Park, which is her place in Shropshire, which had earned for Mr. Triggs the name of The Pobble—you remember Aunt Jopiska's Park, if you read Lear in youth—and which was an expectation of his, if he kept in favour with the old lady. Of course, the Idea didn't depend on Triggs, or any one man. No, thank you! But Triggs had a good business head on his shoulders, and was particularly sound on the subject of Premises. It is a singular and noticeable thing that whenever any great motive or scheme germinates in the human brain, that brain, before it has formulated the conditions thereof, or fully defined its objects, will begin to look at Premises, and while it is examining some very much beyond its means—in Piccadilly, for instance, or Old Bond Street—will feel that the project is assuming form, and that now we shall get on to really *doing* something, and come to the end of this everlasting talk, talk, talk, that leads to nothing, and only sets people against us. So really very little could be done till The Pobble came back from Aunt Jopiska. When he did come back there was some other delay, but it's always well to be beforehand. The enthusiasts of this Idea could look at Premises; and did so.

All this has little or nothing to do with the story. But it serves to individualize Mr. Hughes, who, but for it, would be merely a long artist with a goatee beard, who not infrequently looked in to smoke a pipe on the split wild boar whose head endangered the safety of self-warmers on Mr. Aiken's floor in the Studio near the stove where he found the Vestas that were all stuck together.

Mr. Hughes was standing there, a good many weeks after our last date, chatting with Mr. Aiken, who was becoming quite slovenly and dirty with nobody to look after him—because, of course, Mrs. Parples, who came in by the day, hadn't the sense to see to anything; and, moreover, he was that snappy at every turn, there wasn't, according to Mrs. Parples, many would abear him.

He had been hoping that the first of his advisers whom we cited was right, and that if he waited a reasonable time he would see if his wife wouldn't come round. If they always did, she would. But he was beginning to be afraid they sometimes didn't. He had even impatiently expressed a view equivalent to that which identified her with obstinacy itself, the quality. But this was only temper, though no doubt she might stick out. They might sometimes, those curious examples of a perfectly unique Sex. He really wanted to go to her with persuasive arts and procure a reconciliation. But he was too proud.

Besides, if that was possible now, it would be equally so three months hence. As to the fourth alternative, that of showing he didn't care, that would be capital on the stage, but he wasn't going to burn his fingers with it in real life. So he passed his days working, in his own conceit; and smoking in a chair opposite to his work, in Mrs. Parples'. Perhaps neither conception was quite correct. His evenings he mostly passed seeing bad plays well acted, or good plays ill acted—these are the only sorts you can get free paper for. It was ridiculous for him, knowing such a lot of actors, to pay at the door. Now and again, however, he stayed at home, and a friend came in for a quiet smoke. Even so Mr. Hughes, this evening.

"Things improvin' at all, Crocky?" said he, not exactly as if he thought he wasn't inquisitive.

Mr. Aiken kept an answer, which was coming, back for consideration. He appeared to reject it, going off at a tangent by preference. He had made up his mind, he said, not to fret his kidneys any more over his wife's absence. She would come round before long, and eat humble pie for having made such a fool of herself. He preferred the

expression "damn fool," but chivalry limited its
utterance to a semi-*sotto voce*. "I might get a
letter from her any minute," said he. "Why,
when the post came just now, I fully expected it
was a letter from her." He appeared to confuse
between expectation's maximum and its realiza-
tion. "There he is again. I shouldn't be the least
surprised if this one *was*."

He left the room with a transparent parade of
deliberation. But before he had reached the staircase the postman knocked again, and Mr. Aiken
came back saying: "It isn't her. It's something
that won't go in the box." This was slack language
and slack reasoning—confusion confounded. But
Mr. Aiken retired on it with dignity, saying: "Mrs.
Parples attends to the door."

The something continued to refuse, audibly, to
go in the box, and Mrs. Parples didn't attend to the
door. The postman put all his soul into a final
knock, which seemed to say, "I am leaving, half-
out, what may be only an advertisement, or may
be vital to your hereafter, or somebody's;" and
then washed his hands of it and took up Next
Door's case. Mr. Aiken listened for Mrs. Parples,
who remained in abeyance, and then went out again
and returned with a very ill-made-up consignment
indeed, and a normal square envelope with a be-
spoken "M" embossed on its flap, directed in

an upright hand, partly robust, partly æsthetic, an expression applied nowadays to anything with a charm about it. This handwriting had one.

"Parples is sleeping peacefully," said Mr. Aiken. "It would be a shame to disturb Parples. I know who this is." He opened the envelope with difficulty, but looked stroked and gratified. The latter was from his very sincerely Madeline Upwell. Just you notice any male friend of yours next time you have a chance of seeing one open a letter from youth and beauty which remains—however theoretically—his very sincerely, and see if he doesn't look stroked and gratified.

Mr. Hughes picked up the delivery that had given the letter-box so much trouble, and looked through it at each end. Mr. Aiken was busy reading his letter over and over; so he could only throw out a sideways carte-blanche to Mr. Hughes to unpack the inner secret of the roll. This was what he was reading:

"DEAR MR. AIKEN,

"I think you may like a copy of the photo Captain Calverley (who perhaps you will remember came with me to your Studio) made of this beautiful picture, which I am never tired of looking at. I think it so good. Please accept it from us if you care to have it. Believe me, dear Mr. Aiken, with kind

regards to yourself and Mrs. Aiken, in which my
mother joins,

"Yours very sincerely,

"MADELINE UPWELL.

"P.S.—I know you will be sorry to hear that
Captain Calverley's regiment is ordered out to South
Africa. Of course, it makes us very anxious."

"Transparent sort of gurl!" said Mr. Hughes,
when Mr. Aiken read the letter aloud to him. "Of
course, Captain Carmichael's her sweetheart. Anybody can see that with half an eye."

"Calverley," said Mr. Aiken. "Yes—they get
like that when it's like that." And both pondered
a little, smoking, over the peculiarities of humanity,
especially that inexplicable female half of it.
"Chuck it over here and let's have a look at it," he
added, and Mr. Hughes chucked him over the
photograph. He contemplated it for a moment in
silence; then said: "I expect she wasn't far out,
after all. Euphemia, I mean."

"Chuck it back again and let's have another
look," said Mr. Hughes. Mr. Aiken did so, and let
him have the other look. "Yes," said he. "They
went it in Italy, about that time, don't you know!
Fifteenth or sixteenth century. That sort of
thing!" For Mr. Hughes knew a lot about Italy,
and could quote Browning. He uncrickled a result

of the shape of that letter-box, or tried to, and then stood the photograph so that they could both see it, while they talked of something else, against the grès-de-Flandres straight-up pot that was so handy to stand brushes in, like umbrellas.

They had plenty to talk about, because at this time the Idea of Mr. Hughes that was destined to fill so important an horizon in the History of Modern Art, and was also pregnant with incalculable consequences to several things or persons, besides having an indirect bearing on several others, and challenging the bedrock of Modern Art Criticism— for it had the courage of its convictions, and stuck at nothing—this Idea was taking form slowly but surely, and was already making itself felt in more ways than one. It was easy to laugh at it—this was indisputable—but he who lived longest would see most. It had a future before it, and if you would only just wait twenty years, you would see if it hadn't. You mark the words of its disciple, whoever he was you were talking to—that was all he said—and see if he wasn't right! He was a little indignant—some samples of him—with audiences who decided to wait, his own enthusiasm believing that the results might be safely anticipated. However, the Idea prospered, there is no doubt of that, and the circle of enthusiasts who had leagued themselves together to foster it and promote a true understanding of it had already taken premises, and their telephone number was 692,423 Western.

"It's true," said Mr. Hughes, "that the light in the Galleries is bad, and the hot-air system of warming will destroy any ordinary oil picture in a month. But altering all that is the merest question of money—comes off the guarantee fund, in fact. And one thing nobody but a fool can help seein', at the first go off, is that the Galleries are rum. Rumness is half the battle." This expressed so deep and indisputable a truth that Mr. Aiken could not assent strongly enough in mere words. He nodded rapidly and most expressively, without speech. However, when he had reached the natural limits of a nod's assenting power, he added, "Right you are, Stumpy, my boy. Gee up!" and Mr. Hughes resumed:

"I ain't sayin', mind you, Crocky, that any sort of hocus-pocus is justifiable in any case. When I use the expression 'rum,' I am keepin' in view the absolute necessity for a receptive attitude of mind in the visitor to the Galleries. Tell me such an attitude of mind is possible without a measure of rumness as a stimulant, and I say 'Humbug!'"

Mr. Aiken said again, "Right you are, Stumpy." But he did not rise to enthusiasm—seemed low and depressed.

"It all connects with the fundamental root of

the Idea," Mr. Hughes continued. "No one would be more repugnant than myself to any ramification in the direction of Wardour Street . . . you understand me? . . ."

"Rather!" said Mr. Aiken. And he seemed to do so. It is not necessary for the purposes of this story to prove that either of these gentlemen understood what they were talking about, or anything else, but their conversation has a bearing on their respective characters and their preoccupations at this moment, which are part of it.

Mr. Hughes had mounted a rhetorical hobby, and wished to have his ride. He rigged up three fingers of his left hand, holding them in front of him to check off three heads on, as soon as he should come to that inevitable stage. He did not know what they would be, but his instinctive faith made nothing of that. They would be needed, all in good time.

"I am not saying," he pursued, "that Wardour Street, in its widest sense, has nothing to recommend it. I am not saying that it makes no appeal. I am not disputing its historical and ethical standpoints . . . you see what I mean?" This was a concession to the difficulties that await the orator who expects to round up his sentences. Mr. Aiken interjected, to help this one out of an embarrassment:

"Couldn't be better put! Let it go at that;" and knocked some ashes out of his pipe.

Mr. Hughes was grateful, because he had had no idea what to say next. His indebtedness, however, had to be ignored; else, what became of Dignity? An enlarged manner accepted a laurel or two due to lucidity, as he continued: "But I do say this, that, considered as a basis—perhaps I should say a fulcrum—or shall I say as a working hypothesis of the substratum or framework of the Idea? . . ." The speaker hesitated.

"That's the safest way to put it," said Mr. Aiken, but rather gloomily. He was re-lighting his pipe.

"I think so," said Mr. Hughes judicially. "Considered as . . . what I said just now . . . Wardour Street is, to my thinkin', played out. Quite distinctly played out. . . . What's that?"

"What's what?" The questions seemed to refer to something heard and unheard, by each speaker respectively. Mr. Aiken did not press for an answer, but went to the door, persuading his pipe to draw by the way. "Want anything, Mrs. Parples?" said he, looking out. But no answer came. "Mrs. P. is sleeping happily in the kitchen," said he, returning. "It wasn't her. It was an effect of something."

"I suppose it was. Thought I heard it, too."

Perhaps, if you ever chanced to hear a conversation about nobody could exactly say what, you
noticed that nobody did say anything very exactly,
and everybody talked like these two gentlemen,
who certainly had heard something, but who
decided that they hadn't, because they couldn't find
out what it was.   It was too slight to discuss.

They each said " Rum ! " and settled down to
chat again, after turning down the gas, which made
a beastly glare. Mr. Hughes had forgotten about
the three heads, though, and taken his fingers down.
He did, however, pursue the topic which claimed
his attention, having embarked upon it, and feeling
bound to conduct it to a close.   He said something
to this effect, and we hope our report is fairly
accurate.   He certainly appeared to say that something, which could hardly have been anything,
grammatically, but the close to which he conducted
the topic, embodied the point which underlay the
whole of the extensive area which the Idea opened up
for development, and turned upon the indisputable
truth that the Highest Art—sculpture, music,
painting, poetry—is never intelligible to the ver-
nacular mind. How could any inference be more
incontestable than that no Art could rise above
mediocrity until a quorum of commonplace persons
should be found honestly incapable of attaching
any meaning to it ? By making unintelligibility to

the banal mind a criterion of superiority in Art, we
established a Standard of Criticism, and eliminated
from consideration a wilderness of insipidity which
Mr. Hughes did not hesitate to call a nightmare.
For his part, he was so confident that the system
of Negative Juries, as they had been called, was
sounder than any appeal to popular applause that
he was quite willing that his own work should stand
or fall by the decision of the Commonplace Intelligence as to which side up the picture should be
looked at. He would go that length, and take the
consequences. Let the Selection Committee of their
proposed Annual Exhibition consist entirely of such
Intelligences, and let the Hanging Committee hang
all the pictures they were unable to make head or tail
of, and such a galaxy of productions of Genius would
be accumulated every year on their walls as the World
had never before seen.

"Not work in practice?" said Mr. Hughes, replying to a morose doubt of Mr. Aiken's. "Just
you redooce it to practice. Take the case that
your Jury guesses the subject of a picture. Out
it goes! Did you ever know that class able to
make head or tail of the subject of a work of Genius?
Gradual and infallible elimination, my boy—that's
the ticket!" The speaker, who, though perhaps
rather an idiot—only, mind you, he was subject now
and then to something almost like Inspiration—threw

himself back in his chair as though he had exhausted the subject, and might rest.

"Don't b'lieve it would work," said Mr. Aiken, sucking at his pipe. But he was evidently in a temper this evening, and Mr. Hughes paid no attention to his nonsense. However, it was no use talking about the Idea to him until he was more sympathetic. He would come right presently.

To cajole him into a better frame of mind, Mr. Hughes began talking of something else. "Queer sort of Studio, this of yours, Crocky," said he.

"What do you make out's queer about it, Stumpy?" said Mr. Aiken.

"Such peculiar echoes!"

"I don't hear any echoes."

"Well, when you went to the door—you heard that?"

"Oh, that wasn't an echo: that was somebody spoke outside."

"Somebody spoke outside? What did she say? What was it you heard?"

"Couldn't say. What did you?"

"Well, what I heard sounded like 'Where is Mrs. Aiken?' You shut up and listen a minute." Mr. Aiken accepted the suggestion, and the two sat listening in the half-dark.

Now, whenever sounds are listened for, they show a most obliging spirit, becoming audible where

you thought silence was going on peacefully alone.
The first sound that made Mr. Hughes say " There
now!—what's that?" turned out to be the gas,
which, at a carefully chosen point, rippled. The
next proved to be an intermittent spring fizzing on
the hot stove from a water-jar placed upon it.
The third was a spontaneous insect unknown to
Entomology, which had faced the difficulties of
self-making, behind the skirting, and evidently was
not going to remain a mere cipher. The fourth
was something or other that squeaked on the table,
and if one changed the places of things, noises like
that always stopped. So Mr. Aiken shifted the
things about, and said Mr. Hughes would see that
would stop it. He faced the responsibilities of the
Investigator by quenching the phenomenon, a time-
honoured method. He wrapped up the photograph,
and put it away in a drawer to show to Euphemia.
It would be interestin' to see if she recognized it.
. . . Oh yes! she would be back in the next few
days—sure to!

And Mr. Hughes saw that the shifting about of
the things on the table *had* stopped the noise he
called an echo, and what more could he or anybody
want? So he sat down again and had some toddy,
and talked about the Idea. And towards one in
the morning he got the opportunity of checking off
three heads on his three fingers, and feeling that

he ought to have been in Parliament. He had felt
previously rather like a Seneschal with three spears
vacant over his portcullis, longing for a healthy de-
capitation to give them employment.

The foregoing chapter, apart from the way in
which it emphasizes Mr. Aiken's loneliness and dis-
content as a bachelor, would be just as well left
out of the story, but for the seemingly insignificant
incident of the echo, or whatever it was, which
might have been unintelligible if referred to hereafter, without its surroundings.

CHAPTER VI

EUPHEMIA AIKEN, be it understood, had not
brought definition to bear on her motives for running away to her Aunt Priscilla at Coombe. It
seemed the nearest handy way of expressing her indignation at her profligate husband's conduct—that
was all.

By the time she had got to Clapham Junction her
indignation had begun to cool. But no ruction

would hold out for five minutes if it depended on legitimate indignation. Unfortunately, when that emotion gets up, it always awakens pride, with whom —or which—it has been sleeping. And pride, once roused—and she or it is not a sound sleeper— won't go to bed again on any terms, not even when indignation is quite tired out, and ready for another snooze. So when Euphemia got to Clapham Junction, it was not her drowsy indignation that made up its mind she should take a third-class single ticket, but her proper pride, which said peremptorily that even a weekly return would be absurd. Besides, there weren't any weekly returns. Besides, it was only threepence difference. Anyhow, she wasn't going to come back till she had given Reginald a severe lesson. Her condition of mind was no doubt the one her husband described by an expression obscure in itself, but too widely accepted to be refused a place in the language. He said that her monkey was up.

There is a sense of the irrevocable about the taking of a railway ticket. Even when it is only ninepence-halfpenny—the sum Euphemia paid to go third to Coombe and Malden—one's soul says, as the punch bites a piece viciously out of it, that the die is cast. If you were to hear suddenly that bubonic plague had broken out at, for instance, Pegwell Bay, you having booked to Ramsgate,

would not you feel committed to your visit, plague
or no? Would not your wife say, " But we have
taken our tickets "? Ours would. Was it any
wonder that, with Pride at her elbow and her ticket
inside her glove, Mrs. Reginald Aiken resisted a
faint temptation to get out at Wimbledon and go
back by the next up train that would promise to
stop at Clapham Junction? The story cannot pretend it is sorry she did not, because it would have
lost all interest for the general reader by her doing so.

We ourselves believe that if it had not been for
Miss Priscilla Bax, she might have returned to her
husband next day. The human race has, however,
to stand or fall by its aunts, as it finds them, they
being almost always *faits accomplis* when its com-
ponent individuals are born. Miss Bax had been
one some forty years when her niece Euphemia came
on the scene, and one of the good lady's strong points
was the low opinion she had of persons who married
into her family. She was, however, a kind-hearted
old lady, in spite of her disapproval of her niece's
choice of a husband, and his choice of a profession;
and had not only countenanced the marriage, but
had allowed the couple, as above related, a hundred
a year. Being the only well-off member of her
family, she was expected to do this sort of thing.
Like the well-off members of other families, she

was only permitted to have property on condition
that she did not keep it for herself.

When Euphemia's cab from the station drove her
up to Athabasca Villa, her aunt's residence, this
lady had got through her seven o'clock dinner, and
couldn't imagine who that could possibly be. It
was such a queer time for visitors. It must be a
mistake. She was so satisfied of this that she in-
augurated a doze, listening through its preamble for
something to explain the mistake. She was betrayed
by the doze, which might have had a minute's patience, and was roused from what it insidiously became by a voice, saying guardedly: " Oh dear, I'm
afraid I waked you up ! "

" I was not asleeep," said Miss Priscilla, with
dignity, kissing the owner of the voice. " I was
listening." However, it took time to wake quite
up, and until that happened the old lady did not
fully grasp the surprising character of so late a
visit; and indeed, until she became aware that a
box was being carried upstairs, had but dreamy
impressions of the event. In time reality dawned,
and she showed it by saying: " I suppose, Euphemia,
you will want your bed made up."

As this was the case, and no human ingenuity
could soften the fact, Mrs. Aiken only said: " I
know it's very troublesome."

To which Miss Priscilla replied: " Nothing is

troublesome, so long as you only say distinctly. Now, do you want anything to eat? Because dinner is taken away." Reviving decision, after sleep, became emphatic. Self-respect called for self-assertion.

Mrs. Aiken shuffled. She wasn't hungry, she said.

" Have you *had* dinner? Because if you have *not* had dinner, you *must* have dinner. Ring the bell twice, and Pemphridge will come."

Pemphridge came, and could warm the chicken. Pemphridge did warm the chicken, and Mrs. Aiken hardly touched it. After which she returned, looking extremely miserable, to her aunt in the drawing-room, who said majestically: " And now perhaps, Euphemia, you will tell me what all this means."

" It's Reginald," said Euphemia.

" I am not surprised," said her aunt.

" But you don't *know* yet."

" I know nothing whatever. But I am not surprised. Is it reasonable, Euphemia, to expect me to be surprised? After what I have so frequently had occasion to say. But I am quite prepared to hear that I have said no such thing. Pray tell me anything you like. I will not contradict you." Aunt Priscilla assumed a rigid continuousness, as of one who forms to receive aspersions. Truth will triumph in the end; meanwhile there is no harm in portending that triumph by an aggressive stony patience.

" Only you don't know what it *is*, Aunt Priscey,"
said her niece. No more she did, speaking academically. She was, however, quite prepared for every
contingency.

" I do not think *you* are the person to say *that*
to me, Euphemia, seeing that you have told me
nothing—absolutely nothing! But I can wait."
She waited. As she lay face upwards on the sofa—
the nearest approach to an Early Victorian recum-
bent effigy that the Nature of things permits—she
presented the appearance of a deserving person
floating on her back in a sea of exasperation. Unless this image justifies itself, it must be condemned.
Nothing in literature can excuse it.

Mrs. Euphemia was so used to her aunt, with
whom she had lived since the death of her parents
fifteen years since, that she knew she might never
get a better moment than this for telling the story
of her passage of arms with her husband. She therefore embarked on a narrative of the events we know,
and contrived to get them told, in spite of interruptions, the nature of which, after the foregoing sample
of Aunt Priscilla, we can surmise. Neither need
be repeated.

Thereafter followed a long conversation, the substance of which has already been given. Its effect
was to try Mrs. Euphemia's faith in her husband—
which still existed, mind you!—very severely. Have

you ever noticed—but of course you have—that
when Inexperience testifies to the sinfulness of the
human race *passim,* Average Experience hides her
diminished head, and does not venture on whatever
there is to be said on behalf of the culprit. A
shocking race, no doubt, but scarcely so bad as pure
minds paint it! Old single ladies have pure minds,
as often as not, and wield them with a fiendish
dexterity, polishing off Lancelot and Galahad,
Modred and Arthur himself, all in a breath. Which
of us dares to try a fall with a pure-minded person,
in defence of his sex, or anyone else's? Miss
Priscilla, having a pure mind and getting the bit
in her teeth in connection with her nephew-in-law's
shortcomings, bolted, and dragged her niece after
her through an imaginary Society compounded of
London in the days of the Regency and Rome in
the days of Tiberius, with a touch of impending
Divine vengeance in the bush, justifying reference
to Sodom and Gomorrah. She succeeded in making
the young woman thoroughly uncomfortable, and
causing the quarrel to assume proportions—which is
what things that get bigger are understood to do
nowadays—such as it never dreamed of at first.
For Mrs. Euphemia's scheme of life allowed for everlasting bickerings, never-ending recriminations, last
words *ad libitum,* short tiffs, long tiffs, tempersome-
ness and proper spirit—all, in fact, that makes life

drag in families—but always under chronic conditions that precluded a crisis. If her worthy aunt's suggestion that this incident of Sairah was the merest spark from *ignes suppositos cineri,* and that her husband had never been even as good as he should be—if this indicated a true view of his character, she for one wasn't going to put up with such conduct, Corinthians or no! This *was* a crisis, only it was one that never would have come about but for Miss Priscilla. So, as we mentioned some time since, Mrs. Euphemia cried herself to sleep, and next day, galled by ill-considered moral precepts about the whole duty of Woman, wrote an infuriated letter to her dear Reginald—not her dearest; she might have any number of dearer Reginalds on draught—stating at a very high figure the amount of penance she would make a necessary condition of reconciliation, and even then it would never be the same thing underlined. She was, however, so completely the slave of a beautiful disposition, that no course was open to her but forgiveness, subject only to a reduction of some ninety-per-cent. at the dictation of a rarely sensitive consciousness of obligation to Duty, which she gave him to understand was her ruling passion. The letter demanded the assimilation of an amount of humble pie outside practical politics—so Mr. Aiken said to a friend after reading it; the phraseology is his. He hadn't done anything to deserve the character imputed to him in language he could identify by the style as Aunt Priscilla's, shorn of much of its Scriptural character. It incensed him, and caused him to write a letter which widened the breach between them. Then she wrote back, and the breach fairly yawned. There is nothing so effective as correspondence to consolidate a quarrel.

She had been at all times since her marriage a frequent visitor enough at Athabasca Villa for the inquisitiveness of her aunt's circle of friends to remain unexcited; for a week or so, at any rate. But that good lady's unholy alacrity in disclaiming all knowledge of her niece's domestic affairs stimulated a premature curiosity. When the Peter Dudburys called, Aunt Priscilla might quite easily have said, in reply to Mrs. Peter Dudbury's " And *how* is the Artist?" that she believed the said Artist was enjoying good health. Instead of which she was seized with a sort of paroxysm, exclaiming very often: "Don't ask me! I know nothing whatever about it. Nuth, thing-what, ever!" and shaking her head with her eyes tight shut. Whereupon Ellen Jane Dudbury said, " Shishmar!" and stamped cruelly on her mother's foot. Now really that amiable woman had only expanded into her gushy inquiry after Mr. Aiken because she knew that she and her three daughters had asked more than

once after everyone else. She felt hurt, and resolved to have it out with Ellen Jane, and indeed
began to do so as soon as they were out of hearing.

"Wellmar," said Ellen Jane, "what is one to do
when you won't take the slightest notice?" She
went on to explain that any person of normal
shrewdness would have seen, the moment Mrs.
Aiken made excuses and went upstairs, that there
was something. You could always see when there
was anything if you chose to use your eyes. It was
no use telling her—Ellen Jane, that is—that there
was nothing. She knew better. It was complimentary to Ellen Jane's penetration that her mother
and sisters hoped aloud at the next house where
they called and captured the tenants to inquire
after them, that there really *was* nothing between
young Mrs. Aiken and her husband, and most likely
it was all fancy, because there was nothing whatever to go upon, and such absurd stories did get
about.

To our thinking it is clear that the receptivity
of the Peter Dudburys was caused by that paroxysm
of Aunt Priscilla's. An adoption of a like attitude
with other visitors tended to enrich the gossip of
Coombe and Malden at the expense of Mrs. Euphemia
Aiken.

Miss Priscilla did not have paroxysms of this class
in her niece's presence, so of course the latter had

the less chance of guessing that the cause of her
visit to Athabasca Villa had become common property. She did, however, wake up to the fact that
Coombe and Malden were commiserating her. The
impertinence of those neighbourhoods! She would
have liked to knock their heads together. The worst
of it was that no one put commiseration into a con-
crete form, such as "How is dear Mr. Aiken's
infidelity going on?" or "We are so shocked to
think how your most sacred affections are being
lacerated." Then she might have flown at such
like sympathizers with a poker, or got them down
and cricked their joints by Ju-jitsu. This practice
of talking about everyone else's private affairs to
every-other else, never to their proprietor, is good
for our father the Devil, but bad for his sons and
daughters. Amen.

The truth is that, for some unexplained reason, a
lady who runs away from her husband gets no sort
of credit or glory by doing so, but only puts herself
in an uncomfortable position; unless, indeed, she
takes up with some other male, preferably a reprobate. Then an unhallowed splendour envelops
her, and protects her from the cards of respectability,
which has misgivings about her possible effect on
its sons and husbands. We wonder, is this what
is meant when one hears that some lady is living
under the protection of Duke Baily or Duke

Humphy? Are those—is one of them, we mean—protecting her from Mrs. Peter Dudbury? Honour to his Grace, whichever he is, if he acts up to his description!

With the nobler sex the reverse is the case. Whether deserting or deserted, he is rather looked up to by his more securely anchored male friends as the subject of a wider and more illuminating experience than their own. Of course, the forsaken example does not shine with the radiance of a self-supporting inconstancy. It may be that he comes off best in the end, if he is a man of spirit, and finds consolation elsewhere. For then he can not only crow, farmyard-wise, but he has the heartfelt satisfaction of being an ill-used man into the bargain. If he cottons to someone else's ill-used wife, he has nothing left to wish for.

Nothing of all this has any application in this story, unless it attaches to the fact that Mr. Aiken found some consolation in the company of his friends, while his wife found none in that of her acquaintances. As both parties were perfectly blameless in the ordinary sense of the word—geese are most blameless birds—none of the numerous advantages of wickedness were secured by either. Their interests in Belial never vested. Mrs. Aiken never meant not to go back in the end, as soon as she had made her husband knuckle down, and confess up. And he was consciously keeping his home unsullied by anything too Bohemian, in order that when Euphemia came back—as of course she would—no memory of the interregnum should clash with the Restoration.

Euphemia had the worst of it; but then she was the weaker party. If weaker parties take to expecting the emoluments of stronger parties, what shall we come to next? This feeling of the unfairness of things in general and Destiny in particular, tended towards exasperation and intensification, and the South Cone—metaphors may be fetched from any distance—remained up in the districts of Coombe and Malden. Time passed and Mrs. Euphemia had perforce to endure the commiseration of those districts.

The neighbourhood of Athabasca Villa might be classed as a congested district, and its population as consisting, broadly speaking, of good souls and busybodies. Every resident was both, be it understood.

"Oh yes!" said Euphemia to her aunt, one breakfast time. "Of course the Groobs are goodness itself. But why can't they mind their own business?" For although it may appear incredible, a family residing in the neighbourhood was actually named Groob.

"My dear," said Miss Priscilla, "do not be un-

reasonable and violent. Mr. Latimer Groob is, I
understand, a wine-importer in quite a large way of
business, with more than one retail establishment;
and his son, Mr. Adolphus Groob, has, I am told,
talent. He has had several pictures on the line,
somewhere, and comes down to see his family on
Saturdays, and to stop till Monday."

"Well, then!" said Euphemia. "It wasn't the
Peter Dudburys this time. At least, it needn't have
been, for anything I can see."

"Why not? . . . Do take care of the table-
cloth! Anne has put one of the best out by mistake.
I must speak to her. . . . Why not the Peter Dudburys this time?"

"I am not cutting the cloth. The knife is miles
off. Why not the Peter Dudburys? Why, because I know that odious little Dolly Groob. He's a
friend of Reginald's, and comes to the Studio. I
can *see*. I'm not a baby. Of course, Reginald has
been talking to him." Mrs. Euphemia bit her lips,
and was under the impression that her eyes flashed.
But they didn't really—eyes never do; it's a *façon
de parler*.

Miss Priscilla ignored this petulance. "You had
better let me pour you out some fresh coffee," she
said. "Yours is getting cold. I cannot say, my
dear, that I think ' that odious little Dolly Groob '
is at all the way to speak of an artist who has had

pictures on the line. And his **father**, now I think of it, is in Paris also. Besides, I see he is distinguishing himself by his connection with something."

" With what ? "

" It was in yesterday evening's paper. Perhaps Anne hasn't burned it. Anyhow, I do *not* think the expression ' odious little ' well chosen. . . . Oh yes—that's it! Give it to Miss Euphemia." That is to say, Anne the parlourmaid, not having burned yesterday's evening paper, had produced it as by necromancy, in response. The way Aunt Priscilla spoke of her niece was an accident, not a suggestion that Mr. Aiken was cancelled. It caused " Miss Euphemia," however, a slight twinge of an indescribable discomfort. Possibly, if this is ever read by any lady who has ever been in exactly the same position, she will understand why.

The story knows of it because, when Anne had left the room, Mrs. Aiken looked up from the newspaper, where she had found what she was looking for, to say: " I think, Aunt Priscey, you might be more careful before the servants."

Her aunt replied with dignity: " What you are referring to, my dear Euphemia, I cannot profess to understand." Of course she *did,* perfectly well. What she meant was, " I know you cannot get a conviction, so I can tell a fib." Mankind, securely entrenched, fibs freely.

"Why—'Miss Euphemia,' of course!" said the niece, quoting incisively. "But I know it's no use my asking you to pay the slightest attention." She became absorbed in her paper.

"I think you are nonsensical, my dear," said the aunt. She retired behind something morally equivalent to the lines of Torres Vedras; but was still audible outside, saying: "I think you might say whether you have, or have not, found about Mr. Adolphus Groob."

The niece made no response for a moment, but continued reading; then said, as one who, coming up from diving, speaks without quite locating his audience: "Oh yes—there's about Mr. Groob here. I can't read it all, there's such a lot. Is there some coffee left? . . . Three-quarters of a cup, please!"

Please observe that, although this aunt and niece always conversed more or less as if each was straining the patience of the other past endurance, no sort of ill-will was thereby implied on either part. It may be that it was only that they emphasized the ordinary intercourse of British families. Perhaps you know how much the average foreign family nags, *en famille*. We do not.

Mrs. Aiken read the newspaper paragraph aloud, skipping portions. What she read described the formation of the New Modernism, the Artistic

Society about which so much was being said among
well-informed circles of the Art World, with the
reservation that nothing must be accepted as official.
The Editor was breaking confidence in telling so
much; but then he really was unable, with that
pitiful heart of his, to bear the yearning faces and
heartrending cries for information of his reading
public. The only course open to him was to put
aside all conscientious scruples, and divulge what
had reached him, as it were, under the seal of confession. Such a thirst must be satiated, or worse
might come of it. The object of this Society was
to develop its promoters' ideas, and exhibit their
works in Bond Street. The underlying theory of
their new Gospel of Art appeared to be—only the
writer did not express it so coarsely—that success
in pictorial effort, in the future, must turn on the
artist never having learned to draw, and not knowing how to paint. What was wanted was clearly
his unimpaired Self, unsoiled by the instruction of
the Schools. The near future was entitled to
liberation from the stilted traditions of the remote
past, not only in painting, but in Sculpture, Music,
Poetry, the Drama—what not. Here was an
opportunity to make a beginning, seized by a
brilliant coterie of talented young men, whom a rare
chance had brought together under one roof. If
the writer was not much mistaken, Pimlico Studios

stood a fair chance of becoming the Mecca of the Art World.

"I can't read all this," said the niece. "I don't see where Mr. Groob comes in. Oh yes—it's here! 'The Modern Zurbaran. . . .'" This gentleman was, of course, the artist familiarly spoken of as "Dolly" at the Pimlico Studios. Mrs. Aiken went on reading to herself, and then said suddenly: "I do hope Reginald won't be a fool, and make himself responsible for anything."

"Mr. Adolphus Groob would be able to tell us all about it," said Miss Priscilla. "His sister Arethusa is almost sure to call this afternoon, and you can ask her to find out."

"I shall do nothing of the sort, and I beg you won't say anything to her. I particularly dislike Mr. Groob, and just now nothing could be more unpleasant to me. Please no Mr. Groob on any account!"

"You need not be so testy, Euphemia. Nothing is easier than for me to make no reference to Mr. Groob, who has never so much as called. His sister Arethusa is, of course, not the same thing as he is himself, but no doubt she may know something about this Society."

"I thought her an odious girl. Anyhow, I don't want to know anything at all about the Society, and it's no concern of mine. Reginald must go his own way now, and put his name down for subscriptions just as he likes. . . . Oh yes, I shall answer his last letter, but only to say that, if he wants me to read his next one, the *tone* must be very different."

Her aunt said, as one with whom patience is habitual, and tolerance a foregone conclusion: "It is perfectly useless for me to repeat, Euphemia, what I believe to be your duty as a Christian towards your lawful husband, which Reginald is and continues to be, however disgracefully he may have behaved; and you acted with your eyes open in the face of warnings of his lawless Bohemian habits. *He—is—your—*HUSBAND, and your obvious duty is . . ."

"Oh, do shut up with Corinthians!" was the rude, impatient, and indeed irreligious interruption. "If you mean that a woman is bound to put up with anything and everything, no matter what her husband says or does . . . What?"

"My dear Euphemia, if I have told you once, I have told you fifty times, that it is *not* Corinthians, but Colossians—Colossians three-eighteen. Besides, I'm sure there was a ring at the bell."

There was, and therefore the chronic guerilla warfare—for this sort of thing always went on until visitors stopped it—was suspended until the next opportunity.

The ring at the gate-bell was—or was caused by— Miss Jessie Bax, another niece, who was shy and seventeen. She began everything she said with " Oh! " The first words she uttered were, " Oh, I mustn't stop! " But she had previously said to Anne, at the gate, " Oh, I mustn't come in! " and when overcome on this point by Euphemia, who came out and kissed her, not without satisfaction— because she was that sort—she only just contrived to say, " Oh, I only came to bring these from Volumnia. It's to-morrow night at the Suburbiton Athenæum, where the Psychomorphic meets till the new rooms are ready, and she hopes you'll come."

Miss Jessie explained that she was, strictly speaking, an emanation from her sister Volumnia. That young lady was thirteen years her senior, and was a powerful individuality. She entered into inquiries, and advocated causes. Miss Jessica, on the contrary, flirted.

Was it, this time, advocating causes, or entering into inquiries? Mrs. Aiken, fearing the former, was consoled when she found it was the latter. She would look at the Syllabus tendered, whatever it was, and wouldn't detain Miss Jessie, whose anxiety not to come in need not have been laid so much stress on. It presently appeared that this wish to stop out was not unconnected with Charley Some- body, who was playing with a puppy on the other

side of the road. A suggestion that Charley Somebody should come in too was met with so earnest a
disclaimer of intention to disturb any fellow-creature
anywhere, at any time, that it would have been
sheer downright cruelty to press the point. So the
young lady and Master Charley, whoever he was,
escaped, and were heard whistling for the puppy,
who was getting quite good, and learning to follow
beautifully.

"What is it?" said Aunt Priscilla.

"Oh, some reading papers and nonsense," said
her niece. "I never have any patience with that
sort of twaddle. It only irritates me."

It suited Miss Priscilla to take up a tone of
superiority to such childish petulance, combined
with an enlightened attitude of open-mindedness,
and a suggestion of being better informed than most
people about what is doing. To this end she picked
up the prospectus her niece was ostentatiously
neglecting, and read it aloud in an atmosphere
above human prejudices, specially designed for her
own personal use. It related to a lecture "On the
Attitude of Investigation towards the Unknow-
able," with magic-lantern slides, and a discussion to
follow. "It does not say," said Aunt Priscilla,
"who is the Medium." It is possible that the good
lady had in her own mind confused something with
something else. One does sometimes.

,"I'm not sure that I shan't go, if it isn't the Suffrage," said Euphemia. She took the prospectus, and seemed reassured on re-reading it. Yes, she might go if there were pictures on a sheet. But not if it was to be Women's Rights.

"With your peculiar, new, advanced views, my dear," said her aunt, "it certainly seems to me that you ought to sympathize with your cousin." This, however, was because of Miss Priscilla's exceptional way of looking at Social and Political subjects. She divided all the world—the thoughtful world, that is—into two classes, the one that went in for Movements and things, and the one that consisted of Sensible Persons. The latter stayed at home and minded their own business, sometimes going for a drive when it held up, and, of course, to Church on Sundays, and having hot cross buns on Good Friday, and so on. She made no distinction between Agitators on the score of the diversity of their respective objects. Could she be expected to differentiate between shades of opinion that would now be indicated by the terms—then uninvented—of Suffragettes and Anti-Suffragettes? Volumnia Bax would have belonged to the latter denomination. Women, that young lady said, were not intended by an All-wise Providence to mix in public life. Their sphere was the Home. She belonged to a League whose chief object was to prevent women becoming unfeminine. If it was not Woman's own duty to make a stand against these new-fangled American notions, which could only end in her being completely unsexed, whose was it? If *she* did not exert herself to avert this calamity, who would? So this League consisted entirely of women, pledged to resist, by violence if necessary, but in any case by speaking out at meetings, and getting up petitions, and so on, these insidious attempts to destroy the delicacy of the female character, which from time immemorial had been its principal charm. This was the point on which Aunt Priscilla certainly failed in discrimination, for she drew no distinction between the various shades of political impulse. She objected to anyone leaving the groove, even with the motive of pushing others back into it. Her niece Euphemia shared her views to a great extent, and when she used the expression " Women's Rights," it was probably in a sense much less circumscribed than its usual one. " But," said she to Miss Priscilla, justifying her determination to go on Saturday evening to this lecture, or whatever it was, " it can't be minutes and resolutions and jaw, jaw, jaw, if there's a magic-lantern. So do come, Aunty dear! "

Miss Priscilla gave way, and consented to accompany her niece, but not without a misgiving that she might be compelled to come away in the middle of the entertainment. A reperusal of the Syllabus had engendered in her mind a doubt whether it was quite. That is how she worded it. The story only chronicles; it takes no responsibilities. Euphemia assured her that it could not be otherwise than quite, seeing that so respectable an Athenæum as the Suburbiton would be sure to be most careful. Besides, it was Metaphysical.

So they had the fly from Dulgrove's—as it appears, and we think we know what is meant—and Dulgrove's representative touched one of its hats, which was on his own head, and promised upon the honour of both to return at half-past ten to reimpatriate the two ladies at Athabasca Villa, which is two miles from Coombe proper.

Though Mr. Groob's sister Arethusa did not happen to call, as Miss Priscilla anticipated, Mrs. Reginald Aiken was destined to be brought in contact with her odious brother, the Artist, who was acquainted with her husband. It happened that Miss Bax was desirous that another brother of Arethusa's should come to the lecture. This gentleman, Mr. Duodecimus Groob, had a clear head, and a cool judgment, and belonged, moreover, to a class which is frequently referred to, but whose members cannot always be differentiated with certainty, the class of persons who are not to be sneezed at. Others may be, without offence or injustice.

Now, it chanced that Miss Jessica Bax had been employed by her sister as a species of bait to induce this gentleman to accompany his sister Arethusa—who, of course, was coming to the lecture—by sending her to be driven over in the Groob brougham, she herself accepting a lift from the Peter Tutburys, who had no room for more than one. Miss Volumnia, you see, intended to speak at the discussion, and was naturally anxious that Mr. Groob should bring his clear head and cool judgment to hear and appreciate the powerful analysis she intended to make of the lecturer's first exposition of the subject.

It is impossible in this story to enter at length into the intricate and difficult questions touched upon; but it may be noted that Miss Volumnia, who had read the typed manuscript of this lecture, was prepared to combat its main argument, to take exception to its author's fundamental standpoint, to scrutinize fearlessly his pretensions to Scientific accuracy, and to lay bare its fallacies with a merciless scalpel. She was naturally anxious that a B.Sc., London—for Mr. Duodecimus Groob was so designate—should hear her do it, being so close at hand; and when she said to Jessica, " Tell Arethusa I expect her to bring a brother," she did so with a shrewd insight into the souls of brothers whose sisters very pretty girls accompany to even the humblest entertainments—penny readings and what not. This Mr. Groob came, and what was more, Mr. Adolphus, whom we saw *en passant* at Pimlico Studios, accompanied him. Both had come to stay till Monday at their father's residence—where there were bronzes and Dresden china in the drawing-room, and ruins by Panini all round the dining-room, and a Wolf Hunt, Snyders, in the entrance-hall. We repeat that *both* came, although there was hardly room in the small brougham, and Mr. Adolphus had to go on the box and wrap up. And our belief is that if it had been an omnibus, and there had been young men enough to fill it, they would all have gone to that lecture.

Insignificant as this visit to the Suburbiton Athenæum may seem, it has its place in this story, and that place is given to it by its most unimportant details. As you can scarcely be expected to turn back to it, please note now what it was that really happened.

In the lobby, when Mrs. Aiken and her aunt arrived, Miss Volumnia Bax was, as it were, marshalling Europe. She was a leading mind, over-looking gregariousness through a *pince-nez*. Gregariousness was shedding its fleeces and taking little cardboard tickets in exchange.

"You know Mr. Adolphus Groob," said Miss

Volumnia to her cousin, sternly, almost reproachfully.

" Yes—you know my brother," said Miss Arethusa
Groob, confirmatorily. And Miss Priscilla—oh
dear! one's unmanageable Aunts!—must needs, as it
were, go over to the enemy, saying in honied tones,
with a little powdered sugar over them:

" *You* know Mr. Adolphus Groob, Euphemia."

It was quite the most dastardly desertion on record. There was nothing for it before such an ac-
cumulation of testimony but to plead guilty. What
can you do with such treachery in the camp?
Euphemia admitted grudgingly that she knew Mr.
Adolphus, who had long hair and was like our idea
of a German Student. He, for his part, was horribly
frightened and got away. For, you see, he knew
all about the row between Aiken and his wife; and
although in the absence of that unearthly sex, the
female one, he was ready to lay claim to a deep and
subtle knowledge of its ways, he was an arrant
coward in the presence of a sample.

" I say, Bob," said he aside to his brother Duodecimus, using a convenient, if arbitrary, abbrevia-
tion of that name.

" What's the fun, Dolly? " said Bob, who was a
chap who always made game of everything.

" Why, look here! When a customer you know
quarrels with his wife, and she does a bunk . . . "

" She *what's?* "

" Hooks it, don't you know ! Well, when she runs away, and you come across her, and you know all the story about the shindy, being in the beggar's confidence, don't you see ?—and she knows you know it, only, mind you, there's nothing exactly to swear by, and you know she knows you know it, and she knows you know she knows—up and down and in and out— intersectitiously, don't you see . . . ? " But the heroic effort to express a situation we have all had a try at and failed over was too much for Mr. Adolphus, and his sentence remained unfinished. Consider that he had supplied an entirely new word, and be lenient !

" Want'n'er for yourself, Dolly ? " said that frivolous, superficial beast, Bob. " Don't you, that's my advice ! She's a head and shoulders taller than you. You'll look such an ass ! " Whereupon Mr. Adolphus, not without dignity, checked his brother's ill-timed humour, pointing out that he had done nothing to deserve the imputation of personal motives, and hinting that his well-known monastic bias should have saved him from it.

" Very well, then !—let her alone ! " said Bob.

" But it's very embarrassing, you must admit," said Dolly.

" H'm !—don't see why."

" The position is a delicate one."

" Can't see where the delicacy comes in. You keep out of her way. *She* won't tackle *you*."

This was just about the time when the disengagement of their fleeces had enabled a congestion of the flock to pass on towards the lecture-hall, leaving access clear to Miss Priscilla, her niece, and others. Euphemia's fleece was one that gave trouble; she said it always got hooked. It certainly did so this time, and Mr. Adolphus, passing on after his colloquy with his brother, was able to render squire's service, unhooking it as bold as brass. Whereupon the lady and her aunt gushed gratefully, as in return for life saved. Their rescuer passed on, feeling internally gratified, and that he had shown presence of mind at a crisis—was, in short, a Man of the World. But he did not know that from thenceforward he was entangled in a certain perverse enchantment—a sort of spell that constantly impelled him to dally with the delicate position he was so conscious about. He must needs go and stick himself four seats off Mrs. Aiken, in the two-shilling places, the intervening three seats being vacant.

Now, if only lean men, operating edgewise, had attempted to pass into these seats, things might have gone otherwise. Fate sent a lady over three feet thick all the way down, and apparently quite solid, to wedge her way into one or more of these seats. Mr. Adolphus shrank, for all he was worth, but it was a trying moment. The lady was just that sort the Inquisition once employed so success-fully; one with spikes, that drew blood from any-one that got agglutinated with her costume. She might, however, have got through without accident —you never can tell!—if the trial had been carried out. It was suspended by a suggestion from Mrs. Aiken that Mr. Adolphus Groob should come a little farther along and make room; and when he com-plied, to the extent of going one seat nearer to her, a second suggestion that he should come nearer still, to which he assented with trepidation. Resistance was useless. A galaxy of daughters had already filled in the whole row behind the stout lady, and were forcing her on like the air-tight piece of potato in a quill popgun, only larger. So in the end Mr. Adolphus Groob found himself wedged securely be-tween the stout lady and Mrs. Euphemia Aiken, quite unable to speak to the former, for though they had certainly met—with a vengeance—they had never been introduced This really *was* a very delicate position. Mrs. Aiken might at least have said, " You know Mrs. Godfrey Pybus, I think?" That was the stout lady's name. Then he could have avoided talking with Mrs. Aiken, by becoming absorbed in Mrs. Pybus, and shouting round her to her nearest daughters beyond. As it was, he was fairly forced to make careful remarks to his other neighbour, scrupulously avoiding allusion to husbands, wives, quarrels, studios, Chelsea, London, servant-girls, picture-cleaning . . . this is only a handful at random of the things it would never do to mention in such delicate circumstances. He held his tongue discreetly about every one of these in turn, and talked of little but the weather.

Do not run away with the idea that anything interesting or exciting grew out of this chance meeting, in the story. The introduction of it, at such length, is only warranted by the fact that, without its details, it would have absolutely no relevance at all. Whatever it has will, we hope, be made clear later.

A little conversation passed between the two, but it was of no more importance than the sample which follows.

" Do you know what the lecture is about ? " said Mrs. Aiken.

" Couldn't say," was the reply. " Never know what lectures are about! I'm an Artist, don't you know! My brother Bob could tell you. He's a scientific chap—knows about Telephones and things that go round and burst."

" Is there anything that goes round and bursts in the lecture, I wonder ? "

" Shouldn't be much surprised. Here's the Sylla-bub—I mean Syllabus." Mr. Adolphus handed his information to his neighbour. Caution made him un-communicative. Naturally, he was of a more talka-tive disposition.

Mrs. Aiken studied the heads of the lecture. " What is meant, I wonder, by the Radio-Activity of Space?" said she. Now in asking this question she was deferring to the widespread idea that Man understands Science, and can tell Woman all about it. He doesn't, and can't.

Observe, please, that Mr. Groob was under a mixed influence. He happened to have been rather disgusted because Miss Jessica Bax, instead of appreciating his self-sacrifice in riding outside and wrapping up, had shown a marked preference for a flirtation with his brother. Slightly miffed by this, he had become the victim of a mysterious spell or fascination connected with that hook-and-eye acci-dent, which had caused him—not to sit down beside its victim; he never would have presumed to do that—but to hover near her, and in doing this to be remorselessly forced into her pocket by the dead weight of Mrs. Godfrey Pybus. Things being so, what could he do but rejoice at the Radio-Activity of Space, as a topic surely removed from any wives that had bolted from any husbands? What could be safer? as a resource against embarrassing reference to the painful *status quo?*

He accepted the position of instructor his sex

conferred on him. "It's got somethin' to do with Four Dimensions," he said. "Can't say I've gone much into the subject myself, but I've talked to a very intelligent feller about it. Did you ever see any Radium ? "

"Me? No. My husband saw some, though. He looked through a hole."

"That's it. It destroys your eyesight, I believe, and loses decimal point something of its volume in a hundred thousand years. There is no doubt we are on the brink of great discoveries."

"How very interesting! I wish the lecturer would begin. Oh—here he is ! "

"Very bald feller ! He ought to use petrol. You have to rub it in and keep out of the way of artificial light. This chap's first cousin lost the use of both legs through investigatin'. It was X rays, I believe. You may depend on it we've got a deal to learn." And so on.

Upon the honour of the narrative this sample is a fair one of what passed between this lady and gentleman on this occasion. There was more, but it was exactly the same sort.

In due course the lecture was begun and ended; then the discussion followed, and Mrs. Godfrey Pybus and her six daughters didn't stop to hear Miss Volumnia Bax's analysis and refutation, but went away in the middle and made a noise on purpose. It was just like them and they were perfectly odious people.

It is most extraordinary how Time will slip away when the catching hold of his forelock depends on ourselves. Each morning may bring that forelock again within reach, and each morning the same apathy that made us yesterday too languid to stretch out a hand and grip the old scamp and employ him for our own advantage keeps us in the same stupid abeyance, and we lose the chance for another twenty-four hours. Every postponement makes a new precedent, and every new precedent stiffens the back of inaction.

It was so with Mr. and Mrs. Reginald Aiken. Not a morning passed without an unfulfilled impulse on either part to cross the gulf between them, and terminate their idiotic separation, bridged by correspondence which really did more harm than good. There is one precept which it is quite impossible for the human race to observe too closely—*Never write letters!* If only those words could replace Little Liver Pills and so forth on those atrocities that flank the railways and hide the planet, its inhabitants would be the gainers. Mr. Reginald had an extraordinary faculty for undoing in a postscript any little concession he had made at the outset, and Mrs. Euphemia, for her part, was becoming quite a proficient in sarcasm—three-line whips of scorpions describes her style, or the style she aimed at. For a superficial literary education did not help her up to its perfection.

"Very good, Mrs. Hay!"—thus, on receipt of a letter, would run her husband's commentary, embodying transposed quotation in its text, " 'Pray go my own way': that's it, is it? 'On no account give the slightest consideration underlined to the wishes of your underlined wife.' Oh, very well— I won't. 'If my Conscience with a big C didn't turn a deaf ear to the pleadings of my Better Self with a big B and a big S '—what's all this? can't read it—oh! I see—yes, at least I see what it comes to!—I should come to my sences—spelt wrong— and overcome the ridiculous false pride that stands between me and something or other underlined— h'm! h'm!—' consult my own dignity '—h'm, h'm—something's something else I can't make out in the truest sence of the word, underlined. I dare say. I know what all this rot comes to in the end. I'm to go and ask forgiveness and show contrition, and I shouldn't wonder if I was expected to beg Aunt Priscilla's pardon. And be taken to Church as like as not. I say, Stumpy, that would be rather jolly, wouldn't it? Fancy the Wicked Man turnething away from his Wickedness and Aunt Priscilla taking care visibly not to look at your humble servant, so as not to hurt his feelings!"

"I tell you what, Crocky,"—thus Mr. Hughes, on the occasion the above is chosen from, some time in November—"I tell you what: if I was you, I shouldn't be an Ass. Just you mozey off to Athabasca Villa and make it up. I believe Mrs. Gapp's right."

"That old sot been talking? Parples was the best of the two. I'll have Parples back." For Mrs. Gapp had taken Mrs. Parples' place, under pretence of greater accomplishments and better training.

"At my invitation, Mr. Aiken," said Mr. Hughes with some show of dignity—"at my invitation, observe!—Mrs. Gapp, who has buried three husbands and really ought to know a good deal about connubiosity—conjugosity—what the dooce is the word? . . ."

"Well—married life, anyhow! What did old boozey say?"

"She had great faith in a spirit of mutual conciliation. That is not precisely the way she put it. Her exact expression was 'A good 'ug's the thing, Mr. Stumpy'. . . . Yes—that is what Mrs. Gapp calls me, misled by your example. . . . I must say I think the course she indicated has much to recommend it."

Mr. Aiken looked moody, and did not reply at

once. Then he said: "That's all very fine, Stump, my boy. But—Sairah! Sairah's the point. Now, mind you, I'm not suggestin' anythin'. But just you look at it this way. There was a rather nice lookin' gyairl, with a bird's wing in her hat, came for the place, and Euphemia wouldn't hear of her, don't you know! Suppose it had been her!—puts the matter on a more human footin', shouldn't you say?"

Mr. Hughes reflected, and spoke as one whose reflections had borne fruit. "Not being a married beggar myself, I can't say. Speaking as single cuss, my recommendation to you would be—speaking broadly—not to make an Ass of yourself. See what I'm driving at?"

"That means," said Mr. Aiken, "that you consider I ought to go and beg Euphemia's gracious pardon, and take the blame of the whole how-do-you-do on my own shoulders, and as like as not have to go to Church with Aunt Priscilla. Well—I *won't,* and there's an end of it!"

And Mr. Aiken didn't, and prolonged his uncomfortable circumstances quite to the end of the year. But it is only right to say that his wife contributed all her share to their extension and consolidation. In fact, if this story has achieved the wish of its compiler, ourself, it should be clear to its reader that Mr. Reginald and Mrs. Euphemia Aiken were precisely six of the one and half a dozen of the other.

CHAPTER VII

" *Why* do you want the carriage, darling? "

" To call on a lady somewhere near Richmond, or
Combe, I think it is."

" Won't it do to-morrow? "

" Not so well as to-day."

" Then I suppose you *must* have it, darling."

"Not if you want it, Mumsey!" The speaker
got the head of the person she addressed in Chancery,
to kiss it, using the chair-back of the latter as a
fulcrum.

Lady Upwell, the victim of this manœuvre, said,
" Take care, Mad dear; you'll spoil my ruche and
put your eyes out." So her daughter released her,

and sat at her feet. She had on her tussore in saxe-blue, trimmed with guipure lace, and was as pretty as ever, and as sad.

" *Who* is it you want to go and see, darling?" said her ladyship.

" That Mrs. Aiken," said Madeline.

" Oh," said her mother, " but isn't she rather?" But Madeline shook her head, with her eyes very wide open, and kept on shaking it all the while as she replied, " Oh no, she's not rather at all. It was all her husband." Whereupon her mother said, " Oh—it was her husband, was it?" and put back a loose forehead-lock of hair that was getting in her daughter's eyes.

This wasn't at Surley Stakes. The family had come up to Eaton Place for a week or ten days. And these ladies were sitting in a small jury drawing-room that did duty on flying visits. The real drawing-room was all packed up, and must have been rather savage when the family came to town, yet left it *in statu quo*. And very savage indeed with Madeline, who was begging to be allowed to stop in the country and not come to town this season at all. Indeed, she would have had her way, had not her father said that come she must, to see the new pair of carriage-horses he was thinking of purchasing, whose owner was willing to lend them for a few days on trial, but only on condition that they should not be taken away from London. So the family coachman had accompanied the family, in a certain sense clandestinely. It is needless to tell anyone who knows that of course these ladies were themselves only theoretically in town, with those shutters all up.

Madeline helped to get the lock of hair back, remarking, "It always does," without an antecedent. It was a pity there was no one there—mothers don't count—to see how pretty her wrist looked, with the blue veins in it, as she did so. She continued talking about that Mrs. Aiken, but semi-apologetically, as if she felt abnormal in wanting to see that Mrs. Aiken.

Her mother attempted to rationalize and formulate her daughter's position. "I *can't* understand, dear child," she said. "You only saw this lady that one time, and only for a few minutes then. What makes you want to see her again? She doesn't seem to have produced a—a favourable impression exactly."

"N-n-not very!" is the reply; the prolonged initial conveying the speaker's hesitation to condemn. "But it isn't that."

"What isn't it, child?"

"What she's like. It's because I went there with Jack."

"I see, dear." But it isn't so very clear that her

ladyship does see. For she adds:—" I quite understand. Of course. Yes!" in a tone which seems
to invite further explanation.

Her daughter at least puts this interpretation on
it. " Don't you see, Mumsey dear?" she says.
" It's because I recollect me and Jack, and her
and her husband, all talking together in that muddle
of a Studio, and the lay-figure with its head on
backwards. They seem to come into it somehow."
The further particulars are slight, one would say,
but they carry conviction, for her mother says, " I
understand that, but can you do any good?" as if
the substratum of a debatable point might be considered settled. Madeline goes on, encouraged to
confidence, " I think *perhaps*. Because those Baxes
we met . . ."

" Those *whats?* " her ladyship interrupts; adding,
however, " Oh, I see—it's a name! Go on."

" A grim big one and a little rather jolly one.
That evening at Lady Presteign's. The grim big
one talked about it to me in a corner, because her
sister's too young to know about such things—only
she's nearly my age, and I don't see why—and told
me she believed it was a perfectly ridiculous quarrel
about a horrible maidservant, who was quite out
of the question. And of course this Miss Bax doesn't
know what *we* know."

" My darling Madeline! " A large amused ma-

ternal smile irradiates the speaker. "*Know!* What
a funny child you are!"

"Well, Mumsey, don't we know, or as good as
know? Do you really think Uncle Christopher made
that all up? *I* don't."

"It was the action of his brain, my dear, not his
own doing at all! Let me see—what's it called?—
something ending in *ism*."

"Hypnotism?"

"No! Oh dear, I shall remember directly. . . ."

"Mesmerism?"

"No, no!—do be quiet and let me think. . . ."

"Vegetarianism?"

"You silly girl! I had just got it, and you put
it out of my head . . . There! . . . Stop!
. . . No! . . . Yes—*I've* got it. *Unconscious
Cerebration!* How on earth did I manage to forget
that? Unconscious Cerebration, of course!"

"But it doesn't end in *ism*. It ends in *ation*."

"Never mind, child! Anyhow, I *have* recollected
it, and it's a thing one ought to be able to say.
Don't let's forget it again." To Lady Upwell this
world was a theatre, and the name of the piece was
Society. She was always on the sweetest terms
with the Management, and her benevolence to the
worn-out and broken-down actors was heartfelt.
Still, one had to talk one's part, and dress it. "Unconscious Cerebration" was useful gag. "But,"

said she, returning to the main point, "I don't see what you can *do,* child."

"No more do I, Mumsey dear. But I may be able to do something for all that. I should like to try, anyhow. I'm sure the picture was right. Besides, see what that Miss Bax said. You may say what you like, but she *is* Mrs. Aiken's first cousin, after all!"

"No doubt she's right, dear! And no doubt the picture's right." Her ladyship retires with the dignity of one withdrawing herself from mundane matters, Olympuswards. But one can never touch pitch and not be defiled. Some has clung to her, for she adds, absently, "I wonder where Thyrza Presteign picks up all these odd people." In the end she forsakes speculation to say, "Of course have the carriage, darling; I don't see that any harm can come of it. Only don't get mixed up."

"*I* won't get mixed up," said Miss Upwell confidently, and kisses her mother on both sides, for granting the carriage to go on such a crazy quest. She for the tenth of a second associates the two kisses with the beautiful pair of greys that draw it. She loves horses very much, and gives them too much sugar. If any tongue's tip is ready with a denial of the possibility of such an impression as this, it only shows that the tongue's owner has not had a similar experience. The kisses were cash down for each horse—does that make it clearer?

Anyhow, the greys' eight hoofs rang sweetly next day on a frosty road, going south-westwards, as soon as they left the traffic—that road-spoiler—far enough behind. The sun had taken a mean advantage of its being such a glorious day, to get at nice clean frozen corners and make a nasty mess. But there were many havens of security still where what was blown snow-dust in the early morning might still have a little peace and quiet, and wait with resignation for inevitable thaw.

Such a one was—or had been—on a low window-sill of the Cheshire Cheese, behind the horse-trough which the steaming greys suggested they should empty, but were only allowed to sample. *Had been,* because of a boy. A boy is a reason for so many things in this world. This one, a very nice specimen, coming, well-informed, from a Gothic school near by, was showing how indifferent chubbiness can be to chill February, by using up the snow on this window-sill in the manufacture of two snowballs, of which one was complete. His was a Two Power Standard, evidently.

"Ask that little boy where this place is," says Miss Upwell, from inside furs; because the carriage-lid is set back by request, and the rider is convinced of cold, but won't give in on principle. "He's a native, and ought to know. Ask him, James." "Where's Athabasca Villa, young un? . . . Don't believe he knows, Miss." "Where's Athabasca Villa, little man? . . . Don't you know? Well—where does Miss Priscilla Bax live?"

"Oh—I know *she!* Over yarnder." A vigorous illumination speaks to the force of Miss Priscilla Bax's identity. "Over yonder" is, however, vague: and you may have eyes like sloes, and crisp curly brown hair, and ruddy cheeks, and yet have very small powers of indicating complex routes past Daddy's—not otherwise described—and round to the left, and along to the right, and by Farmer Phipps's barn, and so on. But this is a young gentleman of resource, and he has a suggestion ready: "You let I royd up behind, and *I'll* poyunt out where to drive." The lady accedes to this proposal, though James is evidently uneasy lest a precedent should be established. "Let him ride behind—he won't do any harm——" says Madeline, between whom and this youth a bond of sympathy forges itself unexpectedly. It might have been more judicious to deprive him of ammunition.

For the Two Power Standard, in his case, seemed to involve a Policy of Aggression. His first snowball was aimed too low; and though it struck its object, the Incumbent of the Parish, that gentleman only laughed. The second landed neatly under the back-hair of a stout lady, and probably went down her neck behind, as her indignation found voice proportionate to such a result. Miss Upwell—to her shame be it spoken—pretended not to see or hear; refusing, Gallio-like, to listen—but in this case to Gentiles—and saying to James, " Please don't stop, James—go on quick."

The infant was, however, as good as his undertaking, conducting the carriage intelligently to Athabasca Villa, and taking an unfair advantage of permission to pull its bell; he was, in fact, detached from it with some difficulty. He seemed surprised and pleased at the receipt of a *douceur,* and danced.

" Oh dear! " said poor Madeline to herself, as she heard him die away, with some friends he met, in the distance. " How Jack would have liked that boy! " There was to be no Jack, it seemed, now!

Mrs. Aiken, at one of the bays that flanked the doorway of Athabasca Villa, looked out upon the top and bottom half of a sun up to his middle in a chill purple mist, and waited for tea. Tea waited to be made, like Eve when she was a rib. But with a confidence based on precedent; for Tea was made every day at the same time, which Eve wasn't.

Besides, Miss Priscilla Bax made tea, and wouldn't let anyone else make it. Not that there appears to be any suggestion in the story of Eve that there was ever any talk of underletting the job.

Miss Priscilla Bax had a cap out of last century, about half-way, and the cap had ribbons which had to be kept entirely out of the tea. These ribbons had no function or practical object, though an imaginative mind might have ascribed to them that, being alike on both sides, they helped the sense of equilibrium necessary to safe conduct of the un-made tea from a casket on four gouty feet, whose lid wouldn't keep up, to a black Rockingham teapot, which did for when there was no one.

Only, this time there *was* someone—some car-riage one—and his, her, or its approach caused Mrs. Aiken to exclaim, " Good gracious, Aunty, I'm afraid it's people ! "

Miss Priscilla was watching the tap of the urn run —her phrase, not ours. " How many ? " said she. Then dialogue worked out as follows :

" I think I see who it is."

" How many ? "

" Only one. I fancy it's that Miss What's-her-name. I wish it wasn't. It's too late to say not at home. She's seen me at the window. But you'll have to put in another heaped-up spoonful. When-ever will they stop ringing that bell ? "

At this point presumably the mercenary was strangled off it, and rewarded, for the lady added, "Yes, it's her. She's talking to a boy. What on earth has brought her here? I shall go."

"You can't. You've been seen. Don't be a fool. Who do you mean by 'her'?"

"Oh—*you* know! Miss Upsley Pupsley of Curly something. That place in Worcestershire the picture was to go to. *You* know! They've a house in Eaton Square."

"*Then* we must have the silver teapot, and I shall have to make fresh tea." The house in Eaton Square settled that. A hurried aside caused the appearance of the silver teapot in all its glory and a new ebullition, over the lamp, of a fresh kettle of water at par.

Thereupon Miss Upwell found herself within reach—academically speaking—of talking with this Mrs. Aiken of that lady's private domestic dissensions. But, oh, the impossibility of it! Madeline felt it now, too late. Even getting to speak of the subject at all seemed hopeless. And in another moment she became horribly aware that *she* was inexplicable—couldn't account for her visit at all. Still, she had too much grit in her to dream of giving in. And then, look at the motive! Besides, she had in her heart a strong suspicion that she was a beauty, and that that was why people always gave

way to her. Her beauty was of no use, now that
Jack was gone. Nothing being of any use to *her*,
now, at least let it help her to do a good turn to a
fellow-woman in tribulation. If this picture-ghost
—so she said to herself—had told this Mrs. Aiken
where Jack was, would *she* not come and tell, on
the chance? Of course she would! Courage!

The most terrifying obstacle in her path was
Aunt Priscilla. If this lady had been the in-
offensive tabby Madeline's wish had been father to
her thought of, she could have been treated as a
negligible factor. But what is to be done when
your Aunt, living under an impression that in early
life she mixed in circles, recognizes your distinguished young friend as having emerged from a circle.
This way of putting the case transfers the embarrassment from Miss Upwell to Mrs. Aiken. Probably
that lady felt it, and wished Aunt Priscilla wouldn't
go on so. The fact is she was getting curious to know
the reason of her visitor's unexpected appearance.
There *must* be *some* reason.

It lost its opportunity of being divulged at the
outset. The visitor's parade of the utter indefensi-
bility of her intrusion, and her fib—for a fib it was
in the spirit, however true in the letter—that she
" was in the neighbourhood " worked on the
imagination, and made the position plausible. Mrs.
Aiken dropped all attempts to look amiably sur-

prised, as one courteously awaiting a revelation, and candidly admitted an extremely clear recollection of Miss Upwell's visit to the Studio. Of course she was delighted to see her, on any terms. But the reason of her coming could get no chance of a hearing, when the first flush of conversation had once failed to give it an opening. Miss Priscilla's extraction had to be reckoned with.

If only that appalling old lady had not been there, or would even have been content to play second fiddle! But as soon as she heard the name of the village of Grewceham in Worcestershire mentioned as the nearest township to Surley Stakes, she identified that county as the cradle of her race, saying, "WE came from Sampford Plantagenet, I believe," in a tone suggestive· of remote epochs, and considerable yeomen farmers, at least, vanishing into the mists of antiquity. "But my mother's family," she added, "were all Brocks, of Sampford Pagnell."

Madeline, anxious to oblige as she was, could go no farther than to believe, as an abstract truth, that there were still Brocks in Sampford Pagnell, speaking of them rather as if they ran away when seen, but might be heard occasionally, like bitterns. She could not do any Baxes at Sampford Plantagenet. However, her father would know the name Bax, and his heraldic sympathies would be stirred

by it like the war-horse in Job at the sound of
battle. This anticipation was founded solely on his
daughter's desire to fill out the order for Baxes.
Miss Priscilla always preferred to pour the tea
herself, not without a certain Imperial suggestion
in the preference. Vespasian would have insisted
on pouring out the tea, under like circumstances.

But the tea, when poured, brought with it no clue
to the cause of Miss Upwell's visit. It had furnished
a certain amount of relief, during its negotiation,
by postponing discussion of the point, and by the
claim it made for a chapter to itself. For a short
chapter of your life-story begins when you get your
tea, and ends when you've done your tea. When
Madeline had ceased to be able to pretend that this
chapter had not ended, her suspended sense of in-
comprehensibility cropped up again, and she grew
painfully aware that her hostesses would soon begin
waiting visibly for enlightenment, which she was no
nearer being able to give than at first. How could
she have guessed it would be so difficult? She was
even conscious of gratitude to Miss Priscilla for her
persistency in Atavism, and at heart hoped that the
good lady would not stop just yet.

No fear of that! The Brocks were not nearly
over, and they had to be disposed of before the
Baxes could be taken in hand. Their exponent
picked them up where she had dropped them. "My

Mother's family," she resumed, " were well known
during the Middle Ages. There were Brocks in
Sampford Pagnell as early as fourteen hundred and
four. They are even said to have been connected
with John of Gaunt. Unhappily all the family
documents, including an autograph letter of Alice
Piers to Edward the Black Prince, were destroyed
in the Great Fire of London." On lines like these,
as we all know, a topic may be pursued for a very
long time without the pursuer's hobby breaking down.
It went on long enough in this case for Madeline
to wish she could get a chance of utilizing some
courage she had been slowly mustering during the
chase. This being hardly mature yet, she took another cup of tea, thank you! and sat on, supplying
little notes of exclamation and pleased surprise whenever the manner of the narrator seemed to call for
them.

" It seems only the other day," Aunt Priscilla
continued, with her eyes half-closed to express
memory at work upon the past, " that I was taken
as a little girl of six, to see my great-grandmother,
then in her hundredth year. She was a friend of
Horace Walpole. *Her* mother could remember John
Bunyan."

" Is it possible! " said Madeline, very shaky about
dates, but ready with any amount of wonderment.
She added idiotically, " Of *course* my father must

have known *all* your people, *quite* well." Which
did not follow from the apparent premises.

Mrs. Aiken muttered in a warning voice, for her
visitor's ear only, " When Aunt gets on her grandmother she never gets off. You'll see! " She took
advantage of the old lady's deafness to keep up a
running comment.

Miss Priscilla then approached a subject which
required to be handled with the extremest delicacy.
" I think, Euphemia," she said, " that after so long a
time there can be no objection . . . You know
what I am referring to ? "

" Objection ?—why should there be ? Oh yes, *I*
know. Horace Walpole and your great-grandmother. No—none ! " To Madeline Mrs. Aiken
said in an undertone, " I told you how it would be."
That young lady affected a lively interest in scandal
against Queen Elizabeth, which was what she anticipated.

" I myself," said Aunt Priscilla, in the leisurely
way of a lecturer who has secured an audience,
" have always held to the opinion that there was a
marriage, but what the motives may have been for
concealing it can only be conjectured. . . ."

This was too leisurely for her niece's patience.
It provoked a species of *sotto voce* abstract of her
aunt's coming statement thus, " Oh yes—*do* get
on! You cannot otherwise understand how so

rigid an observer of moral law as your great-grand-
father, however lamentable his religious tenets may
have been, could have brought himself to marry
the widow. *Do get on!*" Which proved to be the
substance of the original, as soon as the latter was
published. But it certainly got over the ground
quicker, and made a spurt at the winning-post, ar-
riving almost before the other horse started.

"This," resumed Aunt Priscilla, after a small
blank for the congregation to sniff and cough, if so
disposed, "was some considerable time before his
accession to the Earldom. The only clue that has
been suggested as a motive for concealment of the
marriage was his unaccountable aversion to the
title, which he could scarcely have indulged if . . .
There's a knock. Do see if it's the Tapleys, and
don't let them go." Mrs. Aiken rose and went out,
reciting rapidly another forecast, "He-never-took-
his - seat - in - the - House - of - Lords - and - signed-
his - letters - 'the - Uncle - of - the - late - Earl - of-
Orford.' She'll have done that by the time I'm
back," as she left the room. Miss Upwell felt a little
resentment at this lady's treatment of her aunt.
After all, is not man an Atavistic animal? Is not
ancestor-worship the oldest of religions?

It *was* the Tapleys, if Madeline had not heard
the name wrong; who had already had tea with the
Outstrippingtons, subject to the same reservation.

But she may easily have got both names wrong. She thought she saw a chance of speaking with the niece by herself, and at any rate appointing a counter-visit before she went back to the Stakes, if she cut her own short before she became involved with the Tapleys, as might happen; and that would be fatal, she felt. So she suddenly perceived that she must not keep the greys standing in the cold, and got past the incoming Tapleys, who seemed to be in mourning for the human race, as far as clothes went; but not sorry at all, if you came to that. She had failed, and must give up the object of her visit, and acknowledge defeat. And, oh dear, how late it was!

She could, however, get a word or two with the niece before departing, unless that young woman consigned her to a servant and fled back to her Tapleys, who were shouting about how late they were, as if they had distinguished themselves. However, Mrs. Aiken had evidently no such intention, but, for some reason, very much the contrary.

The reason came out as soon as the door shut the shouters in, leaving her and her visitor in the passage, with a cap and a white apron hanging on their outskirts, ready for prompt action.

First Mrs. Aiken said, " I am afraid Aunt must have bored you dreadfully, Miss Upwell. She and her family! Oh dear! "

Madeline answered rather stiffly: "It was very interesting. I enjoyed listening." For she would have been better pleased with this young person if she had taken her aunt's part. Her own mother prosed, copiously, about ancestors; but she herself never tried to silence her.

However, her displeasure melted when Mrs. Aiken —having told the cap it needn't wait; she would call—coloured and hesitated, and wanted to say something.

"Yes," said Madeline.

"I was—was so grieved—to see about your friend. . . . Oh dear!—perhaps I oughtn't to talk about it. . . ."

Miss Upwell felt she had to be dignified. After all she and Jack were *not* engaged. "You mean Captain Calverley, Mrs. Aiken," said she. "We are hoping now—I mean his family are hoping—to hear from him every day. But, of course, they are —we all are—*very* anxious."

Mrs. Aiken looked dubiously at her visitor's face, seeming not to see the hand that was suggesting a good-bye shake. Then she said, very hesitatingly, "I—I didn't know—is there a hope? I only see the *Telegraph*." Then, an instant after, she saw her mistake. She might at least have had the sense to say nothing about the *Telegraph*.

Madeline felt her colour come and go, and her

heart getting restless. "A hope? Oh *dear,* yes!"
How bravely she said it! "You know there is no
proof whatever of his . . ." But she could not say
"death."

"Oh no—no proof, of course! . . . I should be
so glad . . . I suppose they only meant . . ."

All Madeline's courage was in the voice that succeeded in saying, "Dear Mrs. Aiken, do tell me
what was said. I daresay it was all nonsense. The
newspapers get all sorts of stories."

Mrs. Aiken would have given something to be
allowed to say no more about it. She stumbled a
good deal over an attempt to unsay her blunder.
She really couldn't be positive. Quite as likely as
not the paragraph might have referred to someone
else. She was far from sure, after all, that the
name wasn't Silverton. Yes, it certainly was, Major
Silverton—that was it!

"You are only saying that," said Madeline, gently
but firmly, "to make my mind easy. It is kind—
but—but you had better tell me now. Haven't you
got the *Telegraph?* I can buy one, of course, on my
way home. But I would much rather know now."

Mrs. Aiken saw no way of keeping it back. "It's
in here—the *Telegraph,*" said she. That is, it was
in the parlour opposite to the one they had left.
There it was, sure enough, and there, in clear print,
was the statement of its correspondent at Something-

fontein or other, that all hopes were now given up of the reappearance of Captain Calverley, who had been missing since the action at Burghersdrift, as some of his accoutrements had been found in the river below Kroondorp, and it was now looked upon as certain that he was drowned shortly after the action.

Madeline knew quite well that she had in herself an ample store of fortitude if only she could get a fair chance to exercise it. But a horrible sort of ague-fit had possession of her, and got at her teeth and spoiled her speech. It would go off directly, and she would be able to know practically, as she now did theoretically, that it was no use paying attention to any newspaper correspondence. She would soon get right in the air. If this Mrs. Aiken would only have the sense to see that what she wanted was to get away and have herself *to* herself until at least her teeth stopped chattering! But instead of that the tiresome young woman must needs say, " Oh dear, you look so ill! Shan't I get you something?" Which was silly, because what on earth could she have got, except brandy, or some such horror?

Madeline made a bad shot at speech, wishing to say that she would be all right directly, but really saying, " I shall be reckly." Collapse into a proffered chair enabled her to add, " Leave me alone—

it's nothing," and to sit still with her eyes shut.
Nervous upsets of this sort soon pass off; and by the
time Mrs. Aiken—who felt that some remedy *must*
be exhibited, for the honour of the house—had got
at one through an emissary, she was able to meet it
half-way. "Oh yes—eau-de-Cologne, please! It's
always delightful!" . Whereat Mrs. Aiken felt proud
and successful, and Madeline mopped her forehead,
feeling better.

But she must get away now as quick as possible.
Her card-castle had collapsed. And, indeed, she
felt too late the absurdity of it all from the beginning.
So far from being able to produce her ghost, or
whatever it could be called, in extenuation of this
young lady's reprobate husband, she had not seen
her way to mentioning him at all, even under a
pretext with which she had flattered her hopes, as a
last resource, that she knew nothing about his quarrel
with his wife and their separation. It might have
brought him on the *tapis*, with a successful result.
There was no chance now, even if she had felt at her
best. And here she was, morally crippled by a severe
shock! For though, of course, she was not going
to pay attention to newspaper stuff, it was a severe
shock all the same.

So she gathered herself up to say good-bye, and
with profusest gratitude for the eau-de-Cologne departed. And Mrs. Aiken, after watching the brisk

start of the greys, and thinking how bored they must have been, went slowly back into the house, to wonder what on earth could have brought an up-to-date young lady out of the Smart Set to such an un-pretending mansion as Athabasca Villa.

She wondered also whether those interminable Tapleys were going to talk like that till seven o'clock, and would Aunt P. go and ask them to stay to supper? Very likely! And she would have to be civil to them all the evening, she supposed.

Reflecting thus, her eye rested on the corner of the mahogany hall-bench, with a roll at each end; to prevent very short people falling over sideways, presumably. What she saw made her say, "What's this, Anne?"

"Which, Ma'am?" said Anne. "Perhaps the Missis knows."

This thing was inside brown paper, and rect-angular. The corners were hard, but the middle clicketted. Probably a *passe-partout*. At least, it could be nothing else. So if it wasn't a *passe-par-tout,* it was non-suited, *quoad* existence. Mrs. Aiken opened the drawing-room door, meeting a gust of the Tapleys, both speaking at once. It didn't matter. Aunt Priscilla heard all the plainer for a noise. There certainly was one.

Her niece said, through it, "Have you ordered a photograph, Aunty?" No, no photograph had been ordered. "Then I shall have to look at it, to see what it is," said Mrs. Aiken. The Tapleys sanctioned and encouraged this course, with loud shouts. And it really is a capital step to take when you want to find out what a thing is, to look at it and see.

It was a photograph, and was recognized at once by Mrs. Aiken as a copy from the Surley Stakes picture. It was a print of the photograph that Madeline had sent a copy of to Mr. Aiken at the Studio, a long time before. You remember how it stood on the table while he talked with Mr. Hughes? "I see," said Euphemia; "Miss Upwell must have left it behind. We must get it back to her." And she was proceeding to wrap it up again; not, however, without seeing enough of it to be sure of its identity.

But she was reckoning without her guests, who pounced simultaneously on the back of the photograph, crying out, "Stop!—it's written on. Read behind." Whereupon it was read behind that this photograph was for Mrs. Reginald Aiken, Athabasca Villa, Coombe. "I suppose she brought it for me," said that lady, rather sulkily.

"Whatever she came for I can't make out," said the niece to the aunt after supper, and indeed after the departure of the Tapleys. For Mrs. Aiken's worst anticipations had been fulfilled, and they had been invited to stay to supper and had done so remorselessly.

The aunt could throw no light on this sudden appearance of Miss Upwell. " She has great charm of manner," she said. " She reminds me a little of the late Lady Betty Dusters. It is in the turn of the chin." But Miss Bax's chin, cited in action to confirm this turn, was unconvincing.

Her niece ignored the late Lady Betty. " I think the girl was going lengths in coming at all," she said. " After all, what did it amount to ? Just that she and this young soldier of hers came to the Studio to see a picture. And supposing it did happen on the day when Reginald behaved so detestably with that horrible girl! Doesn't that make it all the other way round ? " She wished to express that if Miss Upwell had come to know about her quarrel with her husband, she should have kept her distance the more on that account. But she was not equal to the effort, and perhaps acknowledged it when she said, " You know what I mean, so it's no use drum-drum-drumming it all through, like a cart-horse or a barrel-organ. Anyhow, Miss Upsley Pupsley would have shown better taste to keep away, to *my* thinking! "

" I thought you seemed to like her, Euphemia," said the aunt, meekly.

" I didn't say I didn't," said the niece.

"Then I won't speak." Which resolve of Miss Priscilla's is inexplicable, unless due allowance is made for the fact that familiar domestic chat turns quite as much on the way it omits, as the way it uses words. The younger lady's manner was that of one in whom exasperation, produced by unrighteous conspiracy, was being kept in check by rare powers of self-control. That of the elder indicated constitutional toleration of the waywardness of near relations; who are, as we know, a crotchetty class. When one of these, in addition to tapping with her foot and looking flushed and ready to cry on small provocation, bites articles of *virtu,* surely a certain amount of forbearance—an irritating practice—is permissible.

"You'll spoil the paper-knife," said Miss Priscilla. "And it was a present from your great-uncle John Bulstrode, when he came from India."

Mrs. Aiken put the paper-knife down irritably, because she knew, as you and I do, that when those little mosaic pieces once come out, it's no use trying to stick them in again. But she said, "Bother the paper-knife!" And for a few moments her soul was content to find expression in foot-tapping and lip-biting; while her aunt forbore, and took up her knitting.

Then she got up and paced about the room, restlessly. The lamp was going out, or wanted seeing to. She turned it up; but if lamps are going out

for want of oil, turning them up does no good, and
only burns the wick away. They have to be properly seen to. It was too late to be worth putting
fresh oil in, this time. Candles would do, or for
that matter, why not do without? The firelight was
much nicer.

Mrs. Reginald Aiken walked about the room while
Miss Priscilla Bax looked at the fire and knitted.
It was getting on for bedtime.

Suddenly the walker stopped opposite the knitter.
"Aunty!" said she, but in a voice that almost
seemed to add, "Do talk to me and be sympathetic.
I'm quite reasonable now."

Her aunt seemed to accept the concession, skipping ratifications. "Certainly, my dear Euphemia,"
she said, with dignity.

"Do you know how long I've been here?"

Those who know how inconsequent daily famili-
arity makes blood relations who live together, will
see nothing odd in Miss Priscilla's reply: "My dear
niece, listen to me, and do not interrupt. What was
the expression I used when you first announced your
engagement to Reginald? . . . No—I did *not* say
it was a come-down. . . ."

"Yes, you did."

"Afterwards perhaps, but *at first*, Euphemia? Be
candid. Did I, or did I not, use the expression,
'Artists are all alike?' . . . I did? Very well!

And I said too—and you cannot deny it—that any
woman who married them did it with her eyes open,
and had only herself to thank for it. They are all
alike, and Reginald is no exception to the rule."
At this point Miss Priscilla may have had misgivings about sustaining the performance, for she ended
abruptly on the dominant, " And then you ask me if
I know how long you have been here! "

"Because it's six months, Aunty—over six
months! Is it any wonder that I should ask?
Besides, when I first came I never *meant* to stay.
I *was* going back when Reginald wrote that letter.
Fancy his daring to say there was no—what was
that he called it?—you know—'casus belli!'
An odious girl like that! And then to say if I really
believed it I ought to go into Court and swear to
things! How *could* I, with that Sairah? Oh dear
—if it had only been a lady!—or even a decent
woman! Anything one could produce! But—
Sairah!"

This young lady—mind you!—was only trying
to express a very common feeling, which, if you
happen to be a young married woman you will
probably recognize and sympathize with. Suppose
you were obliged to seek legal ratification of your
case against a faithless spouse, think how much
more cheerfully you would appear in court if the op-
position charmer was a Countess! Think how grate-

ful you would be if the culprits had made themselves indictable in terms you could use, and still
know which way to look; if, for instance, they had
had the decency to reside at fashionable hotels and
pass themselves off as the Spenser Smyths, or the
Poole Browns. These are only suggestions, to help
your imagination. The present writer knows no such
persons. In fact, he made these names, out of his
own head.

But—Sairah! Just fancy reading in the *Telegraph* that the petitioner complained of her husband's
misconduct with . . . Oh—it would be too dis-
gusting for words! After all, she, the petitioner, had
a right to be considered a—she detested the expression, but what on earth were you to say?—LADY!
What had she done that she should be dragged down
and degraded like that?

It had been Miss Priscilla's misfortune—as has
been hinted already—to contribute to the pro-
longation of her niece's residence with her by the
lines on which she herself seemed to be seeking to
bring it to an end. Nothing irritated this injured
wife more than to be reminded of feminine subor-
dination to man as seen from an hierarchical standpoint. So when her aunt quoted St. Paul—under
the impression that extraordinary man's correspondence so frequently produces, that she was quoting His Master—her natural irritation at his oriental

views of the woman question only confirmed her in
her obduracy, and left her more determined than ever
in her resentment against a husband who had read
St. Paul very carelessly if at all, and who took no
interest in churches apart from their Music and
Architecture.

Therefore, when Aunt Priscilla responded to her
niece's exclamation, which has been waiting so long
for an answer, with her usual homily, it produced
its usual result. " I can only urge you, my dear
Euphemia, to turn your thoughts to the Words of
One who is Wiser than ourselves. It is no use
your saying it's only Colossians. Besides, it's
Ephesians too. The place where it occurs is absolutely unimportant. ' Wives, submit yourselves
to your husbands, as it is fit in the Lord.' Those are
The Words." Miss Priscilla handled her capitals
impressively. The music stopped on a majestic
chord, and her rebellious niece was cowed for the moment. Not to disturb the effect, the old lady, having
lighted her own bedroom candle, kissed her benedic-
tionally, with a sense of doing it in Jacobean English—or should we say Jacobean silence?—corresponding thereto, and left her, accepting as valid a
promise to follow shortly.

But there was a comfortable armchair still making,
before a substantial amount of fire, its mute appeal,
" Sit down in me." The fire added, " Do, and I'll

roast you for twenty minutes more at least." It
said nothing about chilblains, but it must have known.
Mrs. Aiken acted on its advice, and sat looking at
it, and listening to an intermittent volcano in one of
its corners.

The volcano was flagging, subject to recrudescence
—for a certain latitude has to be given to Derby
Brights and Wombwell Main—before Mrs. Aiken
released her underlip, bitten as a counter-irritant to
Scripture precepts. Aunt Priscey *was* trying! But,
then, how good she was! Where on earth would
she, Euphemia Aiken, have gone to look for an
anchorage, if it hadn't been for Aunt Priscey? She
calmed down slowly, and Colossians died away in
the soothing ripple of the volcano.

But the fire was hot still, and she wanted a screen.
She took the first thing her hand lighted on. It
was the photograph. It would do. But she hated
the sight of it when the volcano made a spurt, and
set the shadows dancing over the whole room. She
turned it away from her towards the fire, to see the
blank back only, and calm down in the stillness, un-
exasperated.

Presently, for some reason, it became irksome to
hold it up. But it must be kept between her face
and the fire. She let it fall forward on her face, still
half holding it, and listened to the volcano. She
could sit and think about things, and not go to sleep.

Of course she could. It would never do to spoil her night's rest.

Was it really six whole months since she quarrelled with Reginald? She recited the months to make herself believe them actual, and failed. It did not really matter, though, how long it was. If Reginald had been ill, she could have gone back any time, and without any sacrifice of pride. Aunt Priscey would have found out a text, proving it a Christian duty more than ever. A little seductive drama crept through her mind, in which Reginald, smitten with some disorder of a good practicable sort for the piece—not a dangerous or nasty one, you know!—had put all his pride in his pocket, and written a letter humbly begging her forgiveness; acknowledging his weakness, his evil behaviour, and acquitting her of the smallest trace of unreasonable punctilio. It was signed, " Your lonely husband, Reginald Hay," that being a form domestic pleasantry in the past had sanctioned. Something choked in her throat over this touching episode of her own creation.

But it dispersed obsequiously when at a moment's notice—in her dream, you understand; dreamt as in the middle of dinner, to establish self-sacrifice as her portion—she started and arrived in time to save Reginald from a sinister nurse, whose elimination made an important passage in the drama. She got as far as the commencement of a letter to her aunt, describing this achievement. At this point drowsiness got the better of her, presumably. For her imaginary pen became tangible, and her paper was beautiful, only it was stamped " At Aunt's," which seemed absurd. And she could only write the words " My pride," which seemed more so.

Then she woke, or seemed to wake, with a start, saying aloud, to no one, " This will never do; I shall spoil my night's rest." But on the very edge of her waking someone had said, in her dream, in a sort of sharp whisper, " Perhaps it is." And it was this voice that had waked her. She found it hard to believe that an outside voice had not spoken into her dream. But no one was there, and had the room been full of folk, none of them could have read the words on her dream-paper. And to her half-awake mind it seemed that " Perhaps it is " could only apply to what she had succeeded in writing. However, there can be no doubt that, at this moment, she believed herself fully awake.

Later she had reason to doubt it. Or rather, she became convinced of the contrary by the subsequent course of events, which need not be anticipated now. During what followed, one would say that she must have had misgivings that she was dreaming. But she seems not to have had many or strong ones; although she may have made use of the expression, " I could hardly believe I was awake," as a mere phrase of wonderment—just as you or I have used it before now. For when next day she described this experience to her cousin Volumnia, who had been much in her confidence during these last months, who said to her, " Of course, you *were* asleep, because that is the only way of accounting for it reasonably," her reply was, " Then we shall have to account for it *un*reasonably, because I *was* awake."

" Well—go on, and tell," was the reply. This cousin Volumnia, the elder sister of that little monkey Jessie, was of course the grim big Miss Bax Miss Upwell had met at Lady Presteign's, and, as we have seen, she was a very determined person, one who would stand no nonsense. " Start from where the voice woke you, Cousin Euphemia," said she. She shut her eyes, and frowned, so as to listen judicially.

" I *laid* the *photo*graph *on* the *table*," said Mrs. Aiken, with circumflex accents over every other syllable, which is how to tell things clearly. But Miss Volumnia said, " You needn't pounce. I can hear." So she became normal. " I was absolutely certain there was no one else in the room. And everything seemed as usual; not the least like a dream. But for all that . . . you won't believe me, Volumnia. . . ."

" Very likely. Go on! "

"For all that I heard a voice—the same voice that waked me up. . . ."

"Of course! You were still asleep. *I* know. Go on! What did the voice say?"

"No, I won't go on at all, Volumnia, if you're going to be nasty."

"Oh yes, do go on. I'm greatly interested. But you must remember that we hear thousands of these things every week at the Psychomorphic. We had a very interesting case only the other day. A man heard a dog barking. . . . However, go on."

"Very well, only you mustn't interrupt. What was I saying? . . . Oh yes—the voice! I heard it quite distinctly, only very small. . . . Nonsense!—you know quite well what I mean. . . . What did it say? What I *heard* was, 'Hold me up, and let me look at you.' Now I know, my dear Volumnia, you will say I am making it improbable on purpose. . . ."

"Not at all, my dear Euphemia! The case is commoner than you suppose, even when the subject is wide awake. Please tell it *exactly* as you recollect it. Soften nothing." The implication was that Psychomorphism would know how much to take, and how much to reject.

"I am telling it exactly as it happened. It said . . ."

"What said?"

"The picture said."

"The picture! Oh, we hadn't come to that. Now what does that mean? The picture said!"

"Volumnia!—IF you interrupt I can't tell it at all. Do let me go on my own way."

"Yes—perhaps that *will* be better. I can analyze afterwards."

"Well—the voice seemed to come from the picture—the photo, I mean. It said quite unmistakably, but in a tiny voice, 'Pick me up, and let me look at you.' . . ."

"You said 'hold' before. Now it's 'pick.'"

"Really, Cousin Volumnia, I declare I won't go on unless. . . ."

"All right—all right! I'll be good." A little pause came here owing to Mrs. Aiken stipulating for guarantees. A *modus vivendi* was found, and she continued.

"I did as the voice said, and held the picture up, looking at it. I can't imagine how I came to take it so coolly. But you know, Volumnia, how it is when a perfect stranger speaks to you in an omnibus, and evidently takes you for somebody else, how civil you are? . . . Well—of course, I mean a lady! How can you be so absurd? I said to it that I had never heard a photograph speak before. The voice replied, 'That is because you never listen. Mr. Perry hears me because he listens.' I asked who this was, and the voice replied, 'The little old gentleman who comes here.' I said, 'No little old gentleman comes here. Do you know where you are?' And do you know, Volumnia, the voice said, 'In the Library at Surley Stakes, over the stoofer.' What could that mean?"

"Can't imagine. But I'm not to speak, you know. That's the bargain. Go on."

"Well—I told the woman in the photograph where she was, and the voice said, 'I suppose you know,' and then asked if this was the place where she saw me before. I said no—that was my husband's Studio. 'But,' I said, 'you were not made.' She seemed not to understand, and persisted that she remembered seeing me there."

"Do excuse my interrupting just this once," said Miss Volumnia. "I won't do it again. I only wish to point out how clearly this shows the dream-character of the phenomenon. Is it credible that, admitting for the sake of hypothesis an independent intelligence, that intelligence would recollect occurrences before it came into existence? It seems to me that the picture-woman's claim to identity carries its own condemnation. How could ideas existing in the mind of the original picture reappear in the mind of a photograph, however carefully made?"

"It was the same woman, Volumnia," said Mrs.

Aiken, beginning to stand on the rights of her Phenomenon, as people do. " I do think, dear, you are only cavilling and making difficulties."

" I think my objection holds good. When we consider the nature of photography . . ."

" Why is it more impossible than the original picture seeing me and recollecting ? "

" The demand on my power of belief is greater in the case of a copy, however accurate. And it would become greater still in the case of a copy of a copy. And so on." This was not original. A paper read at her Society was responsible for most of it. " However," she added, " we needn't discuss this now. Go on."

" Then don't prose. You really are straining at gnats and swallowing camels, Volumnia. Well— where was I ? . . . Oh yes, the Studio! The voice went on—and now this *does* show that it didn't come out of my own head—' I remember the Studio, and I remember a misunderstanding between yourself and your husband that might easily have led to serious consequences.' Now you know, Volumnia, that could *not* have come out of my own—my own inner consciousness. . . . Is that right?—Now *could* it ? "

Miss Volumnia shook an unbiassed head, on its guard against rash conclusions. " The same is true," she said, " of so many dream-impressions.

Did you make the photograph acquainted with the actual position of things? "

Mrs. Aiken seemed to hesitate a moment. " Was I bound to take it into my confidence? " she said. " Anyhow it seemed to me at the time most uncalled for."

" What did you say? "

" I said—because as it was only a photograph I thought it didn't matter—I said that fortunately no such result had come about. I then pressed it to say more explicitly what it referred to. . . . What? "

" Nothing—go on. . . . Well, I was only going to say that in my opinion you were playing with edged tools. The slightest departure from the principle of speaking the Truth is fraught with danger to the speaker. . . . Yes—and then? "

" Well—*did* it matter? Anyhow, let me get on. I asked what it meant—what misunderstanding it referred to. And do you know, Volumnia, the voice began and gave a *most accurate* account of Miss What's-her-name—Pupsley Wupsley's—visit to the Studio, and described that poor young Captain Thingumbob *most accurately*. All I can say is that it did not make a single mistake . . ."

" Of course not! "

" Why ' of course not '? "

" Because it was merely your own Memory unconsciously at work; doing the job on its own, as my young nephew would say. It may have been wrong, but would seem to you right."

" Then why doesn't what followed after I left the Studio seem to me right too? "

Miss Volumnia said, as from the seat of Judgment, " Let's hear it." Thereupon her friend gave, with conscientious effort to report truly, the photograph's version of what passed in the Studio between her husband and the odious Sairah. It corresponded closely with that already given in this story.

As Miss Volumnia's interruptions became frequent towards the close of this narrative, it may be best to summarize it, as near as may be, in the words of the photograph, which had said, or seemed to say: " I did indeed tremble to think what misconstruction might be put on half-heard words of this interview of this young English maiden with your husband. For I could remember well how at the little Castello in the Apennines Icilia Ciaranfi, a girl of great spirit, finding her new-made husband enacting some such pleasantry as this—but quite blamelessly—with Donnina Magliabecchi, stabbed both to death there and then; and her great grief when Donnina's lover Beppe made it clear to her that this was but a foolish jest to which he himself was privy. And thinking of this painful matter I rejoiced that you, Signora, yourself should have been guided by counsels of moderation, at most withdrawing for a term—so I understood—to the house of a relation as to a haven, when no doubt all asperity of feeling would soon give place to forgiveness. I could see that in your case, had you yielded to the mistaken impulse of Icilia, no such consolation as she found could have been yours. For I understood this—though I was young at the time—that so deeply was Beppe touched by Icilia's remorse for her rash action, and she so ready to give her love in compensation for what he had lost, that each flew as it were to the embrace of the other, and the two of them fled then and there, and thence Icilia escaped the officers of Justice. Now this surely would have been an impossible resource to yourself and the lover of *la Sera,* who, unless I am mistaken in thinking that those who 'keep company' are lovers in your land, was the person I heard spoken of as 'The Dust.' Which is in our tongue 'La Mondezza.' But I understood that while he was a man, and in that sense competent for Love, although called by a name fitter for a woman, yet was he socially on a level with those whom we others in Italy call *spazzini,* and no fit mate for a Signora of gentle birth and breeding.

"So that although I heard afar that the Signore and yourself came to high words on this subject, and gathered that you had departed in wrath to seek shelter with an aunt, I thought of this dissension

as one that would soon be forgotten, and a matter
of the past. The more so that your Signore's own
words to his friends reassured me; to whom he said
more than once that you would be the best woman
in the world but for a defect I did not understand
from his description, that when you flew into a
blooming rage you could not keep your hair on, but
that it wouldn't last and you would be back in a
week, because you knew he couldn't do without
you. He set my mind at rest by treating the idea
of any lasting breach between you as something
too absurd for speech. But I tell you this for
certain, that I saw all that passed between him and
la Sera, and that if you are keeping your resentment
alive with the thought that he was guilty of anything
but an ill-judged joke, you are doing grievous
injustice to him as well as yourself. Return to him,
Signora, forthwith; and beware henceforward of
foolish jealousy and needless quarrels!"

The foregoing is a much more complete version
of what the photograph seemed to say than Mrs.
Aiken's fragmentary report to her cousin. She had
not Mr. Pelly's extraordinary memory, and, moreover, she had to omit phrases and even sentences
that were given in Italian. Miss Volumnia Bax,
when not interrupting, checked off the narrative
with nods at intervals, each nod seeming to be
fraught with confirmed foresight of the preceding

instalment. When it ended, she launched at once, without a moment's pause, into a well-considered judgment, or rather abstract of a Report of the Case, which her mind was already scheming to read at the next meeting of the Psychomorphic. This Report, printed recently by the Society, containing all that Miss Volumnia said to her cousin on first hearing the tale, as well as many valuable remarks, commences as follows:

" Case 54103A. Dream or Pseudodream, reported by Miss Volumnia Bax. The subject of this experience, whom we will call Mrs. A., is reluctant to admit that she was not awake when it happened, however frequently the absurdity of this view is pointed out to her. So strong is this impression that if other members of her family had been subject to hallucination or insanity, or even victims of alcoholism, we should incline to place this case in some corresponding class. As it is, we have nothing but the word of the narrator to warrant our assigning it a place outside ordinary Somnistic Phenomena."

This story is not answerable for the technical phrases of what is, after all, merely a suburban Research Society. The Report goes on to give, very fairly, the incident as already narrated, and concludes thus:

" It will be observed that nothing that the dreamer put into the mouth of the photographic speaker was beyond her imaginative powers, subconscious or superconscious. It may be urged that the absurdly romantic Italian story implies a knowledge of Italian matters which the dreamer did not possess, or at least emphatically disclaims. But nothing but the verification of the story can prove that the names, for instance, were not due to subconscious activity of the dreamer's brain. On the other hand—and this shows how closely the investigator of Psychic Phenomena has to follow their intricacies—inquiry has elicited the fact that Mrs. A.'s husband once spent a week in Florence at a Pension in the Piazza Indipendenza and no doubt became familiar with the habits of Italians. What is more likely than that she should unconsciously remember passages of her husband's Italian experience, as narrated by himself? We are certainly warranted in assuming this as a working hypothesis, while admitting our obligation to sift Italian History for some confirmation of the dramatic (but not necessarily improbable) incident of Icilia Ciaranfi and Donnina Magliabecchi—both, by the way, suspiciously Florentine names! We repeat that, failing further evidence, we are justified in placing this story in section M 103, as a Pseudo-real Hypermnemonism."

The Report, of course, said nothing of the advice its writer had felt warranted in giving Mrs. A., as a corollary to her summary of the views she afterwards embodied in it. "If you want my opinion, Cousin Euphemia," she said, "it is that the sooner you make it up with your husband the better! It's quite clear from the dream that you want to do so."

"How do you make that out?" asked Mrs. Aiken.

"Clearly! Your subconscious self constituted this nonsensical photograph the exponent of its automatically cryptic Idea, while you were in a state of Self-Induced Hypnosis. . . ."

"Does that mean while I was asleep?"

"By no means. It is a condition brought about by fixing the attention. You had, by your own admission, been looking at the fire."

"No—I held up the photograph."

"Then you had been looking at the photograph."

"Only the back."

"It's the same thing. I am distinctly of opinion that it was Self-Induced Hypnosis. In this condition the subconscious self may as it were take the bit in its teeth, and energize whatever bias towards common sense the subject may happen to possess. In your case the photograph's speech and its grotesque fictions were merely pegs, so to speak, on which to hang an exposition of your own subconscious cryptic Idea. Does not the fact that you are at this moment prepared to deny the existence of this Idea prove the truth of what I say?"

"I daresay it's very clever and very wise. But I can't understand a word of it, and you can't expect me to. All I know is, that if it's to be submission and Colossians and Ephesians and stuff, back to Reginald I don't go. And as far as I can see, Science only makes it ten times worse. . . . So there!"

"Your attitude of mind, my dear Euphemia," said Miss Volumnia, "furnishes the strongest confirmation possible of the truth of my interpretation of the Phenomenon. But I must go or I shall lose my train."

"How I do hate patronizing people!" said Mrs. Aiken, going back into the drawing-room after seeing her cousin off.

CHAPTER VIII

MRS. AIKEN tortured her speculating powers for
awhile with endeavours to put this curious event on
an intelligible footing, and was before long in a
position to "dismiss it from her mind"; or, if not
quite that, to give it a month's notice. It certainly
seemed much less true on the second day after it
happened than on the first; and, at that rate, in a
twelvemonth it would never have happened at all.
But her passive acceptance of a thing intrinsically
impossible and ridiculous—because, of course, we
know, etc., etc.—was destined to undergo a rude
shock. After taking her aunt's advice about the
duration of the usual pause—not to seem to have too
violent a " *Sehnsucht* " for your card-leavers—the

239

lady paid her visit to Miss Upwell at her parents' stuck-up, pretentious abode in Eaton Square. We do not give the number, as to do so would be to bring down a storm of inquiries from investigators of phenomena.

She gave her card to the overfed menial, who read it—and it was no business of his! He then put it upside down—*his* upside down—on a salver, for easy perusal by bloated oligarchs. The voice of an oligarch rang out from the room he disappeared into, quite deliciously, and filled the empty house. Madeline was delighted to see Mrs. Aiken—had been going to a Bun-Worry. *Now* she should do nothing of the sort; she would much rather have tea at home, and a long talk with Mrs. Aiken. She confirmed this by cancelling her out-of-door costume, possibly to set the visitor at her ease. Anyhow, it had that effect. In fact, if either showed a trace of uneasiness, it was Madeline. She more than once began to say something she did not finish, and once said, " Never mind," to excuse her deficit. Of course Mrs. Aiken had not the slightest idea of what was passing in her mind; or rather, imputed it to a hesitation on the threshold of sympathetic speech about her own domestic unhappiness.

Now the portion of this conversation that the story is concerned with came somewhere near the middle of it, and was as follows:

"I think you said you had met my cousin, Volumnia Bax?"

"At Lady Presteign's—yes, of course I did! With a splendid head of auburn hair, and a—strongly characteristic manner. We had a most amusing talk."

"She has a red head and freckles, and is interested in Psychœopathy." An analogue of homœopathy, which would have stuck in the gizzard of the Clarendon Press, and even the Daily This and the Evening That would have looked at a dictionary about.

"Oh," said Miss Upwell dubiously. "I thought her a fine-looking woman—a—a Lifeguardswoman, don't you know! And her nose carries her *pince-nez* without her having to *pincer* her *nez*, which makes all the difference. She talked about you."

"Oh, did she? I was going to ask if she did. What did she say about me?"

"You mustn't be angry with her, you know! It was all very nice."

"Oh yes, of course! It always is very nice. But—a—what *was* it? You *will* tell me, won't you?"

"Certainly—every word! But I may have mistaken what she said, because there was music—Katchakoffsky, I think; and the *cello* only found he'd got the wrong Op., half-way through."

"I suppose she was telling you all about me and

Reginald. I wish she would mind her own . . . well, I wish she would Psychœopathize and leave *me* alone."

"Dear Mrs. Aiken!—you said you wouldn't be angry. And it was only because *I* mentioned you and talked of that delightful visit—of—of ours to the Studio. . . . Oh no, no!—there's no more news. Not a word!" This came in answer to a look. Madeline went on quickly, glad to say no more of her own grief. "It was not till I myself mentioned you that she said, ' I suppose you know they've split?' "

"That was a nice way to put it. Split!"

"Yes—it looked as if it was sea-anemones, and each of you had split, making four." Miss Upwell then gave a very truthful report of what Miss Bax had told her, neither confounding the persons, nor dividing the substance of her narrative.

When she had finished, Mrs. Aiken began to say, "I suppose——" and underwent a restless pause. Then, as her hostess waited wistfully for more, she went on, "I suppose she said I ought to go back and be a dutiful wife. I'm quite sick and tired of the way people talk."

"She said"—thus Madeline, a little timidly—"that she thought you had acted under a grievous misapprehension. That was what she said—' A grievous misapprehension.' "

"Oh yes!—and I'm to go back and beg pardon. *I* know. . . . But that reminds me. . . ." She reined up.

"Reminds you. . . .?" Madeline paused, for her to start again.

"Reminds me that I've never thanked you for the photograph."

"I thought you might like it. I can't tell you how fond I am of the picture, myself. I wanted to get you to be more lenient to the poor girl. It is the loveliest face!"

"Oh, I dare say. But anyhow it was most kind of you to give it me. Let me see!—what *was* it reminded me of the photograph? Oh, of course,—Volumnia Bax."

"I was wondering why you said ' reminded.' "

Now Mrs. Aiken had two or three or four or five faults, but secretiveness was not among them. In fact she said of herself that she " always outed with everything." This time, she outed with, or externalized—but we much prefer the lady's own expression—what proved of some importance in the evolution of events. "Oh, of course, it was because of the . . . but it was such nonsense!" So she spoke, and was silent. The cat was still in the bag, but one paw was out, at least.

Miss Upwell had her own share of inquisitiveness, and a little of someone else's. "Never mind! Do tell *me,*" she said, open-eyed and receptive. The slight accent on " me " was irresistible.

"It was silliness—sheer silliness!" said Mrs. Aiken. "An absurd dream I had, which made Volumnia say it was evident I was only being obstinate about Reginald, because of Science and stuff. And so going back and begging pardon reminded me. That was all."

" But what had the picture to do with the dream? That's what *I* want to know," said Madeline.

" The picture was *in* the dream," said Mrs. Aiken. " But it was such *frightful* nonsense."

" Oh, never *mind* what nonsense it was! Do—do tell me all about it. I can't tell you what an intense interest I take in dreams. I do indeed! "

" If I do, you won't repeat it to anybody. Now will you? Promise! "

" Upon my word I won't. Honour bright! " Thereon, as Mrs. Aiken really wanted to tell, but was dreadfully afraid of being thought credulous, she told the whole story of the dream, with every particular, just as she had told it to Miss Volumnia Bax.

Her hearer contrived to hold in, with a great effort, until the story reached " Well—that's all! At least, all I can tell you. Wasn't it absurd? " Then her pent-up impatience found vent. *" Now* listen to *my* story! " she cried, so loud that her hearer gave a big start, exclaiming, "What—have *you* got a story? Oh, do tell it! I've told you mine, you know!"

Then Madeline made no more ado, but told the whole story of Mr. Pelly's dream, omitting all but a bare sketch of the Italian narrative—just enough to give local truth.

"Then," said Mrs. Aiken, when she had finished, "I suppose *you* mean that I ought to go back and beg Reginald's pardon, too."

"I *do*," said Madeline, with overwhelming emphasis. "*Now*, directly!"

"But you'll promise not to tell *anyone* about the dream—my dream," said Mrs. Aiken.

That same afternoon Mr. Reginald Aiken had been giving careful consideration to Diana and Actæon, unfinished; because, you see, he had a few days before him of peace and quiet, and rest from beastly restoration and picture-cleaning. One—himself, for instance—couldn't be expected to slave at that rot for ever. It was too sickening. But of course you had to consider the dibs. There was no getting over that.

However, apart from cash-needs, there were advantages about these interruptions. You came with a fresh eye. Mr. Aiken had got Diana and Actæon back from its retirement into the Studio's

picked light, to do justice to his fresh eye. Two
friends, one of whom we have not before seen in his
company, were with him, to confirm or contradict
its impressions.

This friend, a sound judge you could always
rely upon, but—mind you!—a much better Critic
than an Artist, was seated before the picture with
a short briar-root in his mouth, and his thumbs in
the armholes of a waistcoat with two buttons off.
The other, with a calabash straining his facial
muscles, and his hands—thumbs and all—in his
trouser-pockets, was a bit of a duffer and a stoopid
feller, but not half a bad chap if you came to that.
Mr. Aiken called them respectively Tick and Dobbles.
And they called him Crocky.

So there were five fresh eyes fixed upon the picture,
two in the heads of each of these gentlemen, and the
one Mr. Aiken himself had come with.

Mr. Tick's verdict was being awaited, in consid-
erate silence. His sense of responsibility for its
soundness was gripping his visage to a scowl; and
a steadfast glare at the picture, helped by glasses,
spoke volumes about the thoroughness of its source's
qualifications as a Critic.

Mr. Aiken became a little impatient. "Wonder
if you think the same as me, Tick?" said he.

"Wonder if you think the same as 'im!" said
Dobbles.

But Criticism—of pictorial Art at least—isn't a thing to hurry over, and Mr. Tick ignored these attempts at stimulus. However, he spoke with decision when the time seemed ripe. Only, he first threw an outstretched palm towards the principal figure, and turned his glare round to his companions, fixing them. And they found time, before judgment came, to murmur, respectively, "Wonder if he'll say my idea!" and "Wonder if he'll say your idear?"

"Wants puttin' down!" shouted Mr. Tick, leaving his outstretched fingers between himself and Diana. And thereupon the Artist turned to Mr. Dobbles and murmured, "What did I tell you?" And Mr. Dobbles murmured back, "Ah!—what did you tell me?" not as a question, but as a confirmation.

"What I've been thinking all along!" said Mr. Aiken. Then all three gave confirmatory nods, and said that was it, you might rely on it. Diana was too forward. Had Actæon been able to talk, he might have protested against this. For see what a difference the absence of the opposite characteristic would have made to Actæon!

Conversation then turned on the steps to be taken to get this forward Goddess into her place again. Mr. Tick, who appeared to be an authority, dwelt almost passionately on the minuteness of the change

required. " When I talk of puttin' down," said he,
"you mustn't imagine I'm referrin' to any *per-ceptible* alteration. You change the tone of that
flesh, and you'll ruin the picture! "

His hearers chorused their approbation, in such
terms as " Right you are, Tick, my boy! "—" That's
the way to put it! "—" Bully for you, old cocky-wax! " and so on.

Mr. Tick seemed pleased, and elaborated his posi-tion. " Strictly speakin'," said he, " what is needed
is an absolutely imperceptible lowerin' of the tone.
Don't you run away with the idea that you can paint
on a bit of work like that, to do it any good. You
try it on, and you'll come a cropper." This was
agreed to with acclamations, and a running com-mentary of " Caution's the thing! "—" You stick to
Caution! "—and so on. The orator proceeded,
" Now, I never give advice, on principle. But if I
was to do so in this case, and you were to do as I
told you, you would just take the *smallest possible*
quantity—the least, *least*, LEAST touch—no more!
—of . . . ." But Mr. Tick had all but curled up
over the intensity of his superlatives, and he had to
come uncurled.

" What of? " said Mr. Aiken. And said Mr.
Dobbles, not to be quite out of it, " Ah!—what of? "
Because a good deal turned on that.

Mr. Tick had a paroxysm of decision. He seized

Mr. Aiken's velveteen sleeve, and held him at arm's
length. "Look here, Crocky!" said he. "Got any
Transparent Oxide of Chromium?"

"Yes—somewhere!"

"Well, now—just you do as I tell you. Got a
clean number twelve sable? . . . No?—well,
number eleven, then . . . That'll do!—dip it in
Benzine Collas and give it a rinse out. See? Then
you give it a rub in your Transparent Oxide, and
wipe it clean with a rag. What's left will go all
over Diana, and a little to spare. . . ."

"Won't she look green?" Mr. Aiken seemed reluctant.

"Rather! But you do as I say, young feller, and
ask no questions. . . . 'What are you to do
next?'—why, take an absoli-yootly white bit of old
rag and wipe her quite clean from head to foot."
His audience suggesting here that no change would
be visible, he added, "That's the idear. Don't you
change the colour on any account. But you'll see!
Diana—she'll have gone back!"

"There's somethin' in what old Tick says," said
Mr. Dobbles, trying to come out of the cold. He
nodded mysteriously. Mr. Aiken said he'd think
about it.

Mr. Tick said, "I ain't advisin'. I never advise.
But if I was to—there's the advice I should give!"
Then he and Mr. Dobbles went their ways, leaving

Mr. Aiken searching for his tube of Transparent Oxide of Chromium.

Now, Mr. Reginald Aiken always knew where everything was in his Studio, and could lay his hand on it at once. Provided always that you hadn't meddled and shifted the things about! And he knew this tube of colour was in his old japanned tin box, with the folding palette with the hinge broke. It might be difficult to get out by now, because he knew a bottle of Siccatif had broken all over it. But he was keen to make Diana go back, and if he went out to get another tube he would lose all the daylight.

So he sat down to think where the dooce that box had got put. He lit a cigarette to think with. One has to do things methodically, or one soon gets into confusion.

He passed before his mind the epoch-making *bouleversements* of the past few years; notably the regular good clean-up when he married Euphemia four years since, and took the second floor as well as the Studio floor he had occupied as a bachelor.

He finished that cigarette gloomily. Presently he decided that what had happened on that occasion had probably occurred again. History repeats itself. That box had got shoved back into the recess behind the *cassettone*. He would have up Mrs. Gapp, who came in by the day, in the place of Mrs. Parples, who had outstayed her welcome, to help him to shift that great beastly useless piece of lumber. Mrs. Gapp was, however, easier to call over the stairs to than to have up. The number of times you called for Mrs. Gapp was according; it varied with your own tenacity of purpose and your readiness to believe that she wasn't there. Mr. Aiken seemed easily convinced that she was at the William the Fourth, up the street. That was the substance of his reason for not shouting himself hoarse; that is to say, it worked out thus as soliloquy. He went back and tried for the japanned tin colour-box, single-handed.

He had much better have gone out to buy a new tube of this useful colour, as in five minutes he was one mass of filth. Only getting the things off the top of that box was enough!—why, you never see anything to come near the state they was in. And if he had only rang again, sharp, Mrs. Gapp would have heard the wire; only, of course, no one could say the bell wasn't broke, and maintain a reputation for truthfulness. We are incorporating in our text some verbal testimony of Mrs. Gapp's, given later.

But Mrs. Gapp could not have testified—for she was but a recent char, at the best—to the desolation of her unhappy employer's inner soul when, too late for the waning light of a London day, he opened with leverage of a screwdriver the lid of that japanned tin-box, and excavated from a bed of thickened resin which he knew could never be detached from the human hand, or anything else it touched, an abject half-tube of colour which he had to treat with a lucifer-match before he could get its cap off. And then only to find that it had gone leathery, and wouldn't squeeze out.

If we had to answer an Examination question, "When is Man at his loneliest? Give instances," we should reply—unless we had been otherwise coached—"When he is striving, companionless, to get some sort of order into things; working on a basis of Chaos, feeling that he is the first that ever burst into a dusty sea, choked with its metaphorical equivalent of foam. Instance Mr. Reginald Aiken, at the end of last century, in his Studio at Chelsea." Anyhow, if this question had been then asked of anyone and received this answer, and the Examiners had referred back to Mr. Aiken, before giving a decision, he would certainly have sanctioned full marks.

But he gave himself unnecessary trouble. One always does, in contact with disinterred lumber, in which a special brood of spooks lies hid, tempting him to the belief that this flower-stand only wants a leg to be of some use, and that that fashionable armchair only wants a serpentine segment of an arm and new straps under the seat to be quite a handsome piece of furniture. Yes, and new

'American leather, of course! Mr. Aiken had not
to deal with these particular articles, but the
principle was the same. He foolishly tampered
with a sketching umbrella, to see if it would open:
it certainly did, under pressure, but it wouldn't keep
up nor come down, and could only be set right at
the shop, and a new one would be cheaper in the
end. Pending decision, a large blackbeetle, who
had hoped to end his days undisturbed, fell off the
underside as its owner opened it, and very nearly
succeeded in getting down his back.

The things that came out of that cavern behind
the *cassettone!*—you never would have thought it!
A large can of genuine Amber Varnish that had had
its cork left out, and wouldn't pour; the Skeleton's
missing right scapula, only it wouldn't hold now;
and, besides, one never wanted the Skeleton; a
great lump of modelling-wax and apparently in-
finite tools—no use to Mr. Aiken now, because he
never did any modelling, but they might be a
godsend to some art-student; folio volumes of
anatomical steel-plates, that the engravers had
hoped would last for ever—a hope the mice may
have shared, but they had done pretty well already;
Mr. Aiken's old ivory foot-rule, which was the only
accurate one in the British Empire, and what the
dooce had become of it he never could tell; plaster
heads without noses, and fingers without hands,

and discarded fig-foliage, like a pawnshop in Eden; things, too, for which no assignable purpose appeared on the closest examination—things that must have been the lifework of insane artisans, skilful and thorough outside the powers of language to express, but stark mad beyond a doubt. And a Dutch clock that must have been saying it was a quarter-past twelve, unrebuked, for four years or so past.

Mr. Aiken need not have tried to pour out the Amber Varnish; where was the sense of standing waiting, hoping against hope for liquidation? He need not have hunted up a pair of pliers to raise vain hopes in the scapula's breast—or its equivalent—of a new lease of life. He need not have tried to soften the heart of that wax. Nor have turned over the plates to see if any were left perfect. Nor need he have reconsidered the Inexplicables, to find some plausible *raison d'être* for them, nor tried to wind up the Dutch clock with sporadic keys, found among marine stores in a nail-box. But he was excusable for sitting and gloating over his ivory foot-rule, his sole prize from a wrestling-match with intolerable filth—or only tolerable by a Londoner. He was weary, and the daylight had vanished. And even if he had got a squeeze out of that tube, he couldn't have used it. It was much too ticklish a job to do in the dark.

He sat and brooded over his loneliness in the

twilight. How in Heaven's name had this odious
quarrel come about? Nonsense about Sairah!
That absurd business *began* it, of course. Serious
quarrels grow out of the most contemptible nonsense,
sometimes. Oh no—there was something behind;
some underlying cause. But he sought in vain to
imagine one. They had always been such capital
friends, he and Euphemia! It was true they
wrangled a great deal, often enough. But come, I
say! If a man wasn't to be at liberty to wrangle
with his own wife, what *were* we coming to?

He believed it was all the doing of that blessed
old aunt of hers. If she hadn't had Athabasca Villa
to run away to,—why, she wouldn't have run away
at all! She would have snapped and grizzled at
him for a time, and then made it up. And then
they would have had an outing, to Folkestone or
Littlehampton, and it would all have been jolly.

Instead of which, here they were, living apart
and writing each other letters at intervals—for they
kept to correspondence—and, so far as he could see,
letters only made matters worse. He knew that the
moment he took up his pen to write a regular sit-
down letter he put his foot in it. He had always
done that from a boy.

Probably, throughout all the long summer that
had passed since his quarrel with his wife, he had
not once missed saying, as a morning resolution to

begin the day with, that he wouldn't stand this any
longer. He would go straight away, after breakfast, to Athabasca Villa, and beard Aunt Priscilla
in her den, his mind seeming satisfied with the
resolution in this form. But every day he put it
off, his real underlying objection to going being that
he would have to confess to having made himself
such an unmitigated and unconscionable Juggins.
His Jugginshood clung to him like that Siccatif to
his fingers. It was too late to mitigate himself now.
And six months of discomfort had contrived to slip
away, of which every day was to be the last. And
here he was still!

If he had understood self-examination—people
don't, mostly—he might have detected in himself
a corner of thought of a Juggins-mitigating character. However angry he felt with his wife, he
could not, would not, admit the possibility that she
believed real ill of him. His loyalty to her went
further than Geraint's to Enid, for he imputed to
her acquittal of himself, from sheer ignorance of the
sort of thing anybody else's wife might impute to
anybody else's husband. Because, you see, he had
at heart such a very exalted view of her character.
Perhaps she would not have thanked him for fixing
such a standard for her to act up to.

He sat on—on—in the falling darkness; the
little cheerfulness of his friends' visit had quite van-

ished. The lumber he had wallowed in had grimed his heart as well as his garments. He would have liked Tea—a great stand-by when pain and anguish wring the brow. But when you are too proud to admit that your brow is being wrung, and you know it is no use ringing the bell, because Mrs. Gapp, or her equivalent, is at the William the Fourth, why, then you probably collapse and submit to Fate, as Mr. Reginald Aiken did. It didn't much matter now if he had no Tea. No ministering Angel was there to make it.

He sat, collapsed, dirty and defeated, in the Austrian bent-wood rocking-chair. What was that irruption of evening newsboys shouting? Repulse of some General, English or Dutch, at some berg or drift; surrender of some other, Dutch or English, at some drift or berg. He was even too collapsed to go out and buy a halfpenny paper. He didn't care about anything. Besides, it was the same every evening. Damn the Boers! Damn Cecil Rhodes!

The shouters had passed—a *prestissimo* movement in the Street Symphony—selling rapidly, before he had changed his mind, and wished he had bought a *Star*. Never mind!—there would be another edition out by the time he went to dinner at Machiavelli's. He sat on meditating in the gloom, and wondering how long it would be before it was all jolly again. Of course it *would be*—but when?

A sound like a nervous burglar making an attempt
on a Chubb lock caught his ear and interested him.
He appeared to identify it as Mrs. Gapp trying
to use a latchkey, but unsuccessfully. He seemed
maliciously amused, but not to have any intention
of helping. Presently the sound abdicated, in
favour of a subterranean bell of a furtive and
irresolute character. Said Mr. Aiken, then, to
Space, "Mrs. Verity won't hear that, you may bet
your Sunday garters," and then went by easy
stages to the front-door, to see—so further soliloquy
declared—how sober his housekeeper was after so
long an absence. A glance at the good woman convinced him that her register of sobriety would stand
at zero on any maker's sobriometer.

She said that a vaguely defined community, called
The Boys, had been tampering with the lock. Mr.
Aiken, from long experience of her class at this stage,
was able to infer this from what sounded like
"Boysh been 'tlocksh—keylocksh—inchfearunsh."
This pronounced exactly phonetically will be clear
to the student of Alcoholism; be so good as to read
it absolutely literally.

"Lock's all right enough!" said Mr. Aiken,
after turning it freely both ways. "Nobody's
been interfering with it. You're drunk, Mrs.
Gapp."

Mrs. Gapp stood steady, visibly. Now, you can't

stand steady, visibly, without a suspicion of a lurch
to show how splendidly you are maintaining your
balance. Without it your immobility might be
mere passionless inertia. Mrs. Gapp's eye seemed
as little under her control as her voice, and each
had a strange, inherent power of convincing the
observer that the other was looking the wrong way.

"Me?" said Mrs. Gapp.

"Yes—you!" said Mr. Aiken.

Mrs. Gapp collected herself, which—if we include
in it her burden, consisting of some bundles of fire-
wood and one pound four ounces of beefsteak
wrapped in a serial—seemed in some danger of re-
distributing itself when collected. She then spoke,
with a mien as indignant as if she were Boadicea
seeking counsel of her country's gods, and said,
"*Me* r-r-runk! *Shober!*"—the last word expressing heartfelt conviction. Some remarks that followed, scarcely articulate enough to warrant
transcribing, were interpreted by Mr. Aiken to the
effect that he was doing a cruel injustice to a widow-
woman who had had fourteen, and had lived a pure
and blameless life, and had buried three husbands.
Much stress was laid on her own habitual abstention
from stimulants, and the example she had striven
to set in her own humble circle. Her third had
never touched anything but water—a curlew's life,
as it were—owing to the force of this example.

Let persons who accused her of drunkenness look at home, and first be sure of their own sobriety. Her conscience acquitted her. For her part she thought intoxication a beastly, degrading habit— that is to say, if Mr. Aiken interpreted rightly something that sounded, phonetically, like " Bishley grey rabbit." At this point one of the wood-bundles became undone, owing to the disgraceful quality of the string now in use. Mrs. Gapp was dissuaded with difficulty from returning to the shop to exchange it, but in the end descended the kitchen-stairs, lamenting commercial dishonesty, and shedding sticks.

The Artist seemed to regard this as normal charing, nothing uncommon. He returned to the Austrian bent-wood chair, and sat down to think whether he should light the gas. He began to suspect himself of going imbecile with disheartenment and depression. He was at his lowest ebb. " I tell you what," said he—it was Space he was addressing—" I shall just go straight away to-morrow after breakfast to Coombe, and tell Mrs. Hay that if she doesn't come back I shall let the Studio and go to Japan."

But Space didn't seem interested. It' had three dimensions, and was content.

He might as well light the gas as not; so he did it, and it sang, and burned blue. Then it stopped

singing, and became *transigeant,* and you could
turn it down or up. Mr. Aiken turned it down, but
not too much, and listened to a cab coming down
the street. " That's not for here," said he. He
had no earthly reason for saying this. He was only
making conversation; or rather, soliloquy. But
he was wrong; at least so far as that the cab was
really stopping, here or next door. And in the
quadrupedations, door-slammings, backings, re-
proofs to the horse, interchange of ideas between
the Captain and the passengers of a hansom cab of
spirit, a sound reached Mr. Aiken's ear which ar-
rested him as he stood, with his finger on the gas-
tap. " Hullo! " said he, and listened as a musical
Critic listens to a new performance.

When towards the end of such a symphony, the
fare seeks the exact sum he is named after, and
weighs nice differences, some bars may elapse
before the conductor—or rather the driver, else we
get mixed with omnibuses—sanctions a start. But
a reckless spendthrift has generally discharged his
liability, and is knocking at the door or using his
latchkey, before his late driver has done pretending
to consider the justice of his award. It happened
so in this case, for before Mr. Aiken saw anything
to confirm or contradict the need for his close
attention, eight demisemiquavers, a pause, and a
concussion, made a good wind-up to the symphony

aforesaid, and the cab was free to begin the next movement on its own account.

He discarded the gas-tap abruptly, and pounced upon his velveteen, nearly pulling over the screen he had hung it on. " That drunken jade must *not* go to the door," he gasped, as he bolted from the room and down the stairs. He need not have been uneasy. The jade was singing in the kitchen— either the Grandfather's Clock or the Lost Chord— and was keeping her accompanyist waiting, with an intense feeling of pathos. Mr. Aiken swung down the stairs, got his collar right in the passage, and nearly embraced the wrong lady on the doorstep, so great was his hurry to get at the right one.

" Never mind! " said Madeline; and her laugh was like nightingales by the Arno in May. " Don't apologize, Mr. Aiken. Look here!—I've brought you your wife home. Now kiss *her!* "

" You're not fit to kiss anybody, Reginald; but I suppose there's soap in the house." So said Mrs. Aiken. And then, after qualifying for a liberal use of soap, she added, " What *is* that hideous noise in the kitchen ? "

" Oh, that? " said her husband. " *That's* Mrs. Gapp."

CHAPTER IX

"I'M afraid you *did* get mixed up, darling, this
time. But I dare say they're all right." This was
Lady Upwell's comment at breakfast next morning,
when her daughter had completed a narrative of
her previous evening's adventure, which had assumed, between the close of last chapter and the en-
suing midnight, all the character of a reckless
escapade. Indeed, it had long been past that hour
when the young lady, who had wired early in the
evening that she was "dining with Aikens shall be
late," returned home in better spirits than she had
shown for months—so her mother said to sympathetic friends afterwards—to find her Pupsey getting

263

uneasy about her, and fidgetting. Because that was Pupsey's way.

Madeline's parents at this time would probably have welcomed any diversion or excitement for the girl; anything to take her mind away from her troubles. They were not at all sure about these Aiken people; but there!—they would have welcomed worse, to see this little daughter of theirs in such spirits as hers last night. Touching the cause of which they were a little puzzled, as she had stuck loyally to her promise to tell nothing of Mrs. Aiken's dream and the share the Italian picture had in her reconciliation with her husband. All she said was that she had persuaded Euphemia to go back to Reginald; she having, as it were, borrowed from each the name each called the other—in a certain sense, quoting it.

"Euphemia, I suppose, is Mrs. Aiken?" said her ladyship temperately—with a touch of graciousness, like Queens on the stage to their handmaidens Cicely or Elspeth.

"Euphemia's Mrs. Aiken, but he calls her Mrs. Hay as often as not." Perplexity of both parents here required a short explanation of middle-class jocularity turning on neglect or excess of aspirates. After which Madeline said, "That's all!" and they said, "We see," but with hesitation. Then she continued her story. "It was such fun. *I* knocked at the door, and Reginald came rushing out because he heard Euphemia outside, and clasped me in his arms. . . . Oh, well—it's quite true! You see, he was in such a hurry he didn't stop to look, and he took me for Euphemia." For the Baronet had laid down his knife and fork and remained transfixed. But a telegraphic lip-movement of her ladyship reassured him. "This," it said, "is exaggeration. Expect more of the same sort." However, his daughter softened the statement. "It wasn't exactly negotiated, you know. And I don't think it would have been any satisfaction either, because he was so horribly dirty, Reginald was."

The Baronet completed a contract he had on hand with some kippered salmon, and said, before accepting a new one, "Well—*you're* a nice young woman!" But he added, forgivingly, "Go on—gee-up!"

The nice young woman went on. "And do you know, I don't believe that a more filthy condition than that house was in—why, Mrs. Aiken had been away ten months! And there was a drunken cook singing in the kitchen all the while."

"You are an inconsecutive puss," said the Baronet, very happy about the puss nevertheless. "You didn't finish your sentence. 'Filthy condition that house was in'—go on!"

"Bother my sentence! Finish it yourself, Pup-

sey. Well—Reginald and Euphemia made it up like
a shot. Couple of idiots! Then the question was—
dinner. I said come home here, but they said
clothes. There was some truth in what they had
on, so I said hadn't we better all go and dine where
Mr. Aiken had been going. Because I didn't call
him Reginald to his face, you know!"

"And you went, I suppose?"

"I should think so. We dined at Mezzofanti's
in Great Compton Street, Soho—no, it wasn't; it
was Magliabecchi's—no!—Machivaelli's. And I
talked such good Italian to the waiter. It *was* fun.
And what do you think we did next? . . . Give it
up?" Her father nodded. "Why—we went to the
Gaiety Theatre—there! And we saw 'Charley's
Aunt,' and we parted intimate bosom friends. Only
Euphemia is rather fussy and distant, compared to
Us, and I had to stick out to make her kiss me."
A slight illustration served to show how the speaker
had driven a coach-and-six through the bosom-
friend's shyness.

"Well," said the Baronet. "All I can say is—
I wish I had been there with you. If I go to the
play now—there I am, dressed in toggery and sittin'
in the stalls! Lord, I remember when I was a
young fellow, there was Charles Mathews and
Madame Vestris . . . you can't remember
them . . ."

"Of course I can't. I was only born nineteen years ago." The Baronet, however, added more recent theatrical experiences, but only brought on himself corrections from his liege lady. "My dear, you're quite at sea. Fancy the child recollecting Lord Dundreary and Buckstone! Why, she wasn't born or thought of!"

But when this Baronet got on the subject of his early plays and operas, he developed reminiscence in its most aggravated form. He easily outclassed Aunt Priscey on the subject of her ancestors. Her ladyship abandoned him as incorrigible, without an apology, but his daughter indulged him and sat and listened.

All things come to an end sooner or later, and reminiscence did, later. Then poor Madeline ran down in her spirits, and sat brooding over the war news. It was only a temporary sprint. Reginald and Euphemia vanished, and Jack came back.

Madeline kept all this story of the talking photograph to herself. To talk of it she would have had to tell her friend's dream, and that she had promised not to do.

She was so loyal that when a day or two later she met the formidable Miss Volumnia Bax, she kept a strict lock on her tongue, even when that lady plunged into a *résumé* of the dream-story as she had received it, and an abstract of her commentary on it, still waiting delivery at the Psychomorphic.

"I hoped we should meet at Mrs. Ludersdorff Pirbright's," said she, "because I wanted to talk about it. Their teas are so stupid. Ethel Ludersdorff Pirbright said you were coming."

"Oh yes—that was the Unfulfilled Bun-Worry. Mrs. Aiken came in to see me, and I stayed." Then, as an afterthought, "I suppose you know they've made it up?"

Admission that there was something unknown to her did not form part of Miss Volumnia's scheme of life. She left the question open, saying merely, "In consequence of the advice I gave my cousin, no doubt!" Madeline said nothing to contradict this— all the more readily perhaps that she was not prepared to supply the real reason. She, however, could and did supply rough particulars of the reconciliation, giving Miss Volumnia more than her due of credit as its *vera causa*.

That lady then proceeded to give details of her scientific conclusions about the phenomenon. A portion of this may be repeated, as it had a good deal of effect in confirming her hearer's growing faith in its genuineness. "What I rest my argument on," said Miss Volumnia, touching one forefinger with the other, like Sir Macklin in the Bab Ballads, "is the isolated character of this phenomenon. Let the smallest confirmation of it be produced by proof of the existence of analogous phenomena elsewhere, and then, although that argument may not fall to the ground, it may be necessary to place it on an entirely new footing. I would suggest that, in order to sift the matter to the bottom, a sub-committee should be appointed, charged with the duty of listening to authentic portraits to determine, if possible, whether any other picture possesses this really almost incredible faculty of speech. The slightest whisper from another picture, well authenticated by a scientific authority, would change the whole *venue* of the discussion. Pending such a confirmation, we are forced to the conclusion that the subjectivity of the phenomenon is indisputable."

At this point, Miss Upwell, who was really getting anxious about *secondly*—which she was certain the speaker would forget, while it was impossible for her, without loss of dignity, to draw one forefinger from the other—was greatly relieved when the withdrawal was made compulsory by the offer of a sally-lunn, and the resumption of it became unnecessary, and even difficult. For this entertainment was not merely a bun-worry, but—choosing a name at random—a sally-lunn sedative, or a tea-cake lullaby.

It only enters for a moment into this story to show how powerfully Miss Upwell's belief in the picture's personality had been reinforced before the time came for Mr. Pelly to read Professor Schrudengesser's Florentine manuscript.

Perhaps if Miss Volumnia had then been in a position to lay before her friend the results of a subsequent interview with her cousin, in which she elicited some most important facts, this belief might at least have been suspended, and Miss Upwell's attitude towards the pardonable scepticisms of her father and Mr. Pelly might have been less disrespectful. But as a matter of fact Miss Volumnia only came to the knowledge of these facts months later, when she called upon Mrs. Reginald Aiken with the Secretary, Mr. MacAnimus, and Mr. Vacaw, the Chairman of the Psychomorphic; the three constituting a Deputation from the Society, which was anxious for repetition and confirmation of the story before appointing a sub-committee to listen to well-painted pictures. This interview may be given here, for the sake of those curious in Psychological study, but its place in the succession of events should be borne in mind. It is really a piece of inartistic anticipation.

"We shouldn't come pestering you like this, Cousin Euphemia," said Miss Volumnia, after introducing the Deputation, "if it had not been that we have so much trouble in getting volunteers to guarantee the amount of listening which we consider has to be gone through before the negative conclusion, that pictures cannot talk, is accepted as practically established. My sister Jessie has undertaken to listen to any picture at the National Gallery the sub-committee may select, provided that either Mr. Duodecimus Groob or Charley Galsworthy accompanies her, and listens too. I can see no objection to this, but I prefer that they should listen to Gevartius. I think it perhaps better that so young a girl should not hear what the Laughing Cavalier, Franz Hals, is likely to say. Or Charley Galsworthy either, for that matter. Mr. Duodecimus Groob is a graduate of the University of London. . . ."

Mr. Reginald Aiken, who was present at this interview, looked up from his easel, at which he was re-touching a sketch of no importance, to say that he knew this Mr. Groob, who was an awful ass; but his brother Dolly was quite another pair of shoes, of whom the World would soon hear more. The interruption was rude and discourteous, and Mrs. Aiken was obliged to explain to the Deputation that it was quite unnecessary to pay any attention to it. Her husband was always like that. His manners were atrocious, but his heart was good. As for Mr. Adolphus Groob, he was insufferable.

"Shall we proceed to business?" said Mr. MacAnimus, a piercing man, who let nobody off.

"I will, with your permission, run through Mrs. Reginald Aiken's deposition. . . ."

"I never made any deposition," said that lady.

"My dear Euphemia," said her cousin. "If you wish to withdraw from the statement you made to me. . . ."

"Rubbish, Volumnia! I certainly don't withdraw from anything whatever. Still less have I any intention of making any depositions. If we are to be beset with depositions in everyday life, I think we ought at least to be consulted in the matter. Depositions, indeed!"

Mr. Vacaw interposed to make peace. "We need not," he said, "quarrel about terms." He for his part would be perfectly content that the particulars so kindly furnished by Mrs. Aiken should be referred to in whatever way was most satisfactory to that lady herself. He appeared to address Mr. Mac-Animus with diffidence, almost amounting to humility, approaching him with somewhat of the caution which might be shown by a person who had undertaken to encumber a mad cat with a blanket so as to neutralize its powers of tooth and claw. Mr. Mac-Animus conceded the point under protest; and Mrs. Aiken then, who was not disobliging, consented to repeat her dream experience, each point being checked off against the formulated report of her first statement, transmitted to the Society by Miss Volumnia.

It is creditable to that lady's accuracy that very few corrections were necessary, especially as the first narrator seemed in a certain sense handicapped by doubts as to what the exact words used were, though always sure of their meaning. Had Mrs. Aiken understood any Italian, mixed speech on the picture's part might have accounted for this. As it was, an undeniable vagueness helped Miss Volumnia's classification of the incident as a case of Self-hypnosis. That the Deputation was unanimous on this point was soon evident.

It was then that an incident came to light that, at least in the opinion of Miss Volumnia, went far to establish this classification beyond a shadow of doubt.

Mr. Reginald, who had been at no pains to conceal his derision of the whole proceeding, allowed this spirit of ridicule, so hostile to the prosecution of Scientific Investigation, to master him so completely that he quite forgot the respect he owed to his visitors, and indeed to his wife, for she at least deserved the credit which is due to sincerity, even if mistaken. He shouted with laughter, saying did anyone ever hear such glorious Rot? A talking picture—only fancy! Why, you might as well put down anything you heard in your ears to any picture on the walls. One the same as another. Of course everyone knew that Euphemia was as

full of fancies as an egg is full of meat. Just you
leave her alone for a few minutes in a dark room,
or a burying-ground, and see if she didn't see a
ghost!

"That's *quite* another thing," said Miss Volumnia
and Mr. MacAnimus, simultaneously. And Mr.
Vacaw added, as pacific confirmation, "Surely—
surely! Ghosts belong to an entirely different
category." A feeling that Ghosts could not be
coped with so near lunch may have caused an
impulse towards peroration. It was not, however,
to fructify yet, for Mr. MacAnimus appealed for a
moment's hearing.

"With your leave, sir," said he, addressing Mr.
Vacaw as if he was The Speaker, "I should like to
put a question to this gentleman," meaning Mr.
Aiken. Mr. Vacaw may be considered to have
allowed the mad cat's nose outside the blanket, on
sufferance.

Then Mr. MacAnimus, producing a memorandum-
book to take down the witness's words, asked this
question: "What did Mr. Aiken mean by the expression, 'anything heard in your ears'?"

But the witness was one of those people who become diffuse the moment they are expected to answer a question. His testimony ran as follows,
tumbling down and picking itself up again as it
did so. "Oh, don't you know the sort of thing I

mean; a sort of tickle—nothing you can exactly
lay hold of—not what you think you hear
when it's there—comes out after—p'r'aps your
sort don't—it goes with the party—there's parties
and parties—if you don't make it out without a description, it's not in your line—you're not in the
swim."

The members of the Deputation looked at each
other inquiringly, and each shook a negative head,
as disclaiming knowledge of this peculiar phenomenon. They were not in the swim, but could all
say, and did, that this was very interesting.

Mr. MacAnimus struck in with perspicuity and
decision: "Allow me. Will Mr. Aiken favour us
with a case in point? Such a case would enable
the Society to ascertain whether this phenomenon
is known to any of its members." He concen-
trated his faculties to shorthand point, holding a
fountain-pen in readiness to pounce on a clean
memorandum page, virgin but for ⌇⌇⌇⌇⌇ , or
something like it, which meant, "Singular auto-
phrenetic experience of Mr. Reginald Aiken communicated direct to Society at his residence."
Stenography is a wonderful science.

Mr. Aiken complied readily. "Any number of
cases in point! Why, only the other day there was
Stumpy Hughes, sitting on that very chair you're in

now, heard a voice say—where was Mrs. Aiken? What's more, I heard it too, and thought it was Mrs. Gapp in liquor—in more liquor than usual. I told you all about that, Mrs. Hay." Mrs. Gapp was a new general servant, not mentioned heretofore.

Mrs. Euphemia suddenly assumed an air of mystery. "Oh yes," said she. "You told me all about *that*. *I* understood."

"Didn't I tell you?" said her husband, appealing to the company. "Didn't I tell you females might be relied on to cook up somethin' out of nothin' at all?" He had done nothing of the sort, and merely chose this form of speech to fill out his share in the conversation.

His wife was indignant. "I don't know," she said, "what nonsensical imputations you may have been casting on women, who, at any rate, are usually every bit as clever as you and your friends. But I do know this, because you told me, that when that happened you were both close to the *exact duplicate* of the very photograph you are now accusing me of credulity with, and it's ridiculous—simply ridiculous. And it's off the selfsame negative. You know it is."

Mr. Vacaw deprecated impatience. A new avenue of inquiry might be opened up as a consequence of this experience of Mr. Aiken's, provided always that we did not lose our heads, and allow ourselves to be misled by an *ignis fatuus* of controversy into a wilderness of recrimination. Mr. Vacaw's style drew freely on the vast resources of metaphor in which the English language abounds.

Mr. Aiken followed his example so far as to say that he couldn't see any use in flaring up, and that if hair and teeth were flying all over the shop, a chap couldn't hear himself speak. As for the identity of the photographs, he wouldn't have mentioned Stumpy's little joke about where the voice came from if he had thought his wife was going to turn it into a Spirit Manifestation and Davenport Brothers. He saw no use in such rot. This was only an idea, and had nothing supernatural about it.

Mr. Hughes's little joke, whatever it was, did not reach the ears of the story at the time of writing— you can turn back and see—but Mr. Aiken heard and remembered it, and had evidently repeated it to his wife, who had been comparing notes upon it. Her indignation increased, and she would certainly have taken her husband severely to task for his levity and unreason, if it had not been for the sudden animation with which Miss Volumnia cried out " Aha! " as though illuminated by a new idea. She also pointed an extended finger at Mr. Aiken, as it were transfixing him. At the same moment Mr. MacAnimus exclaimed resolutely:

"Yes—stop it at that! 'Identity of the photographs.' Now, Miss Bax, if you please!"

Miss Volumnia accepted what may be called the Office of Chief Catechist, and proceeded on the assumption usual in Investigation, that she was examining an unwilling witness with a strong inherent love of falsehood for its own sake.

"You admit then, Cousin Reginald, that on this occasion a suggestion was made that the voice came from this photograph?"

Mr. MacAnimus nodded rapidly, and said, "Yes —keep him to that!" and conferred a moment apart with Mr. Vacaw, who murmured:

"Yes, yes—I see your point. Quite correct!"

"It was Stumpy's little joke!" said Mr. Aiken. "Not a Phenomenon at all! You'll make anythin' out of anythin'. I shall tell Stumpy, and he'll split his sides laughin' at you."

"Pray do, Cousin Reginald. Only let me ask you this one question—what was the exact date of this occurrence?" Miss Volumnia had abated the pointed finger, but not quite suppressed it. Her colleagues nodded knowingly to each other and each said, "That's the point!"

Mr. Aiken's answer was vague. "A tidy long while ago," said he. "Couldn't say how long. After Stumpy came back from Aunt Jopiska's, anyhow."

" When was that ? "

" Three or four months ago. More! No—less!
Stop a bit. I know what'll fix it. That receipt.
Where the dooce is it ? " Mr. Aiken had a paroxysm
of turning miscellanea over.

" What is it you are looking for, Reginald ? " said
his wife forbearingly. " If you would tell me what
it is, I could find it for you, without throwing everything into confusion. Why can you not be patient
and methodical ? What is it ? "

" Receipt for Rates and Taxes—oh, here it is—
seventh of November—that fixes the time. It was
the day before that." And then Mr. Aiken, in the
pride of his heart at the subtlety of his identifica-
tion of this date, dwelt upon the subject more than
was absolutely necessary. It was because he had
talked—didn't you see?—to a feller who had
sketched a plan of the new rooms in Bond Street
on the back of this very identical receipt—didn't
you know?—telling him of Stumpy and the hearing the voice, the day before—didn't you see?—so
that fixed the date to a nicety. And the feller was
a very sensible clever penetratin' sort of feller—
didn't you see?—and had made some very shrewd
remarks about starts of this sort.

" And who was this intelligent gentleman ? " asked
Mrs. Aiken, not entirely without superiority, but
still with forbearance.

"Not a man you know much of.   Remarkable sort of chap, though!"

"Yes—but who *was* he?   That's what *I* want to know."

"Don't see that it matters. . . .   Well—Dolly Groob, then."

"Mis-ter Adolphus Groob . . ." Mrs. Aiken was beginning, and was going to follow up what her intonation made a half-expression of contempt, by a comment which would have expressed a whole one. Was it Mr. Adolphus Groob all the fuss was about?

But she came short of her intention, being interrupted by Miss Volumnia, whose "Aha!" threw her previous delivery of the same interjection into the shade.   "*Now* we are getting at something!" cried that young lady triumphantly.

"Well, what does that mean?" said Mrs. Euphemia scornfully.   "Getting at something! Getting at what?"

"My dear Euphemia," said her cousin, with temperate self-command—she was always irritating, and meant to be—"I ask you, can you conscientiously deny that Mr. Adolphus Groob sat next you at Mr. Entwistle Parkins's lecture, at the Suburbiton Athenæum, on the Radio-Activity of Space?"

"Well, and what if he did?"

"We will come to that directly, when you have

answered my questions. Can you deny that Mr. Entwistle Parkins's lecture on the Radio-Activity of Space was delivered at least a week after your husband had communicated to Mr. Adolphus Groob the very curious experience he has just related?"

"And what if he did. . . . ?"

"One moment—excuse me. . . . Or that your own very singular—I admit the singularity—Pseudo-dream or self-induced Hypnotism was *subsequent* to this lecture?"

"It was in January. What if it was?"

Miss Volumnia turned with an air of subdued triumph to the other members of the Deputation. "I appeal to you, Mr. Vacaw—to you, Mr. Mac-'Animus. Is, or is not, the conclusion warranted that this Pseudo-dream, as I must call it, had its origin by Suggestion from the analogous experience of Mr. Aiken, who had by his own showing narrated it to Mr. Adolphus Groob?"

"But Mr. Adolphus Groob never said a single word to me about it. So *there!*" Thus Mrs. Aiken with emphasis so distributed as to make her speech almost truculent.

Miss Volumnia's reply was cold and firm. "You admit, Cousin Euphemia, that Mr. Adolphus Groob sat next to you throughout that lecture?"

"Certainly. What of that?"

"Are you prepared to make oath that no part of your conversation turned on Psychic subjects?"

"He talked a great deal of nonsense, if that's what you mean, and said we were on the brink of great discoveries. But I won't talk to you if you go on about being prepared to make oath, like a witness-box."

Mr. Aiken, perhaps with a mistaken idea of averting heated controversy, interposed, saying: "Cert'nly Dolly Groob did say he'd met the missus at a beastly place that stunk of gas out Coombe way, and that she conversed very intelligibly—no, intelligently—on subjects. . . ."

Miss Volumnia interrupted, although the speaker had to all seeming scarcely finished his sentence. "That is tantamount," she said, "to an admission that they had been talking on subjects. What subjects?"

"Sort of subjects they were talkin' on, I s'pose," said he evasively.

"Very well, Reginald," said his wife indignantly. "If you are going over to their side, I give up, and I shan't talk at all." And she held to this resolution, which tended to put an end to the conversation, until the Deputation took its leave, shaking its heads and making dubious sounds within its closed lips. We were on very insecure ground, and

things had very doubtful complexions, and all that
sort of thing.

"What a parcel of fools they were," said the
lady when they had departed, "not to ask about
what the old gentleman dreamed at Madeline's?
That was first hand from the original picture. I
really do think one cannot depend on photographs."

"Must make a difference, I should say. Don't
pretend to understand the subject." Thus the
Artist, absorbed again in retouching the sketch of
no importance. And do you know, he seemed
rather to make a parade of his indifference. In
which he was very like people one meets at Mani-
festations, only scarcely so bad. For a many of
them, face to face with what they are pretending
to think their own *post-mortem,* remain unimpressed,
and cut jokes. Then of course we have to remember
that it is usually a paid Medium—that may make
a difference.

We think, however, it is safe to say that had Miss
Volumnia, when she conversed with Miss Upwell at
the second, or fulfilled, Bun-Worry, been in possession of the facts elicited at this interview, she
might have detailed them so as to induce in that
young lady's mind a more lenient attitude towards
the incredulity of her father and Mr. Pelly about
the picture. As it was—and it is very necessary
to bear this in mind in reading what remains to be

told—this interview had not then taken place, and did not in fact come about till nearly two months later, when the compiling of the Society's Quarterly Report made the adoption of a definite attitude towards the Picture Story necessary.

CHAPTER X

OF course you recollect that Mr. Pelly, when he
came back from his great-grandniece's wedding at
Cowcester, was to read the manuscript Professor
Schrudengesser had sent him from Florence, which
had been the probable cause of all that fantastic
dream-story he wrote out so cleverly from memory?
Dear Uncle Christopher!—how lucky he should
recollect it all like that! Especially now that it had
all turned out real, because where was the use of
denying it after Mrs. Aiken had heard the photograph speak, too? If a mere photograph could

make itself audible, of course a picture could—the original!

Mr. Pelly's reading of Professor Schrudengesser's translation of the Florentine manuscript was fixed for the evening after Madeline's return to Surley Stakes. Uncle Christopher dined alone with his adopted niece and her parents, after which he was to read the manuscript aloud in the library where the picture was hanging. This was a *sine qua non* to Madeline. The picture simply *must* hear that story. But of course she said nothing of the reasons of her increased curiosity on this point to anyone, not even to Mr. Pelly himself.

Behold, therefore, the family and the old gentleman settling down to enjoy the manuscript before the picture and the log-fire beneath it. The reader preliminarizes, of course; wavering, to do justice to his impending start.

"Now, Uncle Christopher dear, don't talk, but begin reading, and let's hear the picture-story." So spoke Miss Madeline when she thought Mr. Pelly had hesitated long enough.

But this did not accelerate matters, for the old gentleman, perceiving that her perusal of his dream-narrative had landed her somehow in the conclusion that the picture and the manuscript must be connected, felt bound to enter his protest against any such rash assumption. "We must bear in mind," he said, " that there is absolutely nothing to connect this manuscript with that picture over the chimneypiece except the name Raimondi. And although the picture was certainly purchased from a castle owned by a family of that name, there is no reason whatever to suppose it to be a portrait of a member of that family. And the fact that a portrait of a lady is spoken of —as we shall see directly—in this manuscript, no more connects the story with this picture than with any other picture. My friend Professor Schrudengesser, although it would be difficult to do justice to his erudition, and impossible to quarrel with most of his conclusions, is impulsive in the highest degree, and no one is more liable to be misled by a false clue. In this case, however, he admits that it is the merest surmise, and that at least we are on very doubtful ground."

Mr. Pelly felt contented, as with a satisfactory peroration, and was going to dive straight into the manuscript which he had really folded to his liking, this time. But the Baronet, to claim a share in erudition for the landed gentry, must needs look weighty with tightly closed lips, and then open them to say, " Very doubtful—very doubtful—ve-ry doubtful!" And this, of course, provoked his daughter to a renewed attitude of *parti pris,* merely from contradiction, for really she knew no more about the matter than this story has shown, so far.

"Don't go on shaking your head backwards and forwards like that, Pupsey dear," said this disrespectful girl. "You'll shake it off. Besides, as to her not being a member of the Raimondi family, isn't it logical to assume that everybody is a member of any family till the contrary is proved? At least, *you'd* say it on your side, you know, if you wanted it, and I should be frightened to contradict you."

This provoked incredulity and even derision. After which, a remark about the clock caused Mr. Pelly actually to begin reading, with a word of apology about the probable imperfection of the translation. Even then he stopped to say that he hoped he had clearly stated the Herr Professor's opinion that the date of the manuscript would be about 1559, as it speaks to the "Duchessa Isabella," to whom it is written, of "your recent nuptials." He added that no doubt this lady was Isabella dei Medici, daughter of Cosimo, the second of the name, who in 1558 married Orsini, Duke of Bracciano.

"Never mind them," said Madeline, interrupting, "unless he poisoned her or there was something exciting and mediæval."

"Well," said Mr. Pelly, rather apologetically, "he certainly *did* poison her, strictly speaking. That is, if Webster's tragedy of Victoria Corombona is historically correct. If you get a conjurer to poison your portrait's lips, with a full knowledge that your wife makes a point of kissing them every night before she goes to bed. . . ."

" That's the sort of thing *I* like. Go on!"

" Why . . . of course you place yourself in a very equivocal position."

" Yes," said Madeline, " and what's more, it shows what pictures can do if they try. Of course he murdered her. What are you looking so sagacious for, Pupsey?" For the Bart.'s head was shaking slowly. He showed some symptoms of a wish to circumscribe the Middle Ages—to stint them of colour and romance.

" It might be a case to go to a Jury," said he grudgingly. Whereupon Mr. Pelly began to read in earnest.

" ' To the most illustrious Duchessa Isabella, most beautiful among the beautiful daughters of her princely father, queen of all poesy, matchless among musicians, mistress of many languages, to whose improvisations accompanied on the lute the stars of heaven stop to listen. . . .' This goes on for some time," said Mr. Pelly.

" Skip it, Uncle Christopher. I dare say she was a stupid little dowdy."

" Very likely! H'm—h'm—h'm! Yes—suppose I go on here: ' In obedience to your highness's august commands I have set down here the full story of my marvellous escape from prison in the

Castello of Montestrapazzo, where I passed a
semestre sotterraneo'—six months underground—
the Professor seems to have left some characteristic
phrases in Italian. I won't stop to translate them
unless you ask—shouldn't like to appear patronizing!
—'now nearly thirty years since, being then quite
a young man—in truth, younger than my son
Gherardo, who is the bearer of this, whom you may
well recognize at once by his marvellous likeness to
his mother, whose affectionate greetings he will
convey to you more readily than I can write them.
For when I look upon his face it seems to me I
almost see again the face I painted thirty years ago,
the *sognovegliante* look '—the Professor fancies the
writer invented this word—*dream-waking,* that sort
of thing—' the *sognovegliante* look of the eyes, the
happy laughter of the mouth. And, indeed, as you
know her now, she is not unlike the boy, and she
changes but little with the years. For even the
beautiful golden hair keeps its colour of those
days. . . .' "

At this point Madeline interrupted: " But that's
the picture-girl down to the ground. How can
anybody doubt it? Why, look at her! "

Mr. Pelly was dubious. " I don't know. I couldn't
say. There's hardly enough to go upon."

" That's exactly like a scholarly old gentleman!
But, Uncle Christopher dear, do just get up a

minute and come here and *look!*" Mr. Pelly complied.

Generally speaking, we thought it might be rash to allow ourselves to be influenced by a description; it was always safest to suspend judgment until after something else, or something still later than something else. We had very little to go upon, independently of the fact that the name Raimondi connected itself with both the portrait and the manuscript.

"Then go independently! However, let's come back and get on with the story." The speaker went back to her place at her mother's feet, and Mr. Pelly resumed.

"Where were we? Oh—'colour of those days'—oh yes!—'and the curvature of the line of his nostril that is all his mother's. . . .'"

Madeline inserted a *sotto voce*: "Of course, it's the picture-girl!" The reader took no notice.

"'. . . That he will prove himself of service to his Excellency the Duke I cannot doubt, for the boy is ready with his pen as with his sword, though, indeed, as I myself was in old days, a thought too quick with the latter, and hot-headed on occasion shown. But him you will come to know. I, for my part, will now comply as best I may with your wish, and tell you the story of my imprisonment and escape.

"'I was then in my twenty-first year; but, young as I was, I already had some renown as a painter. And I think, had God willed that I should continue in the practice of the art that I loved, my name might still be spoken with praise among the best. Yet I will not repine at the fate that has made of me little better than a *poderista,* a farmer, for see now how great has been the happiness of my lot! Figure it to yourself in contrast with that of a man—such a one have I seen, of whom I shall tell you—full of life and health, all energy and purpose, cast into a prison for the crime of another, and unable to die for the little poisonous hopes that would come, day by day, of a release that never was to come itself. His lot might have been mine too, but for the courage and decision of the woman who has been my good throughout—who has been the one great treasure and happiness of my life. Yet one thing I do take ill in my heart—that the picture I painted of her, the last I ever touched, should have been so cruelly destroyed.'" Mr. Pelly paused in his reading.

"The Herr Professor and myself," said he, "are divided in opinion about some points in connection with this—but perhaps I had better read on, and we can talk about it after.

"'For it was surely the best work I had ever painted. And none other can paint her now as I did then. But I must not indulge this useless regret. Let me get to my story.

" ' Know, then, that, being in my twenty-first year, and in love with no woman, in part, as I think, owing to a memory of my boyhood I treasured in my heart—a memory I did not know as Love, but one that had a strange power of swaying my life —that I, being thus famous enough to be sought out by those who loved the art, whether for its own sake, or to add to their fame, was sent for to paint the young bride of a great noble, the Duke Raimondi, at his villa that stands out in the plain of the Arno, nearer to Pistoia than to Firenze. Thither, then, I go with all speed, for the Raimondi was a noble of great weight, and not to be lightly gainsaid. But of this young bride of his I knew nothing, neither of her parentage, nor even of her nationality; indeed, I had been told, by some mistake of my informant, that she was by birth a *Francese*. You may well believe, then, that I was utterly astounded when I found she was . . .' "

Here Mr. Pelly paused in his reading, and wiped his spectacles. " I am sorry to say," said he, " that we come to a gap in the manuscript here—a *hiatus valde deflendus*—and we cannot tell how much is missing. There is, of course, no numbering of the pages to guide us. Italians, it seems, are in the habit of remaining stupefied—a phrase I have just translated was '*ho rimasto stupefatto*'—on the smallest provocation, and the expression might only mean that this bride of the Raimondi was an *Inglese,* and plain."

"We are plain, sometimes," Madeline admitted. "But what geese antiquarians are! You should always have a girl at your elbow, to tell things. Why, of course, this young person was the Memory he had treasured in his heart!"

"I should think it very likely," said Mr. Pelly, "from what follows later. Only, nothing proves it, so far. I should like the arrangement you suggest, my dear Madeline; however, we must get along now, if that clock's right." He nodded at one on the chimneypiece, with Time, made in gold, as a mower of hay; then continued reading:

"'Oh, with what joy my fingers closed on that accursed throat! One moment more, and I had sent my old monster whither go the accursed, who shall trouble us no further, yet shall bear for ever the burden of their sins, a debt whereof the capital shall never be repaid, even to the end of all eternity, Amen! But alas!—that one moment was not for me, for the knave who bore the mace, though he missed my head, struck me well and full, half-way betwixt the shoulder and the ear; and though it was a blow that might not easily kill a young man such as I, yet was I stunned by the shock of it, and knew no more till I found myself . . .' "

" What on earth is all this about ? " said Madeline. " Surely the wrong page, Uncle Christopher."

" Very wrong indeed ! But it can't be helped. We must lump it. It may be one folded page missing or it may be half-a-dozen; we have no clue. We must accept the text as it is." And Mr. Pelly went on reading:—

" '. . . Found myself on the back of a horse, going at an easy amble up a hilly road in mountains. I was bound fast behind a strong rider, of whom I could see nothing at first but his steel cap or morion —and I thought I knew him by it, the basnet thereof being dinted, as the man whose sword my beloved had shed her blood to stop, that else had ended my days for me then and there. For in those days, *Eccellenza,* I had such eyes to note all things about me as even youth has rarely. On either side of us rode another man-at-arms, one of whom I could recognize as him who had struck at me with his mace, also missing of slaying me, by the great mercy of God.

" ' I had little heart to speak to either of them, as you may think, and, indeed, was a mere wreck of myself of two hours ago; for I judged of how time had gone by the last smouldering red of the sundown above the dark, flat, purple of the hills.

My thirst was hard to bear, and the great pain of
my head and shoulder, shaken as both were by the
movement of the horse.   But I knew I might ask
in vain, though I saw where a wine-flask swung on
the saddle-bow of him of the mace.   It is wondrous,
Eccellenza, what youth, and great strength, and pride
can endure, rather than ask a *gentilezza* of an enemy!

" ' Thus, then, we travelled on together, my guards
taking little heed of each other, and none of me
in my agony; seeming, indeed, to have no care
if I lived or died.   They rode as fellows on a journey
so often do when they have said their most on
such matters as they have in common, and are
thinking rather of the good dinner and the bed that
awaits them at their journey's end than of what
they pass on the road, or of what they have left
behind.   One of them, the knave that had struck
me down, who seemed the most light-hearted of the
three, would at such odd times as pleased him break
into a short length of song, which might for all I
know have been of his own making, so far as the
words went; while as for the tune, it was a cadence
such as the vine-setter sings at his work in Tuscany,
having neither end nor beginning, and suited to any
words the singer may choose to fit to it.   Taking note
that he did this the more as the third man, whom I
had not recognized, rode on a short distance ahead,
as he did at intervals, I judged this last one to be

his superior in command; and that, if I could find
voice for speech at all, my best chance of an answer
would be from himself and not from this superior,
who would most likely only bid me be silent at the
best, even if he gave no worse response. So I caught
at the moment when he had ended a rather longer
cadence than usual, judging therefrom that my speech
would reach at most him and the man behind whom I
myself was riding. Where was I being taken so
fast, I asked, and for what? And he answers me
thus:

" ' " To a good meal and a long rest, *mio figlio.*
To the Castello del bel Riposo. They sleep a long
night at that *albergo*—those who ride there as you
ride. I have ridden more than once with a guest
of his Excellency. But there has always been a
good meal for each, *pasta,* and meat, and a flask of
vino buono puro, before he went to rest." Whereon
he laughed, but there was no joy for me in that
laugh of his. I speak again.

" ' " I see what you mean, accursed one! That
flask of wine will be my last on this earth."

" ' " You speak truly, *caro mio figlio.* It will be
your last flask of wine. You will enjoy it all the
more."

" ' " You are a good swordsman——? "

" ' " I am accounted so. But this good Taddeo,
whom you are permitting to ride in front of you—

ho! ho!—he also is a good swordsman. But we
may neither of us grant what I know well you were
going to ask. You will never hold a sword-hilt
again, my son, nor rejoice in face of an enemy. I
could have wished otherwise, for you are a brave
boy; and I would gladly have been the butcher to
so fine a young calf."

"' "You are quick to grip my meaning. But I
could have outmatched you both on fair ground.
Now listen! You have a goodwill towards me—so
I judge from your words. Tell me, then, this:—
how will they kill me?"

"' "I have never said they would kill you, my
son. I have said only this—that you will have a
rare good supper of *pasta* and meat, and a rare good
flask of red wine, before you go to rest. And let
me give you this word of advice. Before you go
to rest at the Castello del bel Riposo, take a good
look at the sunlight if it be day, at the stars of
heaven if it be night, for you will never see them
again, for all your eyes will remain in your head,
even as now."

"'Sometimes, *O Illustrissima,* when I wake in
the night, it comes back to me, that moment. And
there below me is the musical tramp of the horses'
feet on the bare road, and I hear the voice of my
friend sing again a little phrase of song—*che ognuno
tirasse l' acqua al suo mulino*—and I heed him very

little, though I can read in his words a wicked belief about my most guiltless and beloved treasure. I see the sweet light where the sun was, through the leaves of the olive-trees that make a *reticella* (network) against the sky; and the great still star they never hide for long, rustle how they may! But I can but half enjoy the light that is dying, and the star that burns the more the more it dies; for the pain is great in my shoulder where the blow struck, and in my head and eyes, and my body is sore at its bonds and stiff from being held in one position. And yet I may never see that star again—the star we called our own, my Maddalena and I, and made believe God made for us, saying " this star I make for Giacinto *e la sua sorellaccia* "—neither that star, nor its bath of light, nor the sun that will make all Heaven glad to-morrow, unseen by me. For I can guess the meaning of what my friend has said. . . .' "

Here a little was quite illegible. But no conversation ensued on that account, both reader and listeners wanting to hear what followed. Mr. Pelly read on :—

" ' Now I call this man my friend, and, *Eccellenza,* you will see, as I tell my tale, that this is no derisive speech. I think that what showed me he was not all hostility to me in his heart was that he would—I felt sure—if left to himself, have granted the boon

I would have asked of him, and fought fairly with me to the death of one or other. So there was love between us of a soldierly sort. And I, too, could see how it had grown. For I had half suspected him of not showing all the alacrity he might have done with his mace when I had my grip on the Old Devil's throat. . . .' "

Madeline interrupted: " It's perfectly maddening! What wouldn't I give to know what it's all about ? "

" I'll tell you presently the Herr Professor's conjectural history," said Mr. Pelly. But this did not satisfy the young lady.

" Tell us now! I'm the sort that can't wait," said she.

The benignity of Mr. Pelly's face as he replied to her was a sight to be seen.

" The Herr Professor thinks it is quite clear that this young man, on his arrival at the Palace of the great noble whose wife he was to paint, fell in love with some girl of her retinue, possibly having recognized some friend of early childhood; and that the Duchess fell in love with *him*. Naturally—because we must bear in mind this was in the Middle Ages, or nearly—jealousy would prompt assassination of one or both of the young lovers. . . ."

" But who was the Old Devil? That's what I want to know."

" Evidently the wicked Duchess herself."

" What did she want to have her portrait painted for if she was old ? "

" The Herr Professor conjectures that the reason our young painter remained stupefied when he first saw the Duchess was that she turned out not to be young at all, but old and repulsive." Madeline looked doubtful. " Then the idea was that the Duchess personally conducted the assassination of the girl—caught the two young people spooneying, and had her murdered on the spot. And that the young man thereon went straight for her throat. After which she naturally felt that it would be difficult to get on a tender footing with him, as she had wished to do, and had him consigned to a dungeon for life."

Madeline disagreed. " No," said she, " I don't think the Professor's at all a good theory. Mine's better. Go on reading. I'll tell you mine presently."

Mr. Pelly refound his place and went on reading.

" ' . . . Had my grip on the Old Devil's throat. And also I had felt his approval in his hands as he helped to bear me away from the *Stanza delle Quattro Corone,* though my senses failed too fast for me to understand what he said to his comrade. Yet I thought, too, it sounded like *"Un bel giovane, per Bacco!"* So when at last I was unbound, and

stood in the forecourt of a great castle in the middle
of a group of men, some of whom had torches—for
it was then well on into the night—and dogs that I
had heard barking through the last short half-hour
of our approach up the steep and stony ascent to
the great gates that had now clanged to, as I judged
then, for my last passage through them either way
—I, though stiff and in pain, and in a kind of dumb
stupor as I stood there, could still resolve a little in
my mind what might even now be done to help me
in my plight.

" 'I caught the words of the third horseman—
he who had ridden on in front—to a huge bloated
man who seemed to be the seneschal or steward in
charge of the place, who went hobbling on a stick,
seeming dropsical and short of breath.

" ' " We have brought another guest, Ser Ferretti,
for your hospitality. *Sua Eccellenza* hopes you have
room; good accommodation—a clean straw bed or
some fresh-gathered heather. *Sua Eccellenza* would
not have needless discomfort for your guests at the
Castello. A long life to them is the *brindisi* of *sua
Eccellenza—sempre sempre.*" That is to say, for
all time.

" ' And then the fat man answered wheezily, " It
shall be done, *Ser Capitano*. And he shall sup well
and choose his company; it is an old usage and shall
be observed." He then turned to me and said, with

a mock reverence, " Whom does the Signore choose
to sup with before he retires to rest ? "

" ' I turned to the man I had spoken with as we
rode, and laid my hand on his shoulder. *" Sicuro,"*
I said, " with none other than *Messer Nanerottolo*
here." This was my pleasantry, for he was a
monstrous big man, but not ill-favoured. I went
on, " I owe you a supper, my friend, for that *piccolo
vezzeggiamento* you have given me——" ' "

" What does that mean ? " Thus his hearers, in
concert.

" A little caress. I don't know why the Professor
has left some of the Italian words. *Nanerottolo*
means a very little dwarf indeed, and he could
hardly have translated. But he might have said
caress just as well." He resumed reading:

" ' " I can feel it in my shoulder still." At this
he laughed, but said again I was a *bel giovane,* and
molto bravo. " And it is to you," I said, " that I
owe my supper here to-night." But his *Capitano*
gave a laugh, and said, *" Piuttosto a quel piccolo
vezzeggiamento che tu desti alla Duchessa——"* ' "

Here the reader paused to interpret the Italian
again, which was hardly needed; then said, " There
is another gap in the manuscript here, and it is a pity.
The Professor thinks a few more words from what
followed would have made his theory a certainty."

" Why ? " asked Madeline.

"Because ' the caress you gave the Duchess ' could only mean that he owed his supper to having half strangled the old *Duchessa.* They couldn't mean anything else in the context."

"Couldn't they? Never mind, Uncle Christopher! Go on now. I'll tell you presently." Uncle Christopher obeyed, recommencing as before after the gap in the middle of a sentence:

" '. . . Prison for life accords ill with life and hope and youth and the blood that courses in its veins. Whereas despair in an exhausted frame, and pain and hunger, breed a longing for the worst, and if it may be, for an early death. Hence, *Illustrissima,* my good supper, which was given ungrudgingly, while it made me another man, and better able to endure the pain left from the blow of my friend who sat at meat with me, gave me also strength to revolt against the terrible doom that awaited me. Also, hope and purpose revived in my heart, and I knew my last word with the world of living men must be spoken before midnight; for this was told me by the dropsical Castellan, with an accursed smile. So I watch for the moment when my friend, whose name was Attilio, is at his topmost geniality with the good wine, and then I speak, none being there to hear, but only he. I speak as to a friend:

" ' " You love the good red wine, Messer Attilio, and you love the good red gold. Is it not true?

Which do you love the most?" And to this he answered me, "Surely the good red gold, *Ser Pittore.* For wine will not purchase *all* one asks. There is nothing gold will not purchase—enough of it!"

"'"Listen! Where are they going to hide me away? Do you know the Castello?"

"'"I was born here. I can tell you all. There is good accommodation in the *sotterraneo.* It is extended, but it is not lofty. You will have company, but the living is poor, meagre. I have said that you would not see the sun again, but you may! For in one place is a slot, cut slantwise in the stone, that the guests of the Duke who come to stay may not want air. Through the slot, one day in the year only, and then but for a very little space, comes a ray from the sun in Heaven. In the old days of the Warrior Duke, when there would be many prisoners of war, they would count the days until the hour of its coming, and then fight for a good place to see the gleam when it came. But the few you will find there will have little heart for that, or anything else."

"'"Is that the only outlet?"

"'"No! There is the door you go in by. One stoops, as one stoops to enter the little prisons of Venezia, under the Rialto. And there is the *Buco della Fame. . . .*" "That is to say," interjected Mr. Pelly, "The Hunger Hole, or Hunger Pit."

" ' " What is that? " I then asked.

" ' " What they were used to throw bones down, when they had made merry and sucked them dry, to the prisoners below. And there is a drain."

" ' " How large is it? "

" ' " Large enough for the rats to pass up—no larger. I used to watch them run in at the outlet, when 1 was a youngster. But the *Buco*—that is large enough for a man to pass up and down—a sort of well-hole. Not the Ser Ferretti there; he would stick in it. I have seen it all, for my father was the gaoler in old days."

" ' " Listen now, Ser Attilio! You want the good red gold, in plenty. And you shall have it if you do my bidding. When you leave this—are you marking what I say?—go straight to la Marta, she who attends always on the *Duchessa,* and say to her simply this—that on the day I regain my liberty, there will be five hundred crowns for her. Tell her where I am. And for this service to me you shall receive . . ." ' "

Mr. Pelly stopped reading again. There was another gap; a portion of the manuscript was missing as before. He remarked upon the loss to the reader, apparently, of the whole account of the young man's first introduction to the dungeon, in which he seemed to have passed a considerable time—the best part of six months as far as could be made out—before we are able to follow his narrative. He then read on, without comment:

" '. . . Day and night alike for their complete monotony, though, indeed, we could distinguish between them by the light through the air-slot, the only ventilation through all this extent of vaulted crypt. But for incident and change, from day's end to day's end, there was none beyond the daily visit I have spoken of, of Uguccione the gaoler, carrying always his little lamp of brass and a basket of coarse black bread, and a pitcher of water. Is it not strange, *Illustrissima,* that a man should live, should go on living, even when the stupefaction of despair comes to his aid, without light or movement or the breath of Heaven on his face? None the less these others that I told you of had done so, some more, some less; and the very old man who was but as an idiot, and could tell nought of his name and his past, had been there already many years when Uguccione first took the prisoners into his charge. He was a merry, chatty fellow, this Uguccione, and talked freely with me at first, and told me many things. But he said I should not talk for long, for none did. See now, he said, he would speak to the old Alberico, and never an answer would he get. And thereon flashed his lamp across the old man's face, and asked him some ribald question about *la Giustina.* But the old man only shrank from the

light, and answered nothing. Who was la Giustina?
I asked. Nay, he knew not a whit! But he knew
that the former gaoler, old Attilio, from whom he
took the keys, had told him that if he would enrage
old Alberico, he had but to speak to him of la
Giustina. And thereon he flashed his light again
in the old eyes, to see them flinch again; and gave
me black bread and water, and went his way.

" ' But this man told me many things, before
I, too, began to settle into the speechless gloom of
unvarying captivity. He told me that, even now,
the great Duke, after banqueting in the hall above,
would sometimes for his mere diversion have the
trap opened at the top of the *Buco della Fame,* and
throw down what might be left on table, except it
were such as might serve for the cook again, or to
be eaten at the lower table. And he warned me to
be ready and at hand if I should hear any sound
from above, as then I might get for myself the best
pick of the bones or bread-crusts that might come
down in a shower. And I laid this to heart.

" ' And now, as I must not weary your Excellency's illustrious eyes to read needless details
of my sufferings in my imprisonment, I will leave
its horrors to your imagination, saying only this,
that whatever you may picture to yourself, there
may easily have been something still worse. I will
pass on to the moving of the trap-door above me.

" ' Of a sudden, in what I thought was night, but which must have been midday, I hear a sound as of hinges that creak and strain. It comes from the *Buco della Fame;* and I can hear, too, but dimly, what I take to be the murmur of voices in the room it leads to. I rise from the straw I lie on, and move as best I may, for I am free to move about only slowly, because my right hand is manacled to my left foot, and from stiffness and weakness, towards the opening of the hole in the low arch above me. I can touch its edge with my hand. I look up through the long round tube, and can see its length now by the size of the opening at the top. It may be, as I reckon it, at least twenty *bracchie* from the ground I stand on.

" ' As I gaze, a little dazzled by the light, I hear plainly the voices above me of those who are merry with the banquet. And then a face looks down and darkens the opening for a moment; but it is only like a dark spot, and my eyes are thwarted by the change from dark to light, so that I cannot guess if it be man or woman. Then I hear a laugh from above that I compare in my heart to the laugh a Saint in Heaven might give as he looks down a narrow shaft that leads to Hell, and rejoices in his freedom and the great Justice of God. But I myself am nowise better off than the sinners, heretics, and Jews that are consumed in fires

below, yet die not. Then, as I think of this, down
comes a shower of what seems to me good kitchen
stuff. Whereof I secure a piece of turkey for
myself, and of capon for the very old man; but he
shall have his choice, if, indeed, he can eat either.
Then come other prisoners for their share, from afar
off in the crypt, one of whom I had never seen, so
dark was his corner. But I had heard him moan
and mutter. Only, before he comes with the others
I have time to choose somewhat else from the mess,
always sharing as I think fairly. And as I do this
I am taken aback by a sheet of written paper that
has fluttered down the shaft. And I have caught
it, and the trap above closes with a clang, and the
voices die above, and the darkness has come again,
and the silence.

"'Know, *Illustrissima*, that the eyesight that
lives long in darkness may grow to be so keen that
not only the outline of the prisoner's hand that he
holds before him may be seen by him, but even the
seams and lines thereon, by which may be known
the story of his life and the length of his days.
But I had not yet come to that perfection of vision,
and could read nought of the paper in my own place;
for all that the crypt was then at its brightest,
it being late midday, and the gleam from the slot
at the far end strong enough for me to see dimly the
face of the old man as I held out to him in turn the

turkey and the capon. But he would none of either,
and hardly noted what I did, as one in a maze.
So in the end I leave him and go nearer the light, to
read what I may.

"'It is all like a strange dream now. But,
Illustrissima, as I look back to that moment, what
I remember is a huge beating of a heart that will
not be still. It is there, and a gleam of light
through a narrow wall-slot in the masonry is there;
but should you ask me how I read, until I knew by
rote, what was written on that paper, I could not
tell you. Yet I can repeat every word now:

"'" This is to be destroyed, should it reach you,
before the next round of l'Uguccione.

"'" I can get speech of you through the slot.
Watch there always in the early night. It must be
when the old wretch, my master, is in his deepest
sleep.

"'" Your word came to me through la Marta,
months ago, from l' Attilio. They are keen for their
reward. Take heart, oh my dearest one, and watch
for me.

"'" I have sat at the board of my tyrant, and each
day he has taunted me, and pointed down to the
cruel prison of my darling. Oh, if, after all, it is
a lie that you still live! Pray God Attilio is right,
and that this may reach you!

"'" Oh, my beloved, if no better may be, at least

I may compass that you shall receive a tiny flask of poison; whereof I too may take a fatal draught, and each may know of the other that trouble is at an end."

" ' She had signed no name, but none was needed. Hope waked in my heart, for I knew that Attilio . . .' "

Here Mr. Pelly stopped reading. Another hiatus! " The loss of this passage," said he, " is especially irritating, as it might have supplied a clue to the identity of the writer of this letter. The remainder of the story, as I recollect it, leaves us quite in the dark as to who she was, though I am inclined to surmise, from the use of the expression ' my master,' that she was a young person attached to the household of the Duchess." But for all that, Mr. Pelly's dream about the picture disturbed his memory. How could his inner consciousness have concocted it, consistently with this interpretation of the manuscript? Still, he was bound to " dismiss it from his mind," and give his support, provisionally, to the theory of the Herr Professor. How could he cite a mere dream in refutation of it? So he " dismissed it from his mind," and when Madeline said, " Never mind that now, Uncle Christopher! Do go on and see if it doesn't all come right in the end. We'll talk about who she was, after," he was rather glad to resume, without further comment.

" ' ". . . I am hanging in mid-air. Below me is
an awful precipice. If Attilio were to fail me, or the
rope break, what should I do? But I care not; I
care only to succour my darling love, in his dungeon
underground. Do not speak again, dear love, lest
you be overheard within. Attilio says that if I
whisper to you through the little opening no other
prisoner need hear. . . . I will tell you all. Attilio knew from his boyhood that the *sfiatatoio* . . ." ' "

The reader stopped to explain that this appeared
to be a word equivalent to " blow-hole " in English,
used by founders for the opening left for escape of
air when the metal is poured in.

" ' ". . . The *sfiatatoio* opened under the South
Tower in the wall that is flush with the precipice,
that one may see the sun blaze on all day summer
and winter. None can approach it from below; but
Ser Attilio is strong—oh, the strength of his arms!
—and he can let me down from the great high tower
like a child, and then I hang some little space from
the window-ledge. But I swing a little, and then I
hold by the stonework, and I am safe and can speak.
It is bright in the moonlight and still, and I am
speaking to my darling. Stretch out your hand,
my love, without speech, and seek not, I charge
you, to hold my living hand, however great the joy
thereof, but take from it the file I have made shift

to steal from the armourer's boy, who will be
beaten for its loss, but whom I will kiss once
and more for his reward. *Pazienza, carissimo
mio. . . ."'"*

Mr. Pelly put the manuscript on his knee, and
opened his hands out with a deprecating action.

" I'm *very* sorry, Madeline. I really *am!* But I
can't help it. It is, as you say, most aggravating.
Just as we were getting to the interesting bit! But
you understand what happened ? "

" Oh yes! I see it all as plain as a pikestaff.
And, what's more, I saw the very place itself—the
great precipice and the Castle wall that shoots
straight up from it. An *awful* place! But *what
a* plucky little Duchess! "

" Duchess ? I don't quite follow——"

" That's because you are so *stupid,* Uncle Christopher."

" My dear Mad! Really——! " This was the
Bart. and her Ladyship. Because Mr. Pelly wasn't
offended.

" Well, it's true I said I would tell Mr. Pelly all
about it, and then I didn't." She went across to
Mr. Pelly, and leant over him, which he liked, to
get at the manuscript. " Look here! Where is it ?
Oh—the Old Devil! Yes—that wasn't the *Duchessa*
at all! That was her horrible old husband, the
Duke. And she was the Memory of his boyhood,

don't you see? Oh, it's all quite plain. And my picture-girl's her. And it's no use your talking about evidence, because I know I'm right, and evidence is nonsense."

"It certainly is true," Sir Stopleigh said, "that the Castle wall is exactly as Madeline describes it, for I have seen it myself, and can confirm her statement." He seemed to consider that almost anything would be confirmed by so very old a Baronet seeing such a very large wall.

"Suppose we accept Madeline's theory as a working hypothesis, and see how we get on. If we quite understand the last bit, and I think we do, what follows is not unintelligible." And Mr. Pelly continued reading:

"'. . . Working thus patiently in long and dreary hours, and keeping the link of my manacle well in the straw to drown the grating noise, I come to know, on the third day of my labour, that but a very little more is wanted and the ring will be cut through; and then I know the chance is it will spring asunder and leave the two links free. But I do not seek to complete the cut until near the day appointed, for does not Uguccione now and again examine all those fetters, sometimes striking them with a small hammer to make sure they have not been tampered with? So I keep the ring hidden as best I may, and the cut I have made I fill in with kneaded bread. And

one time Uguccione does come and strike the irons,
and I tremble. But by great good luck he
strikes so that they ring, and I am at my ease
again.

" ' Then comes what was my hardest task: the
making of footholes in the shaft that I might climb
and reach the underside of the trap. But first I
must tell you why I need do this. For you will say,
Why could not Attilio let down a cord and pull
me up through the trap? So he could, in truth,
were it possible to open the trap from overhead.
But it was closed with a key from above that came
through a great length to the lock below. Only I
could well understand from the description that this
lock would be no such great matter to prize back
from underneath could I once make shift to reach
it. Therein lay the great difficulty, shackled as I
was, although the links should be parted, to climb
up this long shaft and work at the opening of this
lock, standing on what poor foothold I could con-
trive in total darkness.

" ' Nevertheless, *Illustrissima,* be assured that I
go to my work with a good will, though with little
hope. And on the first night I succeed in loosing
three bricks from their place in the wall, at such
intervals that each gives a foothold I may reach to
from the one below it on the other side. And the
next night again three more. And so on for six

nights, working patiently. And now I can touch
the lock that is above me. But understand that I
did not remove these bricks, else had I been at a
great loss where to hide them from Uguccione. I
left them loose in their places, so that I could twist
them out sideways, and thus make a kind of step.
For you know how strong our Tuscan bricks are.
Yet I had much ado to hide away the loose mortar
that came from between the joints. And had it
not been that the fetter on my wrist, now free, served
to prize out the bricks when the mortar was clear
from the ends, and loosened above and below, I had
been sore put to it to detach them, so firm were
they in their places. And all this work, *Illustrissima*, had to be done in black darkness, by guidance
of feeling only!

"'And now, please you, image to yourself that I
have made my topmost step, and only await a word
of signal through the *sfiatatoio*. And this was, believe me, my worst time of all. For I knew that
the most precious thing to me in all this world, the
life of my Maddalena, must be risked again to give
me that signal! Nay! I did not know, could not
know, that she had not already tried to give it, and,
so attempting it, been precipitated to the awful rocks
below, where whoso fell might readily lie unheeded,
and not be found for years.

"'But I hold to my purpose in a silent despair. I

watch through hours of the still mornings. But
nothing moves again in front of the little stars that
come and go, for many days. I do not let myself
count the days nor the hours, and always strive to
think of them at their fewest. Then one night a
meteor shoots across the span of sky that I can see,
blinding out the little stars, and leaving sparks of
fire to die down as they may. And my heart lifts,
for I count it a harbinger of good. And so it
proves, for I next hear—because, understand me,
this meteor shot across Heaven's vault with a strong
hissing sound, like *fuochi artificiati*—the slack of
the rope that lets my darling down to me with her
message of . . .' "

Another hitch in the narrative. Mr. Pelly stopped
with a humble apologetic expression, having reference rather to the young lady than to her parents.

"Really, my dear," said he, "I feel quite guilty
—as if I was to blame—when these abominable
blanks come."

"Yes! And you know I always think it's your
fault; and I do get so angry. Poor Uncle
Christopher! What a shame! What's that,
Mumsey?"

"Nothing, dear. Only I thought I heard the step
of a horse in the Avenue."

"So did I. Only it can't be anything at this time
of night."

The knowledge that a guest was pending shortly
—one of the sort that comes and goes at will—
caused the Baronet to say: "It might be General
Fordyce—only he said he wouldn't come till
Tuesday." To whom his wife and daughter replied
conjointly:

"Oh no! The General!—not at midnight—well!
—at half-past eleven! Look at the clock. Anyhow,
his room's all ready," etc., etc. After which Madeline spoke alone:

"Now, Mr. Pelly, go on again. I do so hope it's a
plummy bit." Then, illogically, "Besides, it wasn't
a carriage." She silenced a disposition of her parents to interpose on Mr. Pelly's behalf by saying:
"Oh no, we shan't tire Uncle Christopher to death.
Shall we, Uncle Christopher?"

"God bless me, no! The idea! Besides, there's
really not so very much more to read. Unless I'm
keeping you up?"

"Pupsey and Mumsey can go to bed, and leave
us to finish."

"Oh no! We want to hear the end of it." Pupsey and Mumsey were unanimous.

"Very well, then! I can fill up Uncle's glass
and Pupsey's, and we can go on and finish com-
fortably. Now, fire away!" And Mr. Pelly read
on:

"'. . . I can hear them in the room above me.

The voice of my darling herself. But oh—this black darkness! One little gleam of light, and I know I can manage this accursed lock. But I can see nothing; and who knows but by trying and trying stupidly, in the dark, I may not make matters worse? But I will try, again and again, rather than fail now. . . . Oh, she is so near me—so near, I can hear her voice. . . .

" ' All suddenly, a gleam of light from below. A miracle, but what care I? I can see the lock now, plain! Ah, the stupidity of me! I was forcing it the wrong way all the time. Now for a sharp, sharp strain, with all the strength I have left! And back goes the lock with a snap! I can hear its sound welcomed above, and another strain on the trap, and the first creak of its hinge. It will shriek; and they stop, as I think, to make it silent with a little oil.

" ' Then my glance goes down the shaft to ask what was my light, that came to save me in such good time. It was surely the Holy Mary herself, or a blessed Saint from Heaven, that took pity on me. . . .

" ' No! It is Uguccione the gaoler, with his little lamp of brass.

" ' " Aha—ha—ha!—my friend. Come you down —come you down! Or shall I get a little fire and smoke, to tickle you and make you come? It is useless, *caro mio!* The wise player gives up the lost game. Come you down! It is not thus folk say farewell to the Castello del bel Riposo. Come you down, my friend! Or shall I wait a little? I can wait! No hurry, look you!"

" 'I am sad at heart to have to do it, but there is no other way. Whether he lived or died I know not, but I should grieve to think he died. For I had no hatred for Uguccio, who, after all, did but his duty. But there is no other way. I am standing on two bricks that I have placed over against each other, for firmer foothold and better purchase on the lock. One of them I loosen out, standing only on the other and leaning shoulder-wise against the wall. And then I send it down the shaft, with a blessing for Uguccio. I can see his face, turning up to me in the light of his little broken lamp.

" 'The brick strikes him full on the temple, but it also strikes out his light. I hear him fall. I hear a groan or gasp. But I see only black darkness below, and the red wick-spark of the lamp, that grows less and less, and will die. Then only darkness.

" 'Then my last senses fail me. But I know the trap opens, and a strong arm comes down and grips my wrist from above. And then I find myself lying on the floor of a great hall in a dim light. And into my eyes, as I lie there, little better than a corpse, if the truth be told, are looking the sweetest eyes surely God ever made. . . .' "

Here Madeline exclaimed, interrupting, "Oh, how jolly! Now they're there! But do go on; I mustn't interrupt. Go on, Uncle Kit." The reader continued, "'. . . And her two hands stroke my face and hold me by my own. . . .' "

At this point Sir Stopleigh interposed, respectably. "A—really," said he, "we must hope that this young lady, whoever she was, was not the Duke's wife. You will excuse me, my dear Madeline, but that is certainly what I understood you to suppose."

His daughter interjected disreputably, "Oh, bother! Never mind Pupsey—go on."

Then Mr. Pelly said apologetically, "It *was* the Middle Ages, you know. Let's see, where were we? Oh—'hold me by my own'"—and went on reading:

"'. . . And her dear voice is in my ears, and if I die now, at least I shall have lived. So said I to myself, as Attilio worked hard with a file to free my limbs. And they moisten bread with wine, and put it in my mouth. For, indeed, what I say is true, and the last of my strength went in sending that litttle *ambasciata* to the poor Uguccio. Still, revival is in me, though it comes slowly. But I can only

utter the one word " Love," and can only move to
kiss the hand I hold and the pale face that comes
to mine.   Then I hear the beloved voice I had never
hoped to hear again:

" ' " Can we trust that wicked old Marta, Attilio?
If she betrays us we are lost."

" ' " *Che che!*   She owes him an old grudge, and
will pay him—now or later!   And a thousand
crowns, *per Bacco!*   No, no —trust her!"

" ' " But I hear a footstep coming down his stair;
if it is she, it is to say he is waked.   If it is he, she
has betrayed us."

" ' " Neither the one nor the other, I wager.   See,
the Signore is getting the blood in his face.   He will
eat soon, and all will be well."

" ' Then I feel in my neck a dog's nose, that
smells, and the touch of his tongue, that licks.   But
what he would say we know not, though he tries
to speak, too, dogwise.   I know him for the *cagno-
letto* of la Marta, the old woman—for had I not seen
him in the days when I painted my Maddalena in
the *Stanza delle Quattro Corone?* . . .' "

Madeline interrupted again.   " *Now* I hope you're
convinced.   He was sent for to paint the Duchess.
And he painted Maddalena.   Of course, Maddalena
was the Duchess!"

" The Herr Professor's theory is that he painted
two ladies, one of whom was Maddalena, some

beautiful attendant with whom he was in love, the other the Duchess. He may have, you know!"

"He may have done anything, Uncle Christopher! But he didn't. What's the use of being so roundabout? Besides, if she wasn't the Duchess, how did she know the Duke was asleep?"

Her parents may have been anxious to avoid critical discussion, and suggested that perhaps the reading had better go on. It is just possible, also, that Mr. Pelly, who was a typical little old bachelor, saw rocks ahead in a discussion of the Duke and Duchess's domestic arrangements, for he introduced a point of which the Baronet and his Lady did not see the importance.

"Stop a bit, Miss Mad!" said the old gentleman, laying down the manuscript. "I've a bone to pick with you."

"Don't be too long. I want to know what that old woman had been at. It's only some Scientific nonsense, I expect. Go on."

"It's not Scientific this time. It's the other way round." Miss Upwell pricked up her ears. "I want to know, if there was a Duchess named Maddalena, what becomes of the theory that I christened the picture-ghost after you by subconscious cerebration?"

"I see. Of course. I didn't see that." It had produced a visible impression. Madeline appeared to cogitate over it in an animated way, and then to mellow to a conclusion suddenly. " Well—but that proves it wasn't a dream at all, but a genuine phenomenon, and all sorts of things. I'm right, and you're wrong, and the picture was telling the truth all through. I knew she was." Her three hearers smiled from within the entrenchments of their maturity at the youthful enthusiasm of the speaker, and then said very correct things about this coincidence and that being really remarkable, and how we must not allow our judgments to be swayed by considerations, and must weigh everything deliberately, and accept everything else with caution, and hesitate about this, and pause before that, all with a view to avoiding heterodox conclusions. After which Mr. Pelly resumed:

" ' Then, as Attilio holds his hand a moment from filing, as one who awaits some issue before he may begin his labours afresh; and as my darling, whom alone I see—for I see nothing else—awaits it, too, I hear a step that halts, and then a door is pushed from without, and the step halts into the room, as some clocks tick. And it is then I begin to know of a great pain in my right hand.

" ' And here I may say to you, *Illustrissima*, that had this chanced but a few years later, this hand of mine that was my joy to use, the source and very life of all my skill, might even have been saved,

and I might many times again have painted the
dear face of my Maddalena.   For what is there that
is not possible to the skill of the great Francese
Ambrogio ? ' "

" This would be Ambroise Paré," said the reader,
" who would have been about the same age as Cosimo
dei Medici, the father of the lady to whom this is
written . . ."   But he resumed abruptly, in obedience to a shade of impatience in Madeline:—

" ' Yet have I not been altogether disabled.   For
do I not write this with my left hand?   I am, however, but an *egoista*—a selfish person—to dwell on
this; though I know your Excellency will pardon
this fault in an old man.

" ' I hear, then, the halting step approach.   And
both await the words that will follow it in silence.
It is the old Marta Zan.

" ' " *Sta tranquillo—sta tranquillo per bene!* "   He
is quiet—he is quiet for good !   Her voice has a little
laugh in it.   It is not a sweet laugh to hear.

" ' " Does he still sleep—will he sleep?"   It is
my Maddalena who asks.   And la Marta replies,
" *Non c'e pericolo!*   No fear ! "   But I see across
the shoulder of my darling, as she stoops over me
again and tries to clear my brow of tangled hair—
but, you may well think, to little purpose—I see
that the old woman holds somewhat up, hanging
from betwixt her finger and old thumb, to show to

Attilio. And he laughs to see the little knife and
its sharp point, but below his breath, as guilt laughs
to guilt. But this my beloved heeds not; she is
busy with my hair.

"'I can tell but little now from what I saw with
my own eyes of what happened in the sequel, till I
found myself here again in the little old Castello in
the hills where I passed all the early years of my
boyhood, in the family of my wife's father, now
dead; though her mother still lived, and for many
years after that. What I do remember comes to
me as the speech of those about him reaches the
sleeper who half wakes, to sleep and dream again.

"'I can recollect riding, behind Attilio this time,
down the stony road I had come up in such pain
behind his comrade. I can just recollect the barking of the great dogs in the Castle court when we
came away; whereon my Maddalena spoke earnestly
to one of them, Leone, and he went and carried her
speech to the others, and they were silent, though
some made protest under their full utterance. And
though I saw the janitors and porters at the great
gate in deep sleep, I did not then know of the cunning
work of the old Marta, who, indeed, was learned in
the use of drugs, and could as easily have poisoned
them all as made them sleep. Indeed, it was said
by many that the clever Duchess of Ferrara, the
sister of Cesare Borgia, had learned somewhat of the

art of poisoning in her youth from this same Marta Zan. But of this I can say nothing with certainty.

"'But this I do know, that this Marta, who was then near on eighty years of age, having received the reward she had earned of five hundred crowns, and another five hundred for a *buona mano,* did not accompany us, on the score of her age, being unable to mount a horse. But, as you may guess, *Eccellenza,* it was she who had occasioned the old Duke's death, and none of my doing, as was said by some, though the certainty that the knife used was the girdle-dagger of the fat Castellan Ferretti was held a sure proof of his guilt, and led to his being *giustiziato* some months later. And she chose this way of sending her old betrayer to Hell rather than that of poison, seeing that her skill in this last was so well known to all that there was none other in the household on whom suspicion could have fallen. On which account, as I have since understood, she returned again to his bedside to see her work secure, and replaced the knife in the wound, whereby the guilt of his death was fixed on the fat Ferretti. I can in nowise guess why la Marta so long deferred her revenge against the Duke, except it was . . .'"

Mr. Pelly stopped despairingly. "Half a page gone! We must remain unenlightened—as well as on a good many other points. There is not very much more. I may as well finish:—

"'How great my happiness has been with my
Maddalena you, *Illustrissima,* may know from your
most illustrious father, who has known of me
throughout. Life is made up of good and ill, and
what right has one so truly blessed as I have been
to complain of the cruelty of Fate in depriving him
of his right hand and its power of work? Think
of what his lot is to him to whom night and day
alike give the sun in heaven to his soul! Contrast
it with that of the sated blow-fly, of the world-
compelling tyrant, at whose pleasure are all the
contents, at choice, of all the world's treasure-
houses, except Love. That is the one thing wealth
cannot buy, that the behests of kings command in
vain! And that has been mine, in all its fulness;
a fruit whose sweetness has no compeer, a jewel
whose light mirrors back the glow that shines for
ever in the eyes of God. . . .'" The reader
paused, for there was an interruption from without.

"What on earth *can* it be, at this time of night?
I'm sure it's a carriage this time! Do look out and
see—oh no! go on and let's have the rest. It can
only be the General—he changed his mind, and his
train was late. We shall see in a minute—let's
have the last page. . . ." This was collective
speech, which ended when Mr. Pelly said, "There
isn't very much." He went on reading rapidly, subject to a sense of advent, elsewhere in the house:—

"'One only thing, as I have said, is to me a constant thorn of regret—the destruction of the picture I painted in those early days, of my Maddalena. It was all my heart and strength could do, and would have served to tell of all I might have done had God but spared me my right hand. But *fiat voluntas tua, Domine!* None knows for certain how it was destroyed, nor by whom. For the statement of the Old Devil to my Maddalena, that it was burned, for that it was judged worthless by men of great knowledge in Art, and condemned as rubbish, is of little weight. In those last days what could have been the motive of such a statement but to add to my darling's pain? It was averred by the Ferretti, even to the day that he went to the gibbet, that it was removed to a place of safety by order of the Duke; but either he did not choose to say to what place, or possibly did not know. And when all the contents of the rooms the Duke had lived in were removed, and the late Duke, his son, came and took possession of the castle, so deep was his hatred of his father's memory—as, indeed, he believed his mother had been poisoned by his orders—that he had all the furniture removed, and all the pictures that might bring back the wicked old man's memory to his mind. And there was no such picture among them, as I saw myself; for by invitation of Duke Giulio, with whom I have always

been on friendly terms, I inspected every picture
as it was removed from the Ducal apartments, the
walls of which, as you know, were so worthily
decorated afterwards by Francesco Primaticcio, to
whom I would so proudly have shown that one
little work by mine own hand. But, alas! there is,
I fear, no doubt that for once only the old Duke
spoke without lying, and that in truth he had had
it burned, for a *dispetto* to me, and to give a little
more pain to my darling. . . .' "

At this point Mr. Pelly, being close to the end,
read quicker and quicker, to make a finish before
the outcome of the carriage, whatever it was, should
be made manifest and break up the *séance*. But
the time was too short, as Mr. Stebbings the butler
appeared, charged, as it seemed, with some communication, but hesitating about the choice of
language in which to make it.

" General Fordyce, your Ladyship. The General
desired me to say, Sir Stopleigh, would you be so
good as speak to him a half a minute ? " But Sir S.
was slow of apprehension, perhaps sleepy, and said
hay what! Both ladies spoke together. " It *is* the
General! Don't you understand? He wants you
to go out and speak to him."

" Me go out and speak to him—what for ? "

" You'll find that out by going. Look alive,
Pupsey ! "

"I'm coming, Stebbings!   What on earth can the General want to say to me?"

"Do go and see him, and find out."   This was in chorus, from both ladies, as before.   Exit Pupsey.

"I wonder what it can be!   However, we shall hear directly.   Is there any more to read, Uncle Christopher?"

Mr. Pelly read in a slighting, conclusive sort of way:—

"'So now I cannot show you,.*Illustrissima*, as I so gladly should have done, how little change has come in the golden hair of my Maddalena, in all these thirty years!   Nor the painting of that one well-remembered lock that fell all in ripples on the sunflower brocade upon her bosom——'"

Madeline got suddenly up and stood again facing the picture.

"Now," she said, "come here and see and be convinced, Mr. Incredulous."   And Mr. Pelly came, and stood beside her.

"Well, my dear child," said he.   "That certainly *does* look——"

"Very like indeed!   Doesn't it?   But you'll see Pupsey will want to have his own way.   He always does!"

"Whatever can your father be talking—talking—talking to the General about?   Why can't they come in?   What on earth can it be?"   This is

from her ladyship—a semi-aside. She is listening
to the talking at a distance. Then Madeline said,
" I hope you are convinced, Mr. Pelly," and after
one more long look at the picture turned and went
to the door, opened it, and listened through it. Her
mother said maternally, "Madeline—my dear!"
But for all that she stood and listened, as though
she heard something. And Mr. Pelly, following her
mother's eyes, turned and watched her as she stood.
It seemed to him that something like a gasp took
her, as though her breath caught with a sudden
thrill, visible in her shoulders as her dress was cut,
and that her white left arm, that was farthest from
the door, caught up tight, and as it were grasped
her heart. Her ladyship, looking at her over her
shoulder, began, " Why—child——!" and immediately got up and crossed the room to her, saying,
" Is anything wrong?" Then, as the girl closed the
door and turned round, Mr. Pelly saw that she had
gone ashy white, near as white as the clean art-
paint on the door she stood by. But she only said,
" I shall be all right in a minute." Her mother said,
" Come and sit down, darling," which she did; but
sat quite still, looking white. " I wish Sir Stopleigh would come," said her mother. Mr. Pelly was
frightened, but behaved well, for a little old bachelor.

Presently her colour came again, and she said,
" It must have been my fancy," and her mother

said, "*What* must, dear? Do tell us!" But she
only said, "How on earth can I have been such a
fool?" Then her mother said again, "But what
was it, dear?" and she answered uneasily, "Nothing,
Mumsey." Her mother and Mr. Pelly looked at one
another, puzzled.

Sir Stopleigh put his head in at the door, saying
to his wife would she come out for a minute and
speak to him? On which Madeline said suddenly,
"I shall go to bed. Good-night, Uncle Christopher!—Good-night, Pupsey and Mumsey!" and
lit a candle and went away quickly upstairs. "How
very funny of Mad," her mother said, as she followed her husband from the room. "Not at all
like her! I'll say good-night, Uncle Christopher,
but you do as you like." The momentary vision
of Sir Stopleigh—who said he would come back
directly—left Mr. Pelly with an impression that he
was very full of something to tell. And certainly
there came a great sudden exclamation of glad surprise from her ladyship almost as soon as the door
closed behind her.

"I shall hear all about it in good time," said Mr.
Pelly. "At least, I suppose so." He sat down
contentedly in the large armchair opposite the
picture, and looked at the fire. Seventy-seven can
wait.

The murmur of a distant colloquy, heard through

doors and passages, and quenched by carpets, assorts itself into its elements as the silence in the library gets under weigh, and sharpens Mr. Pelly's hearing. He is clear about the woman's voice: his hostess's, of course—no other. But is that George's, or the General's, the unexplained outsider's? Surely that was a third voice, just now? Never mind, Mr. Pelly can wait!

CHAPTER XI

IT is scarcely fair play to make a merit of patience
—isn't cricket, as folk say nowadays—when you
are in a comfortable armchair before a warm fire,
and are feeling drowsy. But, then, Mr. Pelly was
under an entirely wrong impression on this point,
and had scheduled himself as wakeful, but content
to bide his time. Yet he might reasonably have
suspected himself of drowsiness when James, the
young man, coming to wind up the contents of the
room, and revise the shutters, retreated with
apologies. For had he been really awake, he would
certainly have said, " All right, James! Come in.
Never mind me! " As it was, he deferred doing so
a fraction of a second, and the consequences were

fatal. He remained wide awake, no doubt—people always do. But he had not the slightest idea that James had gone, closing the door gently, when the picture said to him from the chimneypiece, in exactly the voice he had heard before, "Is it all true?"

Mr. Pelly found that, mysteriously, he took it as a matter of course that this should be so. "I presume," he said, "that you are alluding to the substance of the manuscript we have just read. I am scarcely in a position to form an opinion."

"Why not?" said the picture. At least, she said "*Perchè?*" and this translates "Why not?" in English.

"Because I am conscious of a strong bias towards accepting it as true, occasioned by the details of your own Italian experience, which you were so kind as to give me—perhaps you will remember?—some while since—let me see?—before I went away to see that niece of mine married at Cowcester. Now, this narrative of yours—so my Reason tells me; and I may add that I have already committed myself to this opinion when awake—can only be regarded as a figment of my own imagination, based on a partial perusal of the manuscript you have just heard—that is to say, *would have* just heard had you been objective. I am borrowing a phrase from my friend, Professor Schrudengesser. I do not see that any harm can come of my speaking plainly, as if you happen to have an independent existence you will appreciate the difficulties of the position, and if you haven't, I don't see that it matters."

"Mr. Pelly," said the picture impressively, " I should like, if you will allow me, to say a serious word to you on this subject. I refer to the reality of our existence, a subject to which the most frivolous amongst us cannot afford to be indifferent. Have you never considered that the only person of whose existence we have *absolute* certainty is *ourself?* Outside and beyond it, are we not painfully dependent on the evidence of our senses? What is our dearest friend to us but a series of impressions on our sight, touch, and hearing, *plus* the conclusion we draw—possibly unsound—that what we touch is also what we see, and that what we hear proceeds from both? Have you attached due weight to . . . ? "

Mr. Pelly interrupted the voice. "You will excuse me," he said, " but in view of the fact that I may wake at any moment, is it not rather a tempting of Providence to discuss abstract metaphysical questions? No one would be more interested than myself in such discussions under circumstances of guaranteed continuity. But . . ." Mr. Pelly paused, and the voice laughed. The picture itself remained unmoved.

" ' Circumstances of guaranteed continuity,' " it

repeated mockingly. " When have you ever had a guarantee of continuity, and from whom? If you were suddenly to find yourself extinct, at any moment, could you logically—could you reasonably —express surprise?—you who had actually passed through an infinity of nonentity before you, at any rate, became a member of Society? Why should not your nonentity come back again? What has been, may be."

Mr. Pelly's mind felt referred to sudden death, but his reply was, " Guaranteed continuity of communication was what I meant." Then he reflected that perhaps sudden death might be only suspension of communication—however, he had had no experience of it himself, and could only guess. The picture continued sadly:

" That makes me think how hard it is that you should wake to live in the great world I cannot join in; to move about and be free, while I must needs be speechless! Give me a thought sometimes, even as the disembodied spirit, as some hold, may give a thought to one he leaves behind. Yet even that one is better off than I; for may not he or she rejoin those that have gone before? While I must grow fainter and fainter, and be at last unseen and forgotten; or even worse, restored! Rather than that, let me peel and be relined, or sold at Christie's with several others as a job lot."

Mr. Pelly endeavoured to console the speaker. "You need not be apprehensive," he said. "You are covered with glass, and in a warm and dry place. Nothing is more improbable than change, in any form, at Surley Stakes. Indeed, the first baronet, over two hundred and fifty years ago, is said to have accepted his new dignity with reluctance, on the score of its novelty. This library is three hundred years old."

"And I," said the voice, "was over one hundred years old when it was built. But tell me—tell me—was it not all true, the story? You know it was!"

"It rests on the intrinsic evidence of the manuscript. There is nothing to confirm it. And, as I have pointed out to you, your own narrative may be a mere figment of *my* imagination—you must at least admit the possibility——"

"I will if you insist upon it; it is of small importance to me what others think, so long as I may hang here undisturbed, and dream over the happy days I must have passed, in the person of my original, four hundred years ago. But oh, to think of that hateful time of bondage, with my darling hidden in the darkness underground, sore with manacles and starved for want of food! Think of my joy when I could see and feel his own dear face, all clammy though it was with the dungeon damps from below!

Think of my exultation at his returning life—life
to be lived for me! And believe me—for this I
can know, for I *was* Maddalena, and now it comes
like a dim memory—that I shuddered when they
told me that the sodden old horror that had been
my owner was well started on his flight to Hell,
sent by the swift little knife-spike of my Marta. Oh,
how often have I seen that little knife itself in the
long girth that could but just span the bloated carcase
of the Ferretti!—for *he* is a clear memory to me.
And to think that that knife—*that knife*—was
to . . ."

Mr. Pelly felt constrained to interrupt. "Pardon
me," he said, "if I venture to recall to you that the
duty of Christians, of all denominations, is to forgive; and besides, entirely apart from that, all this
occurred such a very long time ago."

"How long is needed, think you"—and as the
voice said this, it almost grew cruel in its earnestness—"how long, for a girl, to forgive the utmost
wrong God in His wisdom has put it in the power
of Man to inflict on Woman? Still, I did shudder—
have I not said it?—at what they told me; though
they showed me not the knife, and that was well.
I *did* shudder, it is true; but now, as you say, it
is best forgotten. Better for me to think of our days
that must have been, of the babes that were born to
us that I never saw, of how we watched them growing

in the happy passing hours, in the little old Castello in the hills. Better for me to know, as I know now, that I, while this thing that I am now—this thing of paint and canvas—lay hid in a garret, even I could be to him, my love, a slight half-solace for his ruined hand. How slight, who can tell who does not know what a lost right hand means to the artist whose life is in his craft? . . ."

It seemed then to Mr. Pelly that the voice continued, though he heard it less distinctly, always dwelling on the life of its prototype, as revealed to it by the manuscript, in a manner that the dream-machinery of his mind failed to account for. His impression was that it continued thus for a very long time—some hours—during the last half of which it changed its character, becoming slowly merged in that of another voice, familiar to Mr. Pelly, which ended by saying with perfect distinctness, " The Captain wished his arm to be broke gradual to his family. 'Ence what I say!" And then Mr. Pelly was suddenly aware that he had dropped asleep for five minutes, and had been spoiling his night's rest. Also that he was now quite awake, and that Mr. Stebbings the butler had spoken the last words to Mrs. Buckmaster the housekeeper; and that both were unaware that he was on the other side of the large armchair-back—and, indeed, it was large enough to conceal something bigger than Mr.

Pelly. He abstained from making his presence known, however; more, perhaps, because he thought he was scarcely awake enough for words than to hear what should come next. He fancied the crushed hand incident of the dream had mixed itself into Mr. Stebbings's last speech, and made nonsense of it. But then, how about the sequel?

"'His arm broke gradual,' Mr. Stebbings?" Mrs. Buckmaster repeated. And her perception of the oddity of the speech reassured Mr. Pelly, who began to suspect he might be awake. But he waited for the reply.

"Quite so, Mrs. Buckmaster. Broke gradual. From consideration for family feeling. And that, if an amanuensis, suspicion would attach, and, in consequence, divulge."

Mr. Stebbings's style assumed that if he used the right words, somewhere, it didn't matter what order they came in. It didn't really matter; his respectability seemed more than a makeweight for slighted syntax.

Mrs. Buckmaster was a venerable and sweet institution of forty years' standing, that spoke to every member of the household as "my dear"; and conveyed an impression, always, of having in her hands a key with which she had just locked a store-room, or was going to unlock one. Or, rather, not so much a key, as a flavour of a key. Mrs.

Buckmaster was a sort of amateur mother of several
county families, whose components all but acknowledged her, and paid her visits in her private apartments when they came to call at the Stakes. Her
reply to Mr. Stebbings now was, " Merciful Heaven!
And the girl nursed him. And she a Dutch
woman! "

Mr. Pelly roused himself. His sensitive conscience
recoiled from further eavesdropping. " What's all
that, Stebbings? What's all that, Mrs. Buckmaster ? " he said, becoming manifest, and evoking
apologies. Mr. Stebbings had had no idear!

Mrs. Buckmaster said: " Well, now—to think of
that! " then, collecting herself, added, " Tell Mr.
Pelly, Thomas, what you know. Thomas will tell
you, sir, what he knows."

Thomas perceived distinction ahead, and braced
himself for an effort. " Respecting the actule fax,
sir, they are soon told. After the lamentable dis-
aster to both armies at Stroomsdrift, accompanied
with unparalleled 'eroism on both sides, the Captain's
horse became restive, and ensued. No longer under
the Captain's control, having received a bullet
through the upper arm—unfortunately the right,
but, nevertheless, in the service of his country.
Wonderful to relate, he retained his presence of
mind "—Mr. Stebbings's pride in this passage was
indescribable—" and arrived without further dis-

aster, though unconscious. . . ." It was perhaps as well that the Baronet called Mr. Stebbings away at this point, as Mrs. Buckmaster knew the whole story.

" Why on earth couldn't Stebbings begin at the beginning?" said Mr. Pelly, rather irritably. "Is Captain Calverley alive or dead?—that's what *I* want to know. And who's that outside, talking to Sir George and the General?"

" It's the Captain himself, sir," said Mrs. Buckmaster. " Looking that well—only no arm! His right, too." And then she cleared matters up, by telling how, after the battle, the young soldier, badly wounded in more places than one, had, nevertheless, contrived to keep his seat on a half-runaway horse he could scarcely guide, which carried him away in a semi-conscious state to a lonely farm on the veldt, tenanted only by a Dutch mother and daughter. These two, hating *roineks* in theory, but softening to a young and handsome one in practice, had kept the wounded man and nursed him round, but could get no surgical help advanced enough to save his arm, which he had been obliged to leave in South Africa. The daughter had evidently regarded the Captain as her property—a fair prisoner of war—and had done her best to retain him, writing letters to his friends for him at his dictation, which were never despatched in spite of promises made, and heading off search-parties that appeared in the neighbourhood. Mrs. Buckmaster condemned this conduct on principle, but said: "Ah, poor girl—only think of it," in practice.

That was really the whole of the story, so far. But like a continuous frieze, it would bear any quantity of repetition, as the Captain's reappearance always suggested his first departure, five months ago, and led to a new recital. The frieze, however, was not to remain unbroken; for Mrs. Buckmaster was balked of her fourth *da capo* by the reappearance of the Baronet, with General Fordyce, both of them also knee-deep in recapitulations. Sir George was in a state of high bewilderment.

"Just listen to this, Uncle Kit. . . . Oh, you know—Mrs. Buckmaster's told you. Never mind, General, tell us again how it happened—it *has* been queer! Tell Mr. Pelly how you came to hear of it."

"It was like this," said the General, who was collected. "A month ago I was knocked over by receiving this telegram. Here it is." He produced it from a pocket-book and read: "' Am alive and well if news that am marrying Dutch girl contradict otherwise keep silent till I come Jack.' Well, George, I saw nothing for it but to bottle up, and I assure you I was pretty well put to it to keep my

own counsel. However, I really hadn't any choice.
Very well, then! That goes on till ten days ago,
when another wire comes from Madeira, ' Passenger
by *Briton,* in London this day week, Jack.' And
sure enough my young friend bursts into my cham-
bers four days ago, with, ' Tell me about Madeline—
is she engaged?' ' Not that I know of, my dear
boy,' said I. ' And I think I should know if she
were.' Then says he, ' Oh, what a selfish beast I
am! But you'll forgive me, General, when you
know.' However, I didn't want to know, but forgave
him right off."

"And then I suppose he told you all he's been
telling us downstairs—about the Dutch girl and the
farmhouse on the veldt?"

"Yes, he seems to have known very little from
the moment he was struck until his senses came
back to him at the farm. I must say they seem to
have behaved wonderfully well to him. . . ."

" I can't say I think burning his letters and cutting
him off from all communications was exactly good
behaviour." Thus the Baronet. But the General
seemed doubtful.

" We-e-ell!—I don't know. I shouldn't quite say
that. Remember it was only this poor girl that did
it, and one sees her motive. No—no! All's fair in
love, George. I'm sorry for her, with all my heart."

Mrs. Buckmaster murmured under her breath,

"What was I saying to Mr. Christopher?" and
thereon Mr. Pelly felt in honour bound to testify
to her truthfulness. "Yes—Mrs. Buckmaster
thought so." Nobody was very definite.

"But did he come here with you, General?"
asked Mr. Pelly, who was gradually toning down to
sane inquiry-point. Mixed replies said that the
Captain had not been long in the house. Lady Upwell was interviewing him—they were, in fact,
audible in the distance. The General supplied
further information.

"You see," he said, "Master Jack and I had just
arranged it all beautifully. I was to come here to
let it out gently and not frighten Miss Upwell, and
also to find how the land lay. Because, you see,
after all, they were not engaged. . . ."

"Oh no! They were not *engaged*." This was a
kind of chorus; after which the General continued:

"Anyhow, Miss Upwell might have picked up with
some other young fellow. However, she hasn't.
Well!—I was to come here and take the sound-
ings, and his ship was to follow on; he meanwhile
going down to inflict a full dramatic surprise on
his own family at Granchester Towers. He said
their nerves were strong enough, and it would do
them good. He was to come on as soon as he could
unless he heard to the contrary. And then, as he
was riding through Sampford Pagnell on his way

here, what must he come upon but a man of his own
company, who had been invalided home after
enteritis, who had been drinking and got into a row?
He stopped to see him out of his difficulties—had
to go bail for him—and then came on here. But
it made him late. And I should have been here
sooner myself, only something went wrong with the
trains. It made me so late that I almost made up
my mind, if Jack wasn't here, to go back to the inn
at Grewceham, so as not to frighten you all out of
your wits."

"There's my wife coming up. I wonder what
they've settled." Thus the Baronet.

Then her ladyship came in, and following her,
in tiptoe silence, the young soldier himself. But
alas!—it was all true about the arm. There was the
loose right sleeve, looped up to his coat. But its
survivor was still in evidence, and Mr. Pelly, as
he took the hand that was left in his own, wondered
if he was not still dreaming, so full was his mind of
the story of that other hand, lost four hundred years
ago. He could not dismiss the picture from his
thoughts; and as he stood there talking with the
young soldier, in whom he could see the saddening
of his terrible experience through all the joy of his
return, he was always conscious of its presence,
conscious of its eyes fixed on all that passed before
it—conscious of its comparison between the lot of

its original, and Madeline's. And it made the old
gentleman feel quite eerie and uncomfortable. So
he resolved to say good-night, and did so as soon as
a pause came in an earnest conversation aside between the Baronet and his Lady, who seemed to be
enforcing a view by argument. Mr. Pelly heard the
last words:

"I have told this dear, silly fellow Mad must
speak for herself. I won't say anything. . . .
No—not to-morrow; she had better be told and come
down now." Here a subcolloquy. Wouldn't she
have gone to bed? Oh no, Eliza said not. Besides,
she could slip something on. And then the main-
stream again. "You must give me a little time to
tell her, you know. One o'clock, isn't it? That
doesn't matter. Just think if it was a party!
You'll find I'm right, George." For when Lady
Upwell is pleased and excited she calls her husband
by his Christian name without the Sir.

When she had departed the General went back
on a previous conversation. "But we can't make
out yet, Jack,. how we came not to get any wire
about it—as soon as it was known you were alive.
It ought to have been in the papers a month
ago."

"Nobody knows out there yet, except Headquar-
ters. Don't you see? As soon as I was fit to get on
a horse, I rode all night across the veldt, and re-

ported myself in the early morning. I begged them to keep me dark for a bit, and old Pipeclay said he could manage it. . . ."

"But why did you want it kept dark?"

"I'll tell you directly. When I had settled that, I made a rush for Port Elizabeth, and just caught the *Briton*. Do you know, I was so anxious nobody should know anything about it till I knew about Madeline that I travelled as Captain Maclagan. And when I got to Southampton there was a Mrs. Maclagan and two grown-up daughters inquiring for me! So really no one knew anything at all about me till you did."

Then the Baronet would know more of Jack's two months of nursing at the Dutch farm. He thought he could understand about the girl; and he wouldn't ask any questions. But why had Jack thought Madeline was engaged to Sir Doyley Chauncey? *He* was engaged to another girl? Yes, he was; but that was just it. It *was* another girl, of the same name— another Madeline. Master Jack coloured and was rather reserved. Then he spoke:

"I'll tell you if you like. I told the General." Who nodded. "But you mustn't blame poor Chris. Remember she was brought up a Boer, though she had some English education. It was a newspaper notice—Court and Fashionable game—' A marriage is arranged between Sir Doyley Chauncey of Limp

Court, Gloucestershire, and Miss Madeline . . .'
and there the paper was carefully cut away between
the lines with scissors—one can always tell a scissor
cut. I was sure poor Chris had done it, for her own
reasons. I had told her all about Mad. There was
no humbugging at all."

"But, you silly boy," said the General, "don't you
see what I told you is true? If she had seen the
name Upwell, on the next line, she *wouldn't* have cut
it. Of course, she wouldn't leave the name Farrant
—it's Lina Farrant, George; old Farrant's daughter
at Kneversley—man thinks Bacon wrote Shakespeare——"

"Of course not! I see that all now. But one
isn't so cool as one might be sometimes. I got
quite upside down with never hearing, and, of course,
I couldn't write myself. I was quite dependent on
poor Chris. But I was going to tell why I wanted
to keep it dark that I was alive. You see, if Mad
had got engaged—to *anyone*—well, I don't exactly
see how to tell it. . . ." He hesitated a good deal.
"Well, then . . ."

"Well, then what?"

"Do you know, I think I would almost soonest
not try to talk about it. But there was nothing
wrong, you know, anywhere."

"Oh no! Nothing wrong. We quite understand."

"Only when a girl has nursed you like that—even if . . ."

"Even if you don't love her—is that it?"

Jack was relieved. "Yes—that's about it! All the same, if Madeline *had* been engaged, I *might* have gone back and married her—to do the poor girl a good turn."

"In spite of her squelching your letters?" said Sir George.

"Why, ye-es! Look at why she did it!"

"There, they are coming down," said the General. "Come along, George! We aren't wanted here. Good-night, Jack!"

And then off they go, leaving the young man alone, pacing backwards and forwards between the door and the picture. There is but one lamp left burning, on a small table near, and it is going out. He picks it up and holds it nearer to see the picture. But his hand shakes; one can hear it by the tinkle in its socket of the ring that carries an opal globe that screens the light. And he does not see much, for he can hear, a long way off, Madeline's voice and her mother's—a mere murmur. Then the murmur flashes up a little louder for a moment, and the voices of the Baronet and the old General are bidding each other good-night, a long way off. Then a girl's footstep on the stair.

The tinkle of the lamp stops as the young soldier

puts it back on its table. That lamp will go out very soon. But a log on the fire, that seémed dead, breaks out in a blaze, and all the shadows it makes on the walls leap and dance in its flicker. For the lamp is making haste to die.

That is a timid touch upon the handle of the door. The young soldier's face of expectation is a sight to see, a sight to remember. His one hand is bearing on the table where he placed the lamp—almost as though he were for the moment dizzy. Then, in the wavering light he can see the loose, many-flowered robe of Madeline, such a one as she wears for the toilette, and her white face, and her cloud of beautiful hair that is all undone. They are all there in the leaping light of the fire, and he hears her voice that says, " Oh, Jack—oh, Jack—oh, Jack! " and can say no more. And he, for his part, cannot speak, but must needs grieve—oh, how bitterly!—for the loss of the one strong arm that is gone. How he would have drawn her to him! But he still has one, and it is round her. And her two white arms are round his neck as their lips meet, even as those arms in the picture must have met round the neck of *her* beloved, even as their lips must have met, when the dungeon closed again on the dead gaoler and its prisoners, in that castle in the Apennines, four hundred years ago!

The picture still hangs over the chimney-shelf in the library at Surley Stakes, and you may see it any time if you are in the neighbourhood. Mr. Stebbings will show it to you, and give you an abstract of the *cinquecento* in Italy. But he sometimes is a little obscure; so our recommendation to you is, to ask for Mrs. Buckmaster, who can never tire of talking about it, and who will strike you as being the living image of Mrs. Rouncewell in "Bleak House." Make her talk freely, and she will tell you how whenever "our young lady," otherwise Lady Calverley—for our friend Jack unexpectedly came to the inheritance of Granchester Towers two years since—visits the Stakes she always goes straight to the picture and looks at it before anything else. And how she tells little Madeline, her eldest girl, who is old enough to understand, that pictures can really see and hear; and, indeed, has told her the story of the picture long ago. Of which the crown and summit of delight to this little maid of four seems to have been its richness in murder. Chiefest of all, the impalement of the old Raimondi on Marta's knife. You will gather that requests are made for a recital of this part of the story at untimely moments—coming home from church on Sunday, and so on. She is going to tell it to Baby herself as soon as he is old enough. But he isn't one yet;

he has to be reckoned in months. To think of the
joys there are before him!

Mrs. Buckmaster will tell you too—if you work
her up enough—of the Dutch girl, and the miles
of veldt Sir John bought and gave her as a wedding
present. But to get at all this you must first get
her out of the library, for while she is there she can
talk of little but the picture.

"I always *do* have the thought," she will very
likely say, as she has said it to us, "that the picture
can as good as hear us speak, for all the world as if
it was a Christian, and not an inanimate object.
Because its eyes keep looking—looking. Like
reading into your mind, whatever Mr. Stebbings
may say! We must all think otherwise, now and
again, and Mr. Stebbings's qualifications as a butler
none can doubt." Mrs. Buckmaster will then tell
you of the three different artists three separate
eminent critics have ascribed it to. But there can
be no doubt that the family incline to Boldrini, on
the strength of Mr. Pelly's dream. To be sure,
no such artist is known to have existed. ' But is
not the same true of the *nipote del fratello di latte
del Bronzino,* whom the Coryphæus of these Art
Critics invented to father it on?

Anyhow, there hangs the picture, night and day.
If it sees, it sees its owners growing older, year by
year. It sees their new grandchildren appear mys-

teriously, and each one behave as if it was the first new child in human experience. It sees a one-armed soldier keen on organization of territorial forces, and a beautiful wife who thinks him the greatest of mankind. And it sees, too, now and again, a very old, old gentleman whom Death seems to overlook because he is so small and dry; whom you may see too, by-the-by, if you look out sharp at Sotheby's, or Wilkinson's, or Puttick's, or Simpson's, or Quaritch's, or the Museum Reading Room. Some believe Mr. Pelly immortal.

If it hears, it hears the few sounds the silent north has to show against the music and the voices of the south. It can listen to the endless torrent of song from its little brown-bird outside above the meadow, poised in the misty blue of a coming day, or the scanty measure of the pleading of the nightingale, heard from a thousand throats among the Apennines in years gone by, welcome now as a memory that brings them back. It can hear the great wind roar in the chimney at its back through the winter nights, and the avalanches in miniature that come falling from the roof above when the world awakes to fight against its shroud of snow. But there is one thing it heard in our story it may listen for in vain—the bark of the great dog Cæsar. For Cæsar died of old age at eighteen, the age at which many of us fancy we begin to live, and the great bark shakes the Universe no more. Other dogs eat small sweet biscuits now from the hand of the mistress who loved him with precisely the same previous examination of them, with the identical appearance of condescension in taking them at all. But Cæsar lies—his mortal part—in a good-sized grave behind the lawn, where it can be pointed out from the library, and his *hospis comesque corporis* may be among the shades, may have met for anything we know the liberated soul of Marta's poodle, and they may have considered each other sententiously, and parted company on the worst of terms. Cæsar never could have stood that poodle, on this side.

But the picture is there still, for those who are curious to see it. Whether it would not hang more fitly in the little Castello in the hills, if it could be identified, is matter for discussion. If pictures could really speak, what would this one say?

THE END

AN APOLOGY IN CONFIDENCE

THE present writer has a weight upon his conscience. But he has no desire to disburden himself at the expense of the future reader of his works. This is addressed solely to those whom he has acquired the right to apostrophize as "My readers"; and, indeed, properly speaking, only to such of them as were misled, by a too generous appreciation of his first four novels, into purchasing his fifth. For he cannot free himself from a haunting sense that he was guilty of a gross neglect in not giving them fuller warning that the said fifth volume was not Early Victorian, either in style or substance.

It is well understood nowadays—and it is not for so humble an individual as the P. W. aforesaid to call in question the judgments of everybody else—that each living author, whether he be painter or writer, shall produce at suitable intervals, preferably of twelve months, a picture or volume on all fours with the work from his hand which has first attracted public attention. And the P. W. cannot conceal from himself that in publishing, without a solemn warning addressed to possible purchasers, such a novel as his last ("An Affair of Dishonor": Henry Holt and Company), he has run the risk of incurring the execration or forgiveness—the upshot is the same—of many of his most tolerant and patient readers, to remain on good terms with whom is, and always will be, his literary ambition.

For the "Affair" is certainly not an Early Victorian story in the ordinary sense of the words. A certain latitude has been claimed by some critics in the choice of names for the periods treated of in the other humble performances of its author; but so far no commentator has called its epoch—that of Charles II.—"Early

359

Victorian." It has been spoken of freely as sixteenth and eighteenth century; but that is immaterial. In fact, it is difficult to resist the conviction that in what may be called sporting chronology—a system which seems to have a certain vogue of its own—so long as the writer says "century," one number does as well as another to make the sentence ring. The expression "Early Victorian," however, is embarrassingly circumscribed in its meaning. It cannot be applied at random to any period whatever, without danger of the Sciolist, or the Merest Tyro, going to the British Museum and getting at Haydn's "Dictionary of Dates," and catching you out. Still, it does not do to be too positive; seeing that the P. W. has here—and can show it you in the house—what seems a description of the Restoration as "Pre-Cromwellian." There it is, before him, as he presently writes on the shiniest paper that ever made an old fogy wish he had been born fifty years earlier.*

To fulfil the conditions which literary usage appears to dictate, and to signalize his conformity with public opinion, there is no doubt that the writer of "An Affair of Dishonor"—or, shall I drop the thin veil adopted to avoid egotism, and say I myself?—should have made that work not only Early Victorian, but Suburban. For, as I understand, I am expected to be Suburban. This is

---

* I will be just and generous to this writer simultaneously. The Protector was born in 1599. Pre-Cromwellian days were the sixteenth century, clearly. In the sixteenth century St. James's and Piccadilly would not be includable in residential quarters, because the latter was not born or thought of. If by Pre-Cromwellian this writer means Pre-Commonwealth, the inclusion of Piccadilly in the description of a country girl's conception of swell London, written a hundred years later, when Piccadilly was "fait accompli," seems to me not unnatural. I am bound to say, however, that when I first read the passage (p 181)—immediately after I had written it—I thought "those days" meant the days of the story. Analysis of London topography would have been out of place in treating of the cogitations of a country girl unfamiliar with the metropolis.

less difficult, as suburbs do not depend on chroniclers, like periods, but remain to speak for themselves. One knows when one is being Suburban. Among epochs one treads gingerly, like the skater on ice that scarcely bears him. I may take as an instance a book I wrote, called "Somehow Good," whose cradle, as it were, was the Twopenny Tube. The frequent reference to this story as an "Early Victorian" tale has impressed me that Early Victorianism is an abstract quality, which owes its fascination neither to its earliness, nor to its epoch. I am stating the case broadly, but as this is entirely between ourselves, very great niceties are hardly called for. We may leave the Sciolist, and the Merest Tyro, to fight about niceties. On the other hand, outside opinion, though a little vague about Early Victorianism, has not been inconsistent about Suburbanity. It has shrewdly identified, in my first four novels, the Suburban character of Tooting, Balham, Hampstead, Putney, Shepherd's Bush, and Wimbledon; and I now perceive that my reader was entitled to expect Clapham Junction or Peckham Rye, at least. Nothing would have pleased me better, when writing my last book, than to supply the nearest practicable Carolean equivalent, had I seen more clearly how the land lay. However, it's done now and can't be helped.

Broadly speaking, then, non-Victorianity and defective Suburbanity seem to be responsible for my slump in conformity. And, though I have to go to America for distinct proofs of it, I am obliged to recognize suggestions of the same critical decision nearer home. The first three of the following American reviews appeared at intervals in the same journal, showing how deeply the writer had taken my delinquency to heart:

"*Probably written years ago, and found in an old desk.*"

"*A totally uncharacteristic and thoroughly disappointing 'historical romance.'*"

"'*A perfectly good cat,' that I have found in the literary ash-pan . . . . differs from everything that has come to us previously from the author's pen, as lifeless clay differs from living spirit."*

" Wherein lies the superiority of fiction that can give us nothing better than this ? "

" It is not, in itself, worth reading . . . being an unpleasant unexciting, and unoriginal experiment in historical romance . . . leaving us disappointed of what we hoped for, and unedified by what we get."

" The ghosts of ' David Copperfield ' and ' Joseph Vance,' ' Alice-for-Short ' and the ' Little Marchioness,' may together weep pale spirit tears, or nobly repress them, in the hope that ' It Never can Happen Again.' "

" We can but hope for a return from this invented matter and artificial style to an unabashed Victorianism, from which it should appear the author is trying to escape."

There is something spirited in a selection of quotations which begins and ends with such different conjectures as to the genesis of their subject. There can be no doubt about the earnestness of the hope expressed in the last one, for it is confirmed in the same words by more than one American journal.*

Another accusation against me is that I have given up nice people, and only write about nasty ones. Is this true? I myself thought Lucinda a nice enough girl, particularly when she was fishing in the sea for the phosphorescence. All the same, the following seemed to me quite a just comment, and very well worded: "There must have been something of Phaedra in Lucinda for her to act as she did, unless we are to revert to the belief in a baneful Aphrodite no human will

* The force of the unanimity of two or three American papers grows less when their reader perceives the verbal identity of the article throughout—and that their writers are not only unanimous, but unicorporeal. Numbers are impressive, but when they play fast and loose with plurality in this way, all their edge is taken off.

*can resist." Something of Phaedra—but still, I sub-
mit, not much, for Sir Oliver was passionately urgent;
while Hippolytus—to borrow a phrase from Mrs. Steptoe, a quarter where I have unlimited credit—didn't
want to any such a thing.*

*Every book has a right to an assumption intrinsically
improbable, to make the story go. What a flat tragedy
Hamlet would have been without its fundamental ghost!
And my "quidlibet audendi" is a small presumption
compared with my giant namesake's. Of course, I have
no right to the comparison unless you grant like
rights to tittlebat and leviathan. "Semper fiat aequa
potestas," for both. Indeed, the dwarf needs artificial
latitude more than the giant.*

*In my capacity of tittlebat in an estuary of
Leviathan's great sea—or, should I not rather say, a
sandhopper on its coast?—I have assumed that this
baneful Aphrodite no human will can resist had possession of Lucinda; who was, and continued to be, a
very nice girl for all that. Phaedra was not nice, because of the attitude of Hippolytus, as sketched by Mrs.
Steptoe; and even more because of the fibs she told
when she found the young man blind to the attractions
of his stepmother. Lucinda was not a bit the less nice
because she was swept away by, absorbed into, crushed
under, a passion of which she only knew that it was the
reverse of hate, and of which few of us know much
more. Indeed, all male persuasions get so very mixed,
owing to the Nature of Things, that they are almost
a negligible factor in the solution of the problem. Now
and again, however, it is hinted at by thoughtful male
persons—Shakespeare and Browning, and the like. Read
this, for instance:*

> *"But, please you, wonder I would put*
> *My cheek beneath that lady's foot;*
> *Rather than trample under mine*
> *The laurels of the Florentine,*
> *And you shall see how the Devil spends*
> *A fire God gave for other ends.*

> *" I tell you, I stride up and down*
> *This garret, crowned with Love's best crown,*
> *And feasted with Love's perfect feast*
> *To think I kill for her at least*
> *Body and soul and peace and fame,*
> *Alike youth's end and manhood's aim."*

    *   *   *   *   *   *

Perhaps you will say that no ladylike, well brought up girl, ever feels so explosive. About a Man too—the idea! But for my part, I don't see that Browning's chap need have been a nasty chap. Nevertheless, my sense of the proprieties—which is keen—compels me to admit that if I had a daughter, and she were to go on like that, I should feel it my duty to point out to her that if she continued to do so, she would run the risk of being taken for a suffragette, or something. I might get no farther, because I word things badly.

Lucinda, you see, might have gone on like that about Oliver; only no doubt the memory of old precepts hung about her, and acted as I trust my remonstrance would have done in the case of my hypothetical daughter. Anyhow, I do think that the time-honoured usage which keeps girls as ignorant of life as possible, so that they shall be docile when a judicious Hymen offers them a marriage with a suitable " parti," ought at least, as a set-off, to go hand-in-hand with leniency towards this ignorance when it betrays its possessor into an indiscretion she has no means of gauging the dangers of. For my belief is that the wickedness of her action seemed purely academical to Lucinda. And Oliver knew how to manage cases of this sort, bless you!

As for him, I readily admit that he was not nice, but I take the testimonials to his nastiness as complimentary. When an Italian audience pelts Iago with rotten eggs, it is accepted by the actor as heartfelt praise. And you must have Devils, as well as Fairies, when it's in a Pantomime, as we all know. An unhappy author whom lack of material for copy has nearly qualified for Earls-

wood cannot go on for ever writing about good people.
He must have a villain, please, sooner or later!

Nevertheless, some of my correspondents want to
deprive me of this innocent luxury. Such an appeal
as the following makes me feel that I may have to " leave
the killing out, when all is done."

> " Dear sir, can any ' success ' that meets your latest story
> compensate for the pain, and—so personal have you made
> our relations to you—the humiliation so many of us feel?
>
> " Why leave the heights—the sunny hill-slopes—where we
> met you as a wise, sweet older brother, and lingered long
> after your story was over, with stilled and strengthened
> hearts?
>
> " I am sure none of us is happier, and none certainly is
> better for breathing the sickening air into which you have
> led us . . ."

Now, if I had published this story after a manifesto
warning, cautioning, and earnestly entreating all readers who expected it to be Victorian and Suburban to keep
their money in their pockets, I should not be feeling, as
I do now, that the writer of the above letter had been
entrapped into reading it under false pretences. I can
only offer humble and heartfelt apology to the writers,
English as well as American, of the many letters I have
received, practically of the same tenor as the above.

But I am left in a dilemma. I cannot consider myself bound to make my next net volume exclusively
Victorian, Suburban, kindly, gossipy, button-holy—I
rather like that word—in the face of some very strong
encouragements to have another go-in at Barts, or their
equivalents, of evil dispositions, or, perhaps I should say,
of Mediæval dispositions; for I am countenanced by
many sporting chronologists in attaching a meaning to
this word at war with my boyish understanding of it,
which stopped the " moyen âge " at the Reformation.
However, it doesn't matter; this is all in confidence. I
cannot very well cite these encouragements. They form
part of a most liberal and intelligent series of reviews—
not unmixed praise by any means—which I am sticking

*at odd times in a big book, to which I shall have to
allude more particularly presently. It is enough for us
now that several of them speak of " An Affair of Dishonor" as its author's best production, so far. After
that I must really be Mediæval, or Marry-come-up, or
whatever one ought to call it, a little more. There is no
way out.*

*A reviewer of an isolated and forcible genius also has
a share in inducing me to try the same line again. I
want to be reviewed by him, please, as often as possible.
There is a healthy and bracing tone in his lightest word.
Listen:*

"*A story-teller ought to be able to tell a story. There is
a story in 'An Affair of Dishonor,' but I pity the reader who
tries to excavate it. He must tie a wet towel round his head,
and clench his teeth, and prepare to face hours of digging
and scraping. And when he has excavated the story from
the heavy clay of the style, he will ask why the author took
so much trouble to bury it so deep in affectation. . . . Mr.
De Morgan tries to copy the language of the seventeenth century, but he copies it like a schoolboy. . . . To make the
mess complete, the last chapter is taken from a manuscript.*

"*If Mr. De Morgan desired to imitate Esmond he ought
to have stuck to the Esmond method. If he wished to tell
a melodramatic story he ought to have told it plainly. The
story is stale. . . . I suppose the rake is meant to be a Love-
lace, and Lucinda a Clarissa Harlowe. The whole thing is
artificial, there is no illusion, and the characters are all sticks.
The battle is bad, and the duels are bad, and the dialogue is
very bad. And how it bores one!*"

*Can you wonder that I look forward to being reviewed
again by this gentleman? I shall feel an eager anticipation as I search among my press-cuttings, after the appearance of this present volume, for the name of his halfpenny journal. I can fancy his indignation at a picture that speaks—a completer mess even than the
dragging in of a manuscript at the end of Lucinda!
This was shocking—at least, it must have been, as otherwise this gentleman would have been talking nonsense.*

But my button-holed readers must be expecting me to

come to the point.   It is this.   " A Likely Story " is an honest, if a humble, attempt to satisfy all parties— except, indeed, the last party just cited, whom I should be sorry to satisfy.   It combines on one canvas the story of a family incident that is purely Victorian— though, alas, the era came to an end so shortly after- ward—with another, of the Italian cinquecento, with- out making any further demand on human powers of belief than that a picture is made to talk.   I have also introduced a very pretty suburb, Coombe, as the residence of the earliest Victorian aunt, to my thinking, that my pen is responsible for.   I like this way of shift- ing the responsibility off my own shoulders.

However, it is fair to admit that the expedient of making the photographic copy talk, as well as the original, may outrage the sense of probability of some of my more matter-of-fact readers.   I shall be sorry, be- cause modification in a second edition will be difficult, if not impossible.

If I do not succeed in pleasing both sections of my Public, I am at least certain of the approval of a very large number of readers who have found my previous productions too long.   The foregoing is even less than the 100,000 words which seem to recommend themselves as the right length, " per se," for a net volume.   A slump from a quarter to a tenth of a million words marks a powerful self-restraint on the part of my " cacoethes scribendi"—an essay towards conformity which seems to me to deserve recognition.   I do not understand that anyone has, so far, propounded the doctrine that a story cannot be too short.   If that were so the author would save himself a world of trouble by emulating the example of the unknown author of the shortest work of its kind on record—the biography of St. James the Less.   But perhaps I am mistaken in supposing that Jackaminory and the Apostle were one and the same personage.

I am personally more interested in the length of re- views than of books, in connection with the volume men- tioned just now, in which I am collecting my press-

cuttings. The page of this volume is fourteen inches by eight, and three reviews thirteen inches long exactly cover it, leaving a little space for the name of the journal and the date. It is too small to accommodate more than three normal press columns in the width. So that a review thirteen inches long is from my point of view the most suitable for my books. Of course, twenty-six and thirty-nine inches are equally acceptable. The difficulty only begins when accommodation of fractions becomes necessary. I account that review ill-written which perplexes me with the need for such accommodation.

I am prepared to accept six shilling volumes of 100,000 words, with reviews thirteen inches long, as the true and perfect image of Literature indeed.

Man, male and female, is a reading animal: or, what is perhaps more to the purpose, believes himself one. He may be divided into two classes—the Studious Reader and the General Reader. The former never skims books. If he dips into them at all he takes long dips, and when he comes out, leaves a bookmark in to show where he was, or which was his machine. He goes steadily and earnestly through the last, last, last word of Scientific thought—say, for instance, "An Essay towards a fuller Analysis of the Correlation between Force, Matter and Motion, with especial reference to their relations in Polydimensional Space"—and wants to just finish a marginal note upon it in pencil when the dinner-gong gets a rumble. He knits his brows and jumps and snorts when he peruses a powerful criticism, with antitheses and things. He very often thinks he will buy that book, only he must just glance at it again before he sends the order. Nevertheless, his relations with Fiction lack cordiality. They do not go, on his part, beyond picking up the last net volume from the drawing-room table, reading the title aloud, and putting it down again. And he only does this because it's there, and looks new. He wouldn't complain if no Fiction came into the house at all.

*Not so the General Reader. His theory of Literature
is entirely different. Broadly speaking, it is this: that
books are meant to be read, up to a certain point, but
that, as soon as that point is reached, it is desirable
that they should be returned to Mudie's or the " Times,"
and something else got, with a little less prosywozying
in it; and bounceable young women who ought to know
better, but don't; and detectives if possible, and motors
and aeroplanes anyhow. The exact definition of this
point is difficult, but it lies somewhere about the region
in which the General Reader gets bored to death, and
can't stand this dam rot any longer. It does not matter
to him that he may be the loser by his abrupt decisions;
if anything, he takes an unnatural pleasure in straining
the capacity of his Circulating Library to the full extent of its contract. He has paid his subscription, and
may change whenever he likes. That's the bargain, and
no humbugging!*

*So he goes on slap-dashing about, shuttle-cocking back
every new delivery, saying " Pish! " over this and
" Tush! " about that; writing short comments on
margins such as, " Vieux jeu! " or " No Woman
would"; only occasionally going carefully through a
book to find the chapter that reviewer-fellow said was
quite unfit for the girls to read, because one really ought
to keep an eye on what comes into the house nowadays.
His decisions can, however, scarcely be accepted as un-
failing guides to a just discrimination of literary merit,
as those who know him are never tired of insisting on his
inattentive habits, his paroxysms of electric suddenness
in action, and, above all, his insatiable thirst for something new. As for me, I am like Charles Lamb, when
he was told there was a gentleman in the room who ad-
mired " Paradise Regained." I should like to feel his
bumps.*

*Nevertheless, he is a personage for whom Authors have
a great and natural respect. He is so numerous! And
just think what fun it would be if each of him bought a
copy of each of one's immortal works! Consequently, I*

*wish to consult his liking, and am prepared—within rea-
son—to defer to his opinion of what length a book ought
to be.   It is no doubt quite otherwise with those Authors
who may be said to belong to the school of Inspiration-
alism—really one feels quite Modern, writing such a
word—who claim for each of their stories the position or
character of a sneeze—an automatic action which its
victim, perpetrator, executant, interpreter, proprietor,
promoter, parent, mover, seconder—or whatever we
choose to call him—has absolutely no control over.*

*But I am wandering away from the point of this
apology, which is really to say " peccavi," and, please, I
won't do so any more.   So far, that is, as is practicable.
If I drop into a prehistoric problem novel, by way of a
change, or have a try at an autobiography of Queen
Nitocris—just possibilities at random—I will do what I
can to head off readers who want one sort only, and
know which it is.*

*As for the foregoing story, it is just as Victorian as
it is anything else, though not, perhaps, Early enough to
give entire satisfaction.   One can't expect everything,
in this imperfect world.   To my thinking the shortness
of the story should cover a multitude of sins.*